SCIENCE
COMICS

TREES
Kings of the Forest

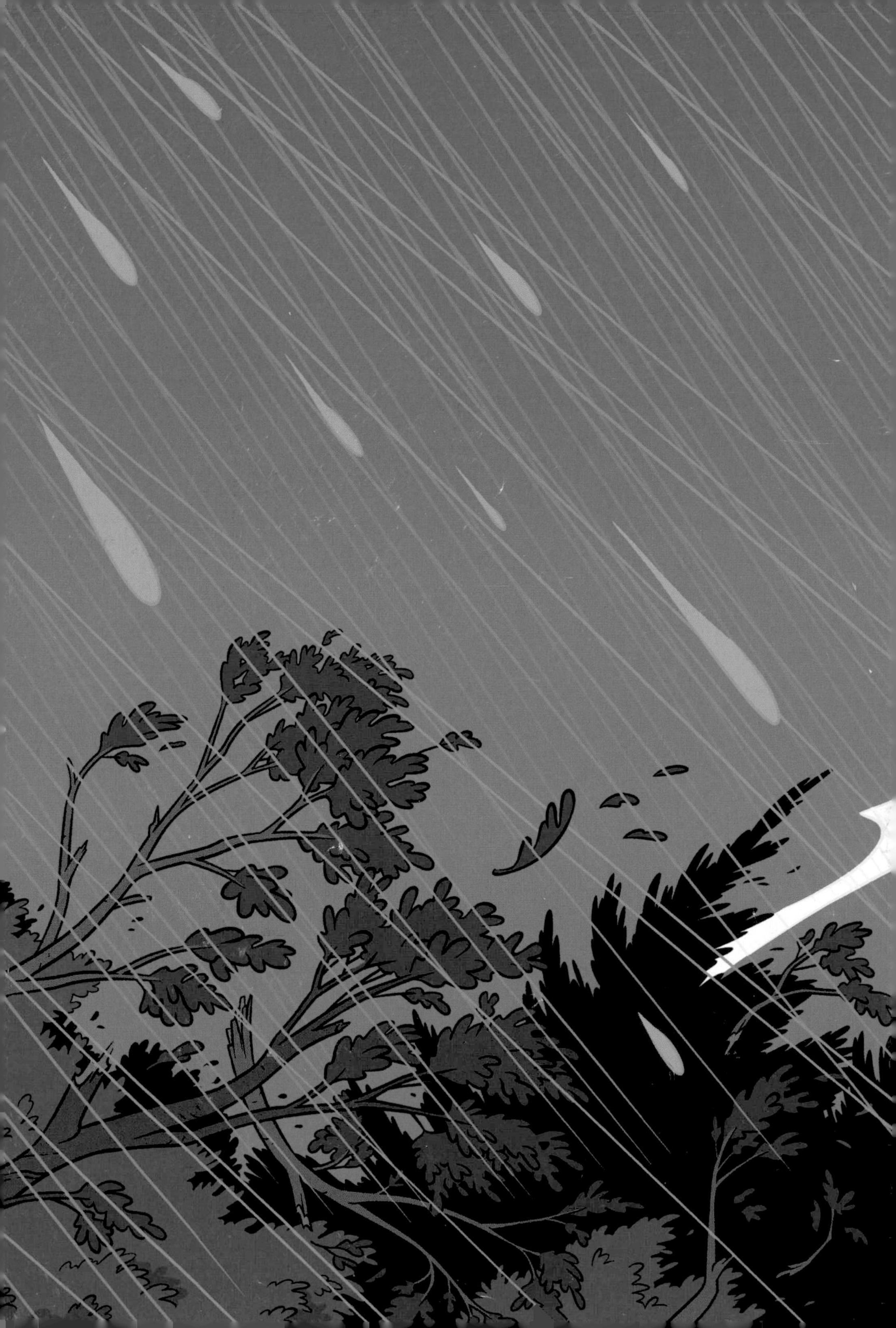

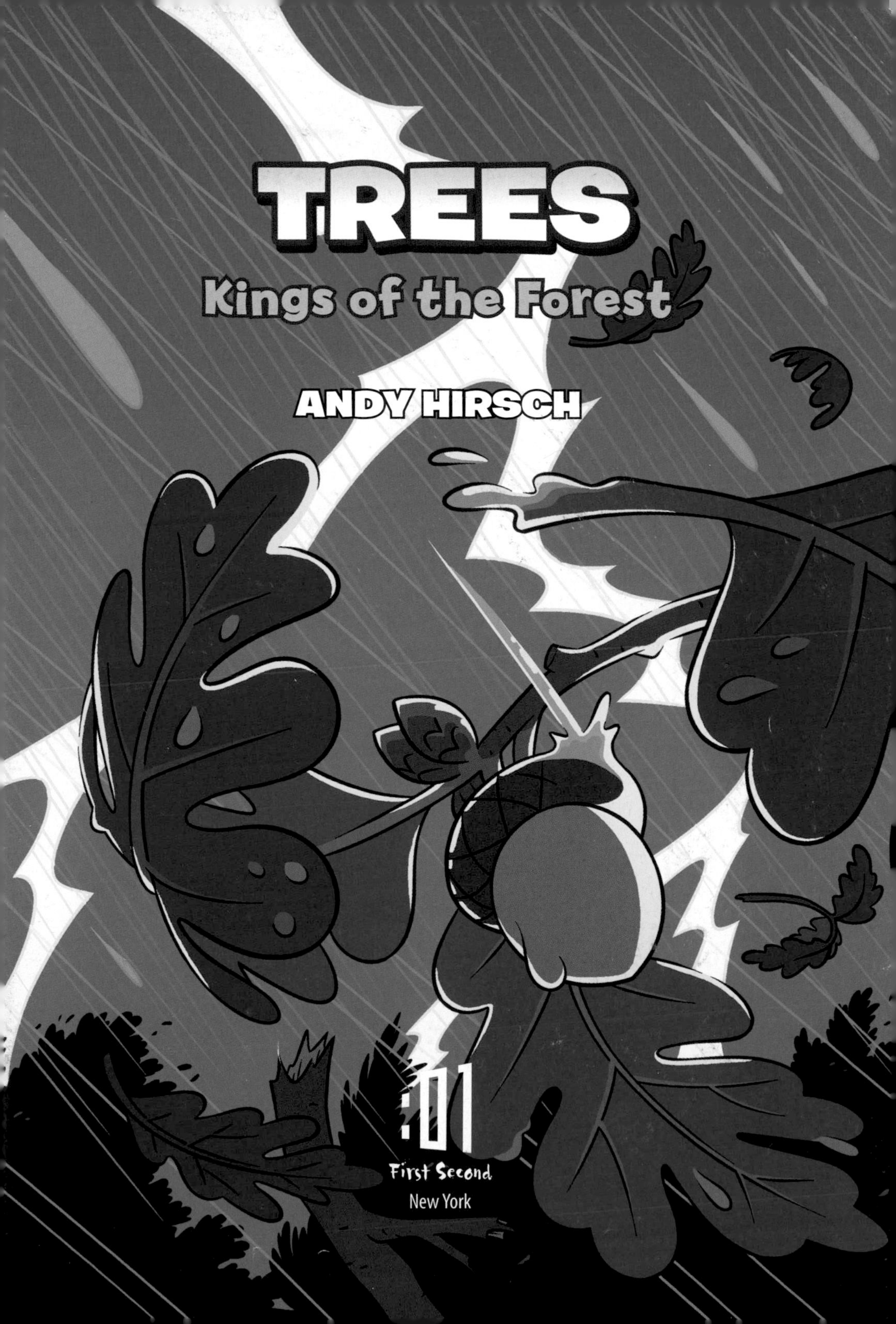

TREES

Kings of the Forest

ANDY HIRSCH

:01 First Second
New York

For the tree huggers

First Second

Copyright © 2018 by Andy Hirsch

Drawn in Clip Studio Paint EX. Colored in Adobe Photoshop CC. Lettered with Comicrazy font from Comicraft.

Published by First Second
First Second is an imprint of Roaring Brook Press,
a division of Holtzbrinck Publishing Holdings Limited Partnership
175 Fifth Avenue, New York, NY 10010

Library of Congress Control Number: 2017946156

Paperback ISBN: 978-1-250-14310-5
Hardcover ISBN: 978-1-250-14311-2

Our books may be purchased in bulk for promotional, educational, or business use. Please
contact your local bookseller or the Macmillan Corporate and Premium Sales Department
at (800) 221-7945 ext. 5442 or by e-mail at MacmillanSpecialMarkets@macmillan.com.

FIRST

EDITION

First edition, 2018
Edited by Dave Roman
Book design by John Green
Trees consultant: Lewis J. Feldman

Printed in China by Toppan Leefung Printing Ltd., Dongguan City, Guangdong Province
Paperback: 10 9 8 7 6 5 4 3 2 1
Hardcover: 10 9 8 7 6 5 4 3 2 1

Whan most people think of trees, they don't picture a lot of action. Trees seem to be stuck in place, unaware of what's happening around them and unable to do much about it. This impression is completely wrong!

Even though plants have no eyes, they are very aware of the amount of light and the colors around them. They grow in the direction of more light and can tell the difference between green plants and other objects, like rocks. They can also anticipate when they are about to be shaded before it actually happens!

Even though plants have no mouths or tongues, they grow more roots in the places where soil contains the nutrients they want. And they can produce chemicals that make them more efficient at taking up those nutrients.

Even though plants have no noses, they can sense chemicals in the air that tell them when their neighbors are being attacked or eaten. They can then respond by ramping up their own defenses.

Even though plants have no ears, they can sense vibrations caused by feeding insects and then protect themselves.

Even though plants have no hands, they can interact with objects that they contact. This lets them grow around rocks or attach to useful structures if they are climbing vines.

All of these cool and sophisticated behaviors happen even though they have no brain.

This comic introduces you to some of the amazing things that trees can do. When I was a child, I first became fascinated with trees by making collections of leaves in the fall. I collected the most colorful leaves I could find and placed them to dry between pages in a big book. I was always disappointed that it was so hard to find perfect leaves—they all seemed to have a few holes in them. It made me wonder why almost all leaves had bites taken out of them but very few were eaten completely. Only years later, when I was officially working as a scientist, did I get interested in this observation again. The answer to this riddle seems to be that when an insect takes a bite out of a leaf, the tree responds by changing that leaf in many ways. Some of these changes make the leaf a less desirable meal for that insect. So the insect moves to another leaf that hasn't had a bite taken out of it yet. By the end of the season, almost every leaf has a bite or two missing. These changes are similar to an immune response by the tree.

There are still many things that we don't know about trees. For example, we don't know much about the language that trees use to communicate with one another. How do they understand that an insect is attacking their neighbor? Do all trees use a similar language? How do plants perceive chemicals in the air or vibrations in their shoots? How do they make decisions when there are conflicting signals?

Anyone can think like a scientist. It is not about knowing all the facts but more about being curious and allowing yourself to wonder, less about being an expert or a true believer and more about being open to the evidence. Your observations may provide us with the scientific breakthroughs of the future!

—Richard Karban,
professor of entomology, member of the
Center for Population Biology at the University of California, Davis,
and co-author of *How to Do Ecology: A Concise Handbook*

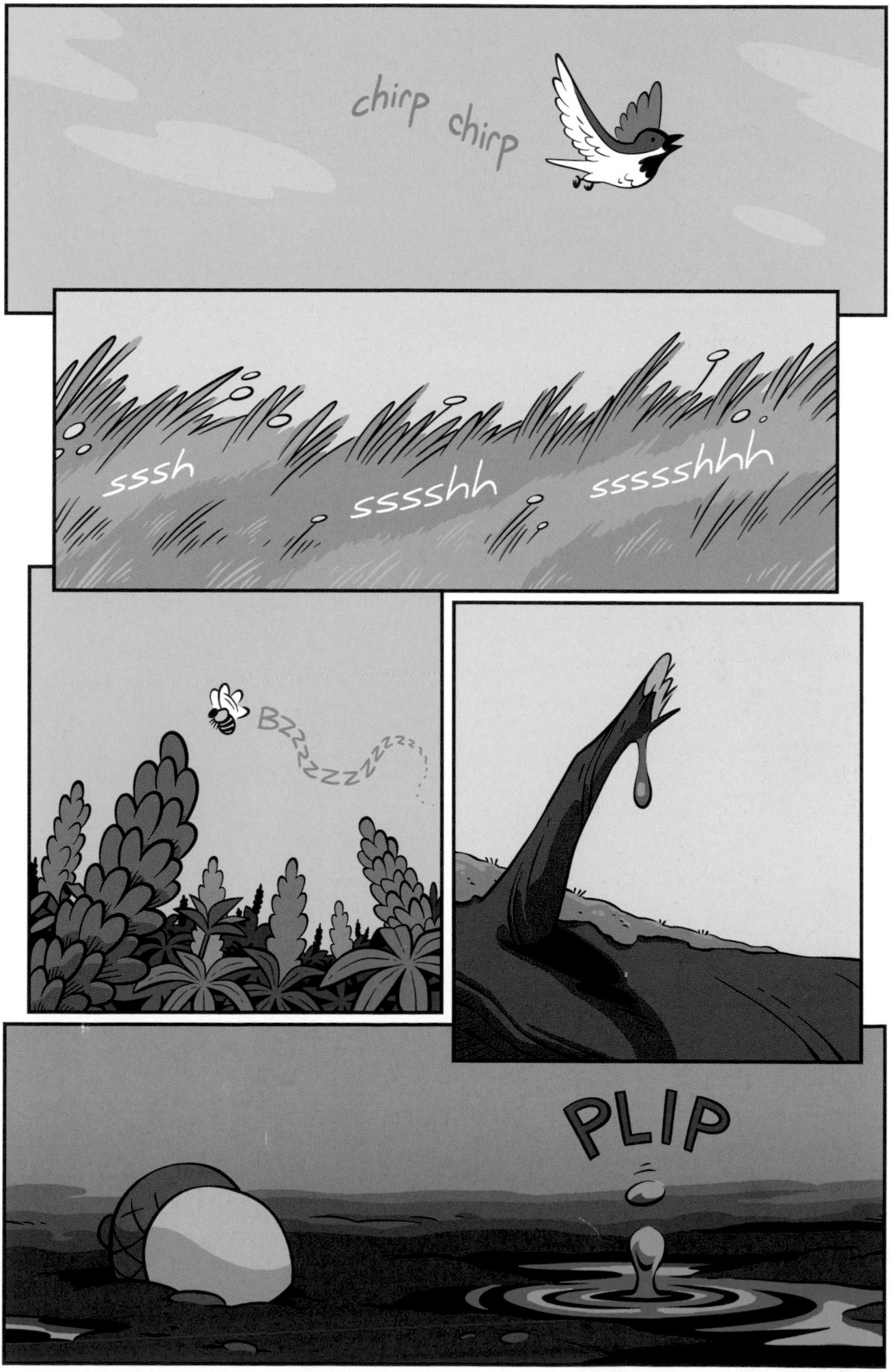
chirp chirp
sssh
sssshh
ssssshhh
Bzzzzzzzzzzzz
PLIP

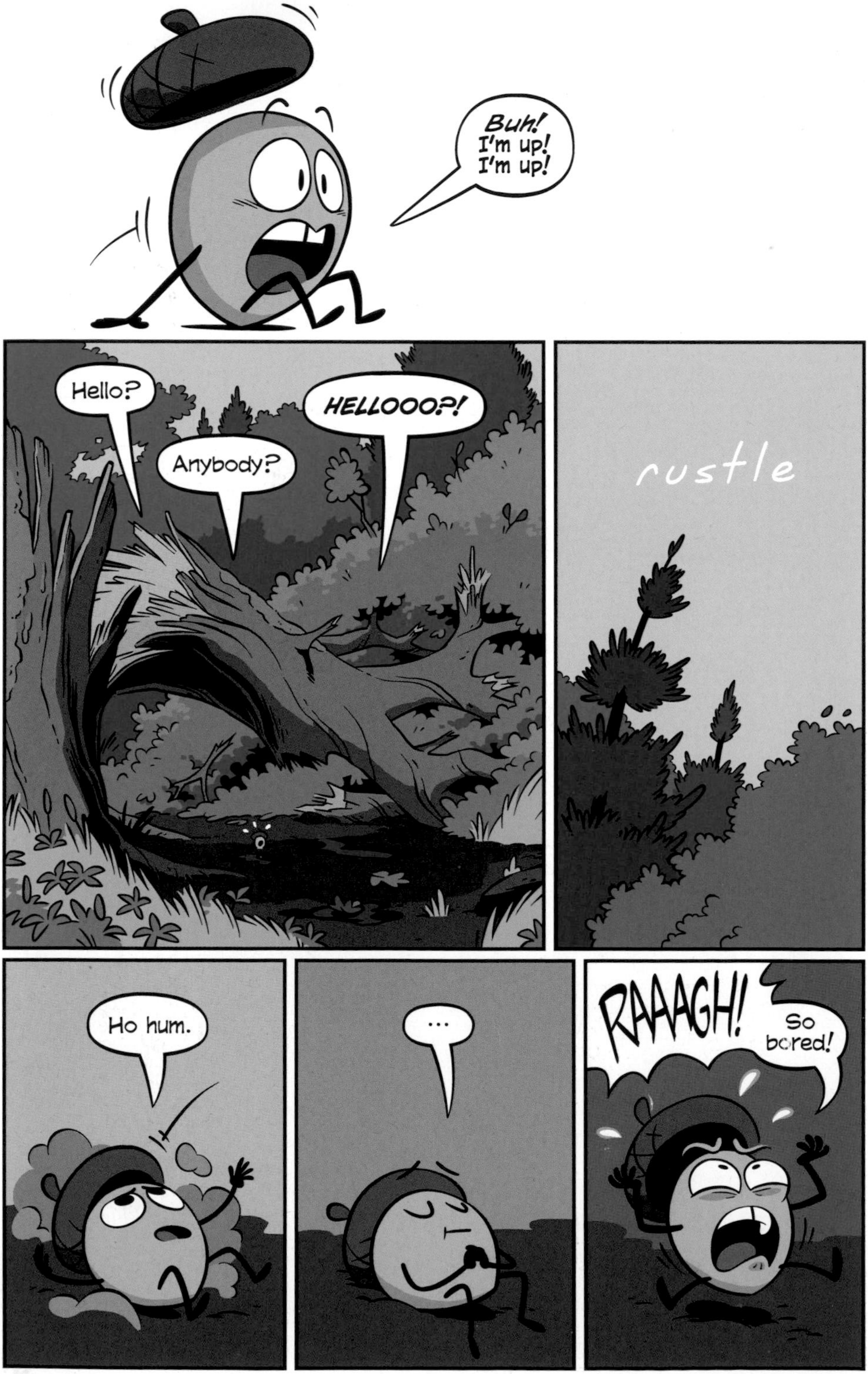
Buh! I'm up! I'm up!
Hello?
Anybody?
HELLOOO?!
rustle
Ho hum.
...
RAAAGH!
So bored!

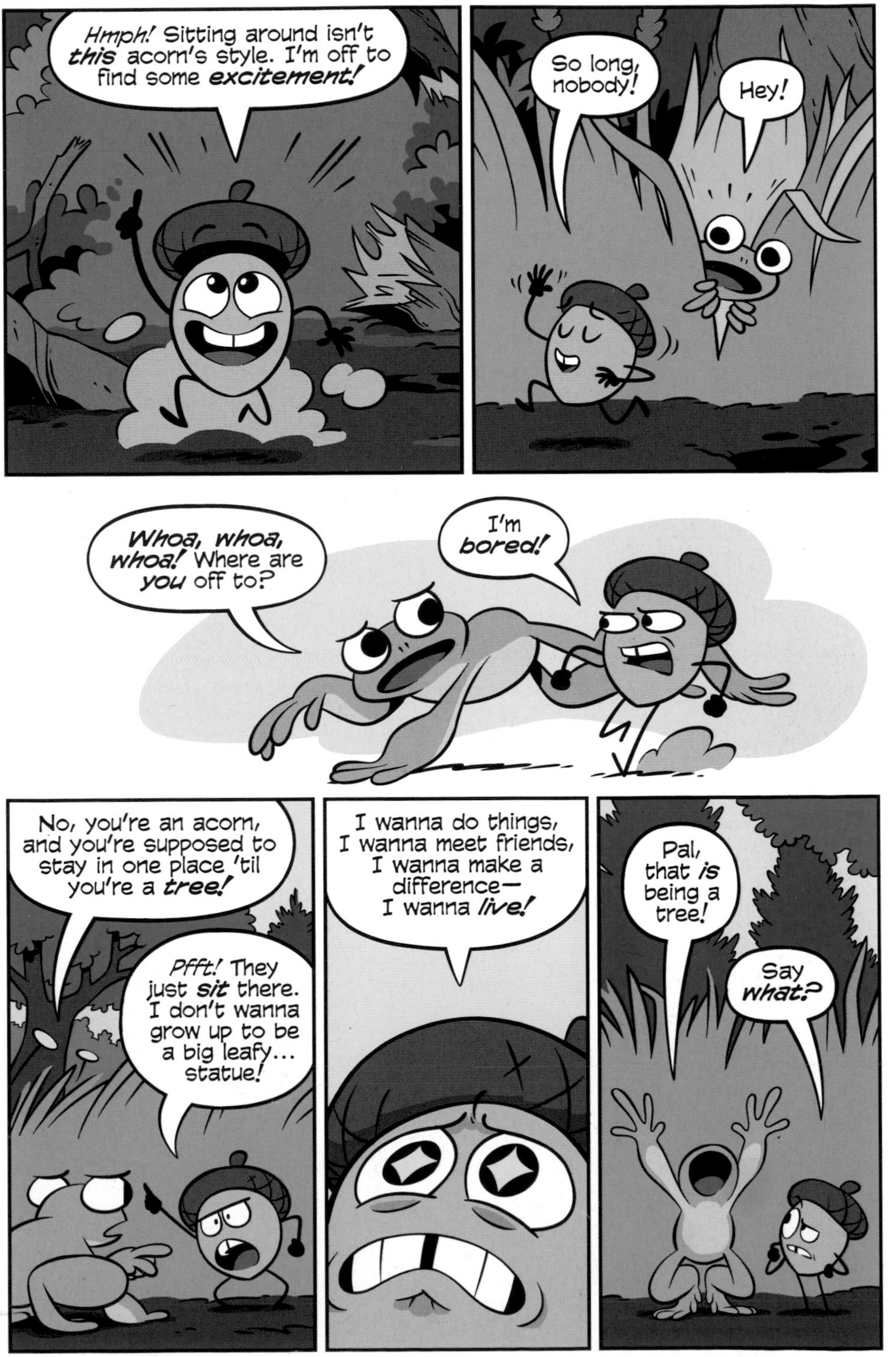

Hmph! Sitting around isn't ***this*** acorn's style. I'm off to find some ***excitement!***
So long, nobody!
Hey!
Whoa, whoa, whoa! Where are ***you*** off to?
I'm ***bored!***
No, you're an acorn, and you're supposed to stay in one place 'til you're a ***tree!***
Pfft! They just ***sit*** there. I don't wanna grow up to be a big leafy... statue!
I wanna do things, I wanna meet friends, I wanna make a difference— I wanna ***live!***
Pal, that *is* being a tree!
Say ***what?***

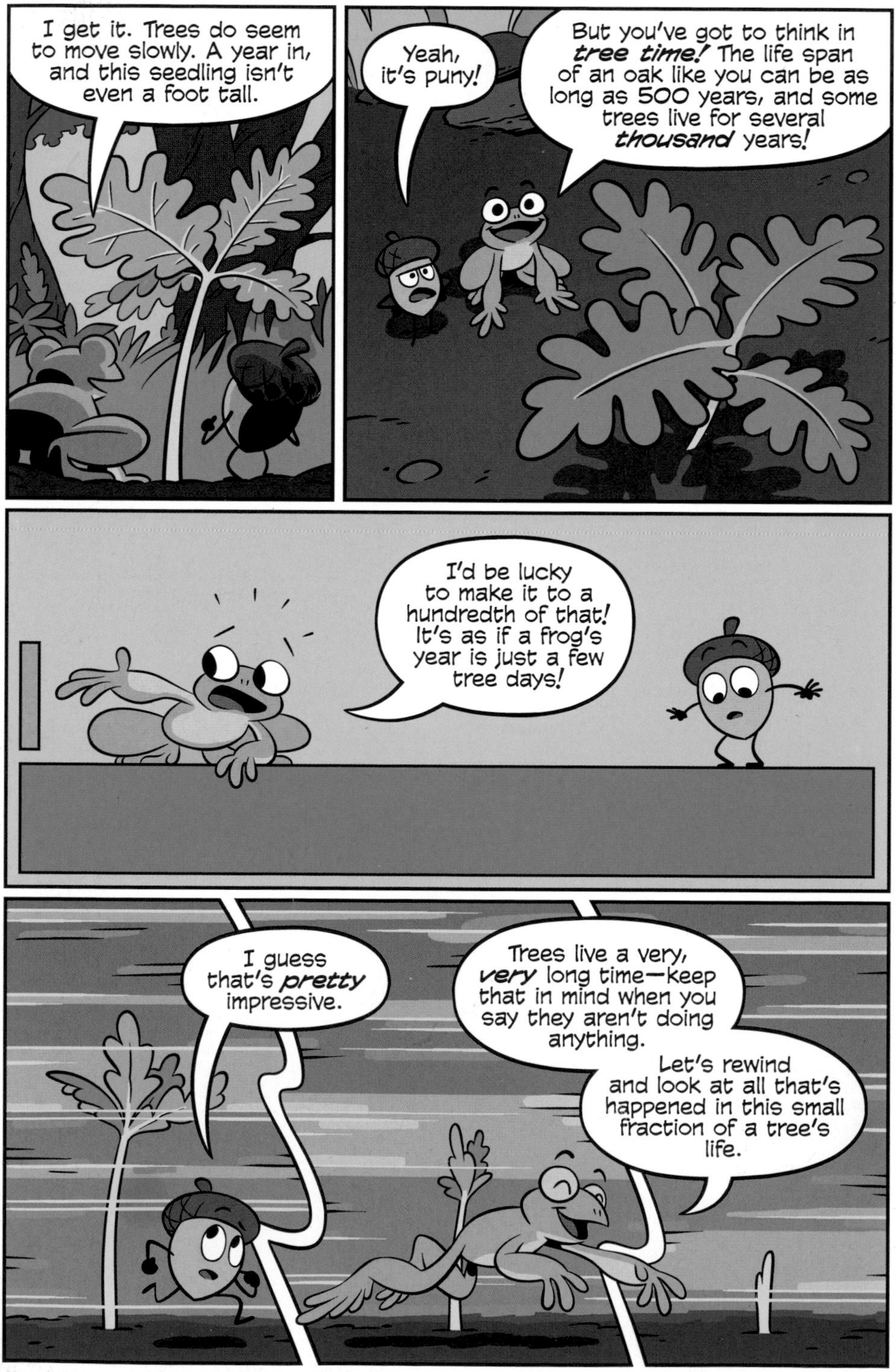
I get it. Trees do seem to move slowly. A year in, and this seedling isn't even a foot tall.
Yeah, it's puny!
But you've got to think in *tree time!* The life span of an oak like you can be as long as 500 years, and some trees live for several *thousand* years!
I'd be lucky to make it to a hundredth of that! It's as if a frog's year is just a few tree days!
I guess that's *pretty* impressive.
Trees live a very, *very* long time—keep that in mind when you say they aren't doing anything.
Let's rewind and look at all that's happened in this small fraction of a tree's life.

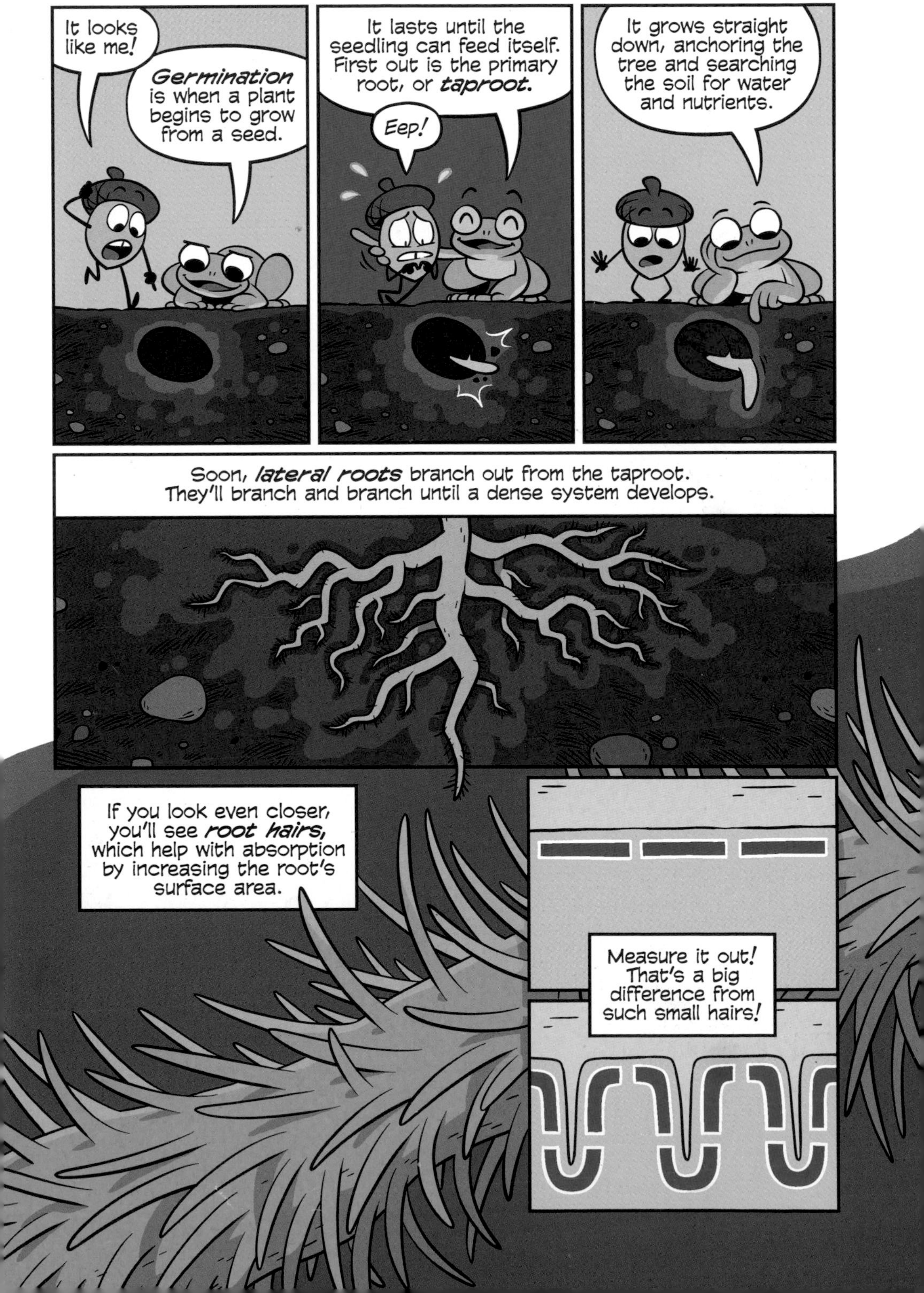
It looks like me!
Germination is when a plant begins to grow from a seed.
It lasts until the seedling can feed itself. First out is the primary root, or taproot.
Eep!
It grows straight down, anchoring the tree and searching the soil for water and nutrients.
Soon, lateral roots branch out from the taproot. They'll branch and branch until a dense system develops.
If you look even closer, you'll see root hairs, which help with absorption by increasing the root's surface area.
Measure it out! That's a big difference from such small hairs!

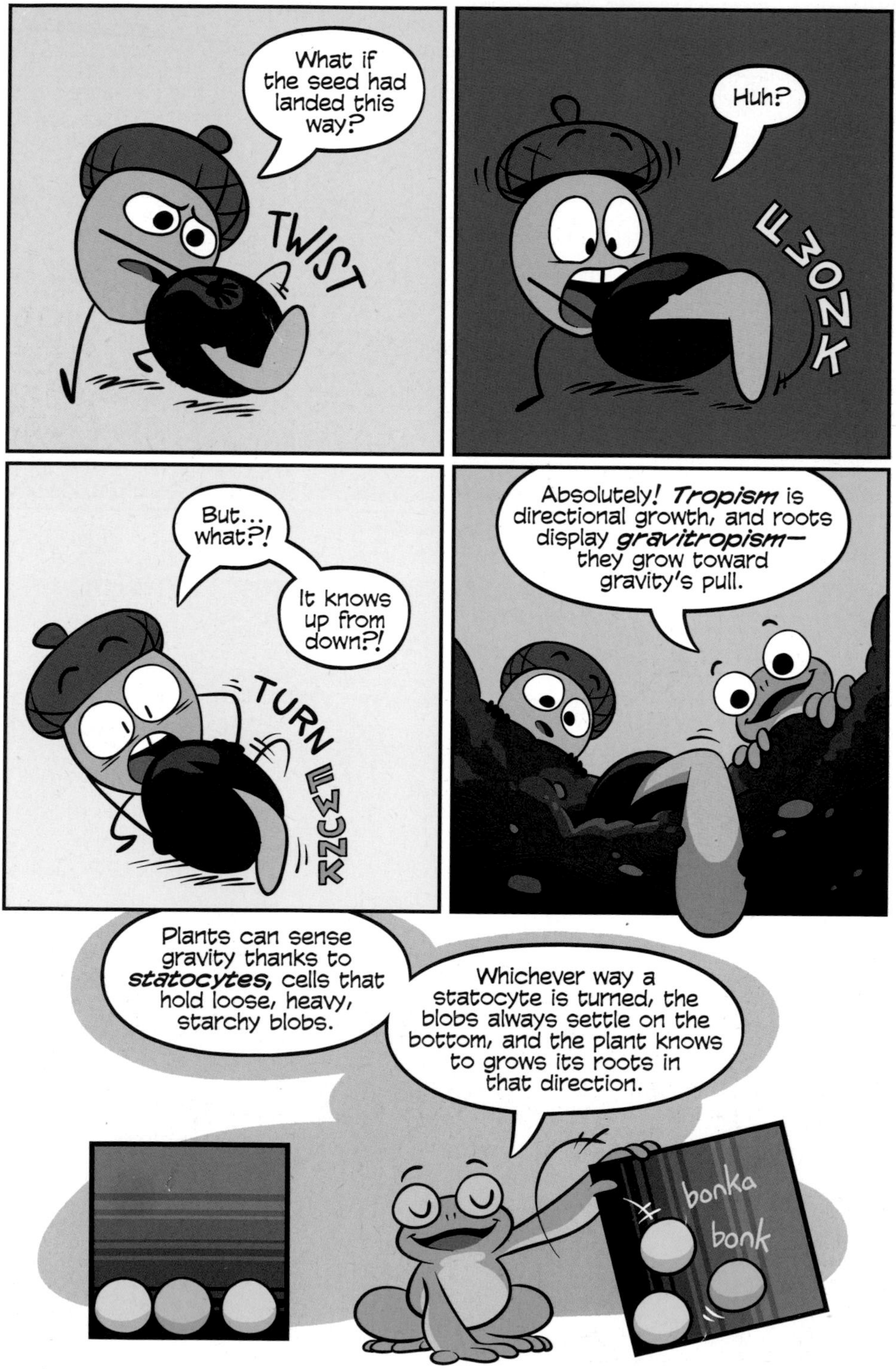
What if the seed had landed this way?
TWIST
Huh?
FWONK
But... what?!
It knows up from down?!
TURN
FWUNK
Absolutely! *Tropism* is directional growth, and roots display *gravitropism*— they grow toward gravity's pull.
Plants can sense gravity thanks to *statocytes,* cells that hold loose, heavy, starchy blobs.
Whichever way a statocyte is turned, the blobs always settle on the bottom, and the plant knows to grows its roots in that direction.
bonka
bonk

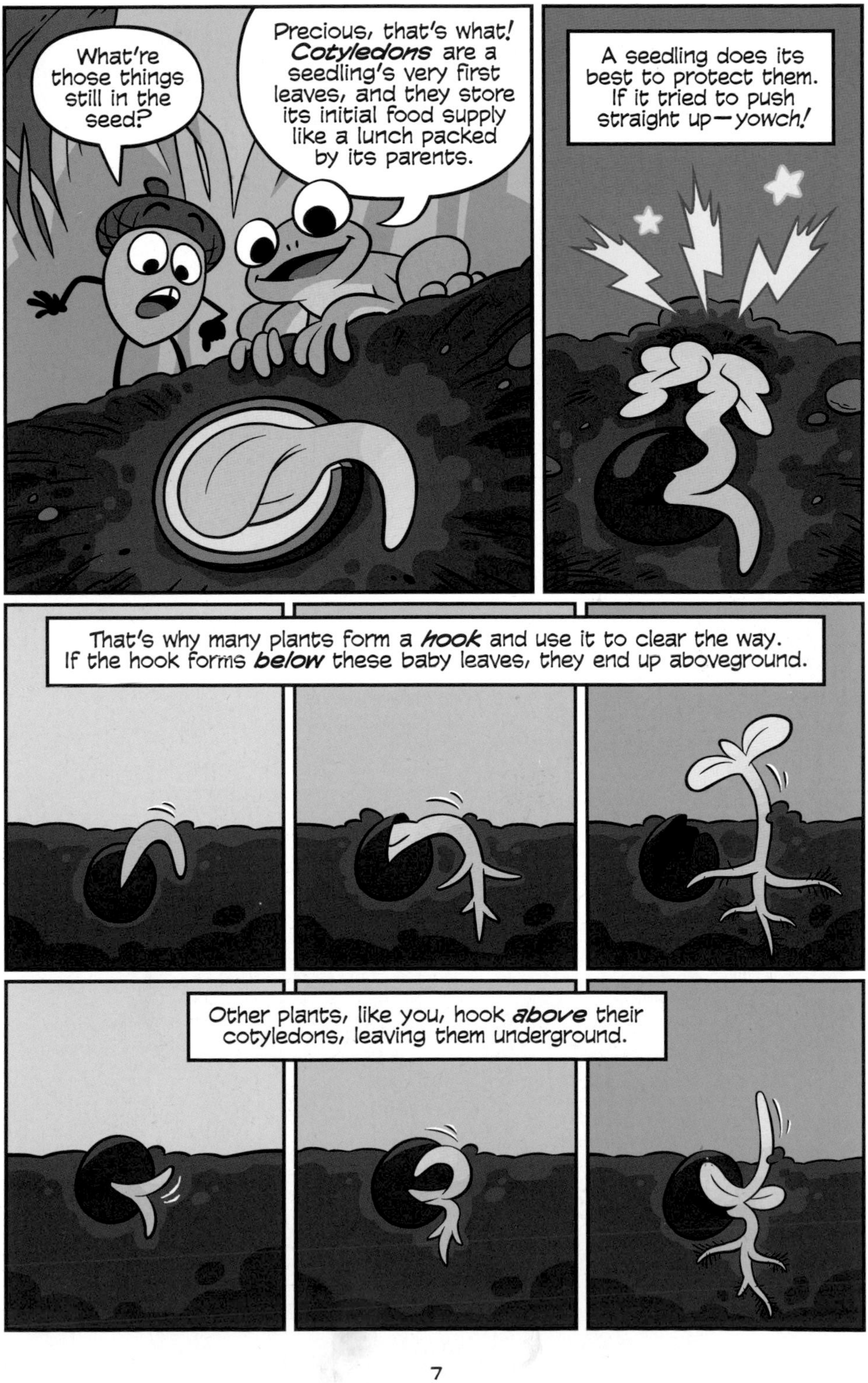
What're those things still in the seed?
Precious, that's what! *Cotyledons* are a seedling's very first leaves, and they store its initial food supply like a lunch packed by its parents.
A seedling does its best to protect them. If it tried to push straight up—*yowch!*
That's why many plants form a ***hook*** and use it to clear the way. If the hook forms ***below*** these baby leaves, they end up aboveground.
Other plants, like you, hook ***above*** their cotyledons, leaving them underground.

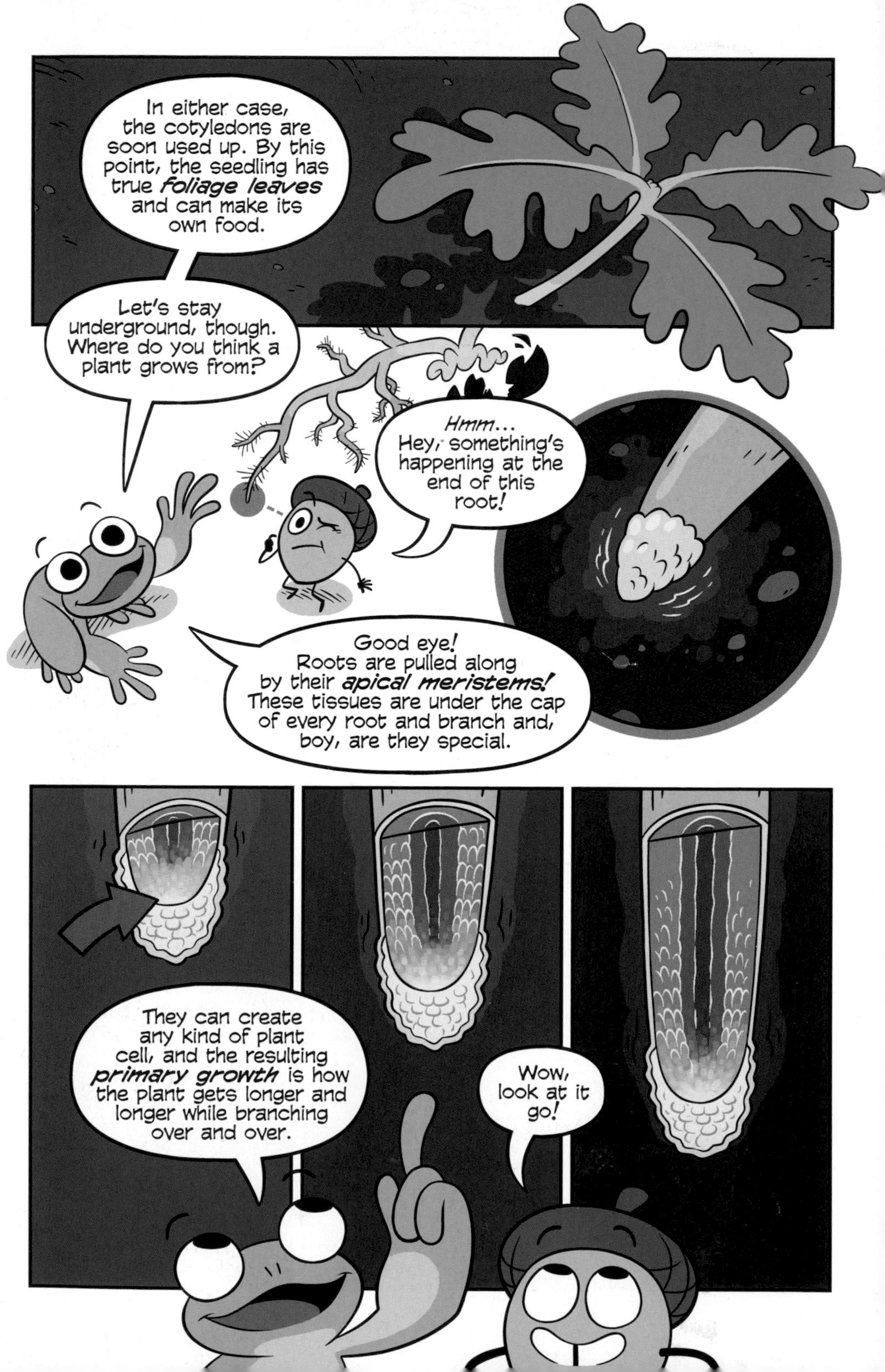

In either case, the cotyledons are soon used up. By this point, the seedling has true *foliage leaves* and can make its own food.
Let's stay underground, though. Where do you think a plant grows from?
Hmm... Hey, something's happening at the end of this root!
Good eye! Roots are pulled along by their *apical meristems!* These tissues are under the cap of every root and branch and, boy, are they special.
They can create any kind of plant cell, and the resulting *primary growth* is how the plant gets longer and longer while branching over and over.
Wow, look at it go!

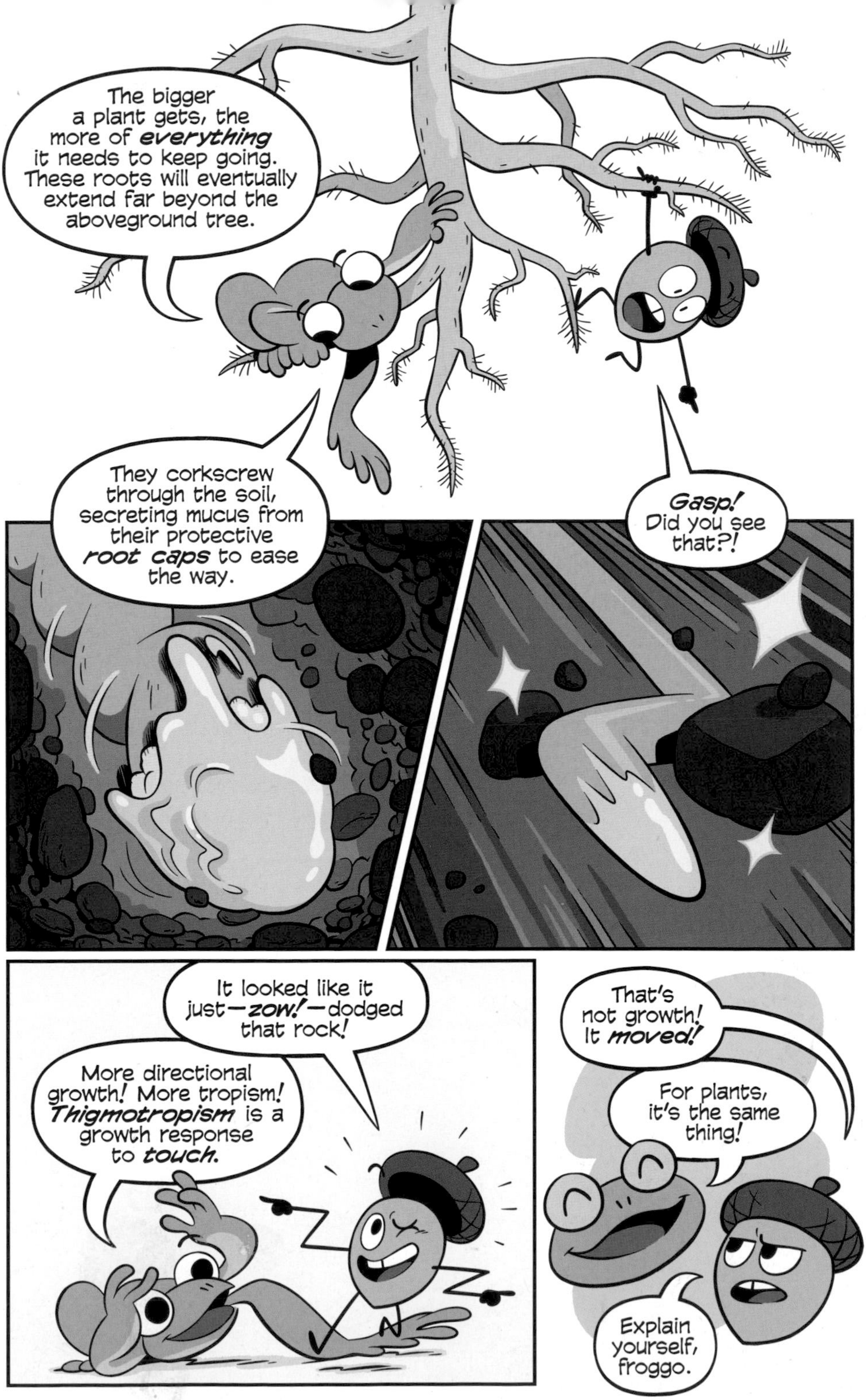
The bigger a plant gets, the more of *everything* it needs to keep going. These roots will eventually extend far beyond the aboveground tree.
They corkscrew through the soil, secreting mucus from their protective *root caps* to ease the way.
Gasp! Did you see that?!
It looked like it just—*zow!*—dodged that rock!
More directional growth! More tropism! *Thigmotropism* is a growth response to *touch.*
That's not growth! It *moved!*
For plants, it's the same thing!
Explain yourself, froggo.

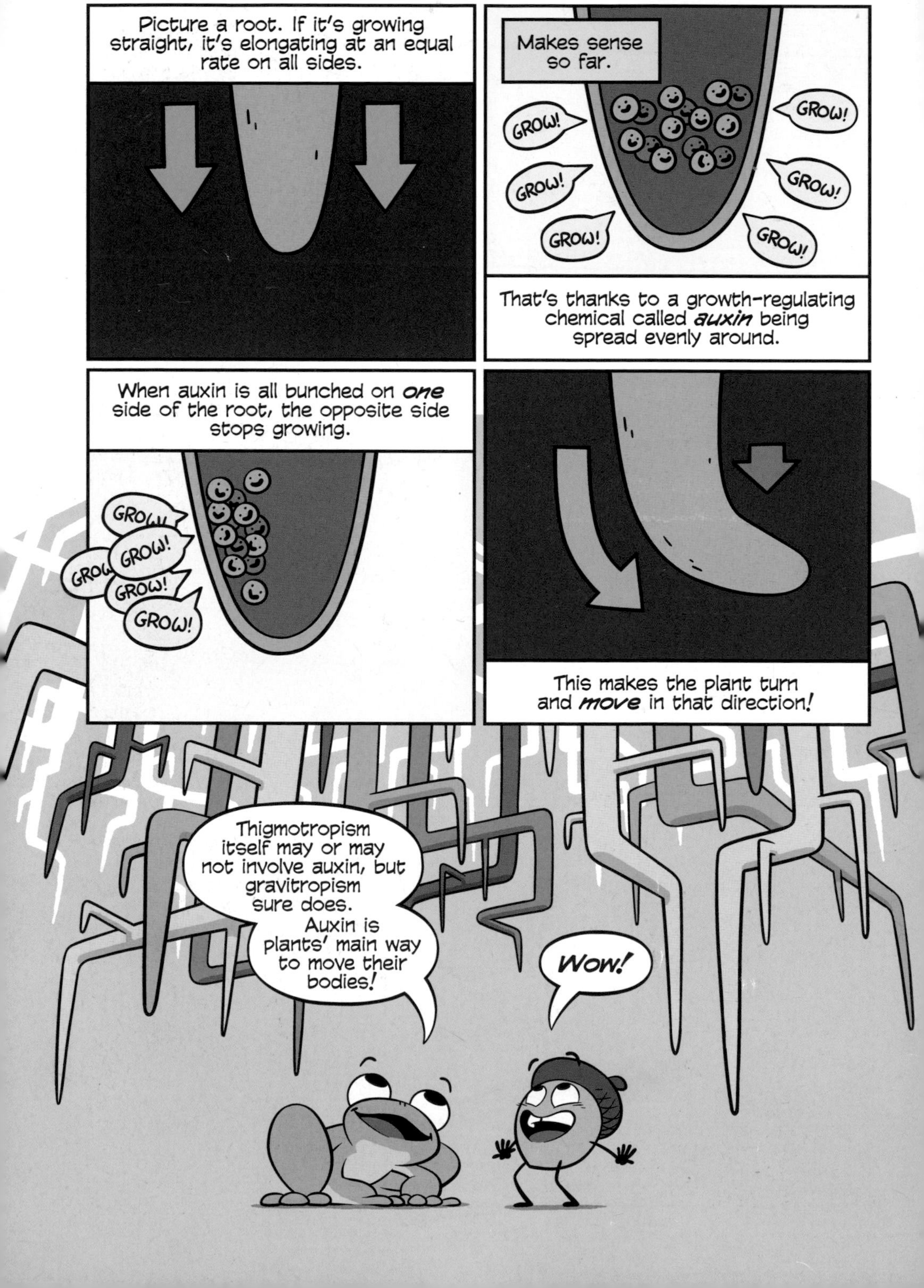
Picture a root. If it's growing straight, it's elongating at an equal rate on all sides.
Makes sense so far.
GROW!
GROW!
GROW!
GROW!
GROW!
GROW!
That's thanks to a growth-regulating chemical called *auxin* being spread evenly around.
When auxin is all bunched on *one* side of the root, the opposite side stops growing.
GROW!
GROW!
GROW!
GROW!
This makes the plant turn and *move* in that direction!
Thigmotropism itself may or may not involve auxin, but gravitropism sure does.
Auxin is plants' main way to move their bodies!
WOW!

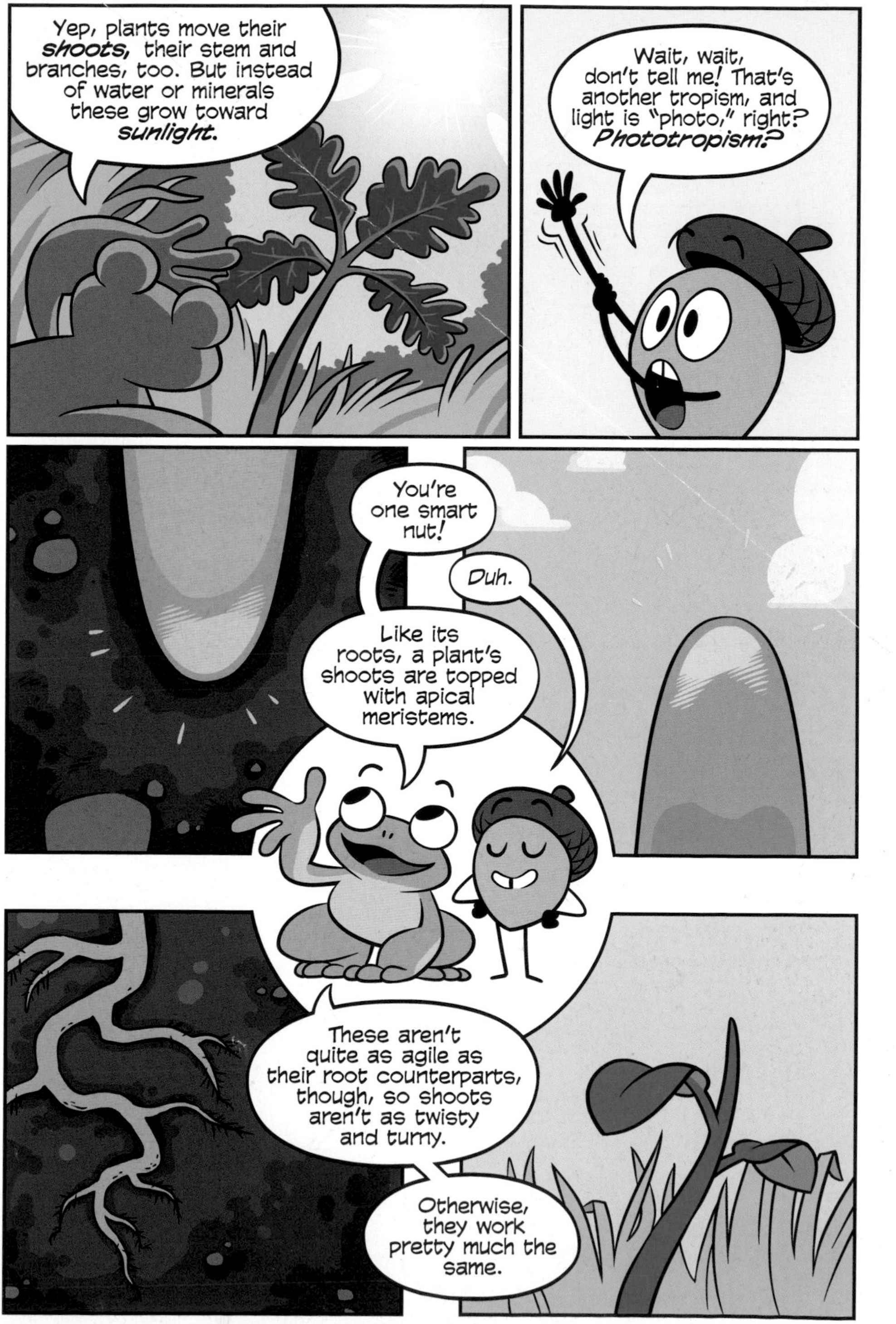

Yep, plants move their ***shoots,*** their stem and branches, too. But instead of water or minerals these grow toward ***sunlight.***
Wait, wait, don't tell me! That's another tropism, and light is "photo," right? ***Phototropism?***
You're one smart nut!
Duh.
Like its roots, a plant's shoots are topped with apical meristems.
These aren't quite as agile as their root counterparts, though, so shoots aren't as twisty and turny.
Otherwise, they work pretty much the same.

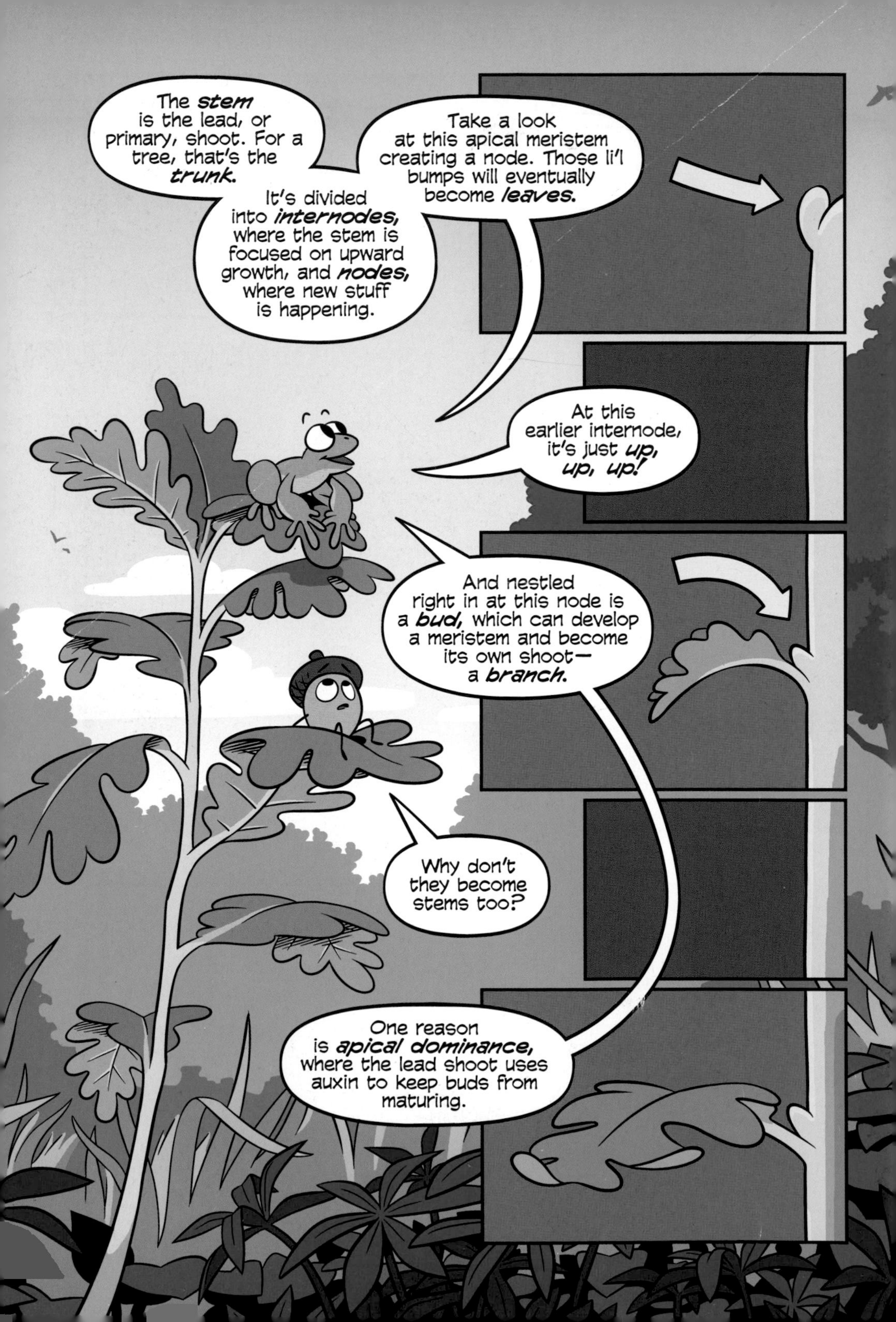
The *stem* is the lead, or primary, shoot. For a tree, that's the *trunk*.
It's divided into *internodes,* where the stem is focused on upward growth, and *nodes,* where new stuff is happening.
Take a look at this apical meristem creating a node. Those li'l bumps will eventually become *leaves.*
At this earlier internode, it's just *up, up, up!*
And nestled right in at this node is a *bud,* which can develop a meristem and become its own shoot— a *branch.*
Why don't they become stems too?
One reason is *apical dominance,* where the lead shoot uses auxin to keep buds from maturing.

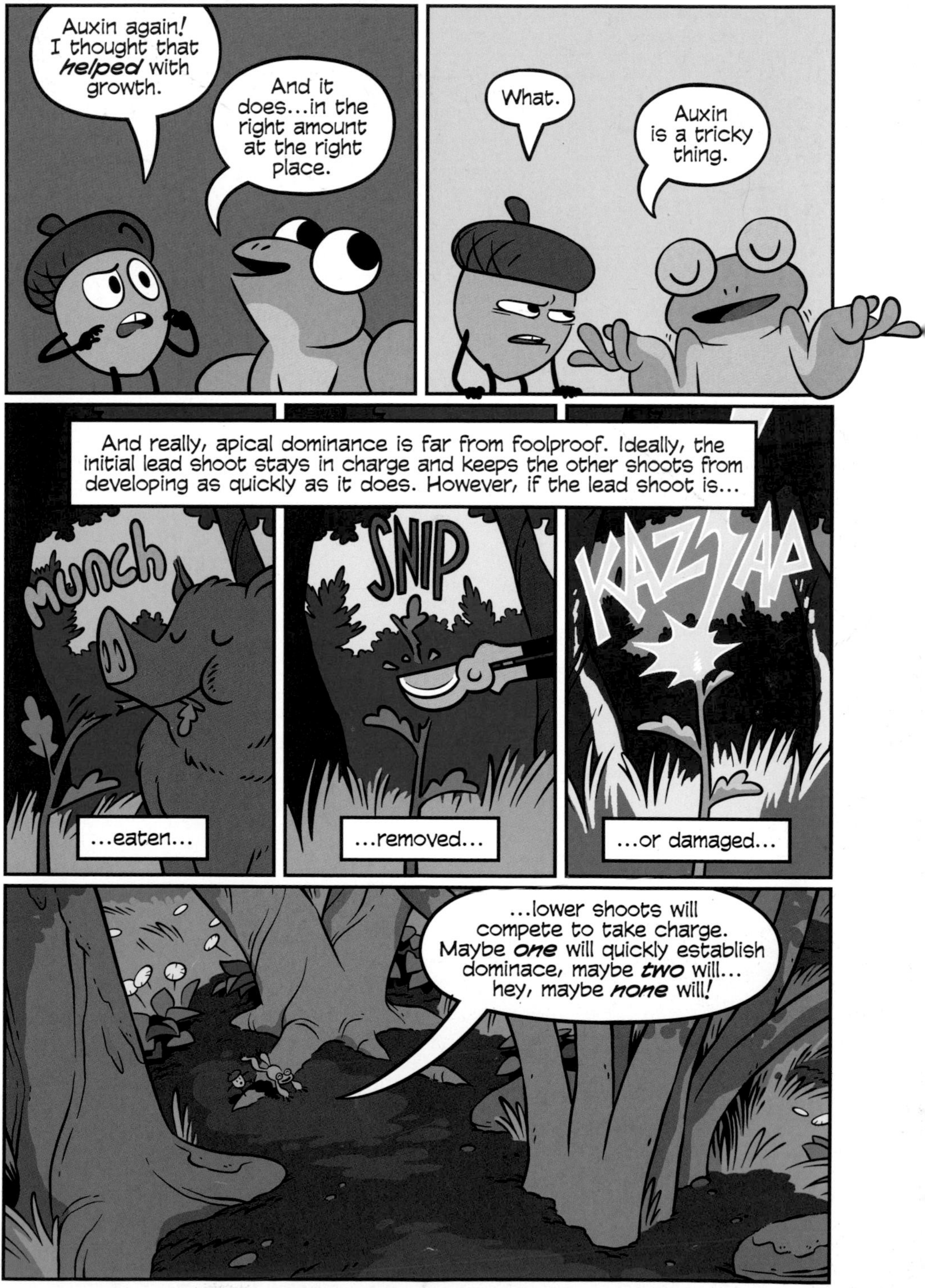
Auxin again! I thought that *helped* with growth.
And it does...in the right amount at the right place.
What.
Auxin is a tricky thing.
And really, apical dominance is far from foolproof. Ideally, the initial lead shoot stays in charge and keeps the other shoots from developing as quickly as it does. However, if the lead shoot is...
MUNCH
...eaten...
SNIP
...removed...
KAZ'AP
...or damaged...
...lower shoots will compete to take charge. Maybe *one* will quickly establish dominace, maybe *two* will... hey, maybe *none* will!

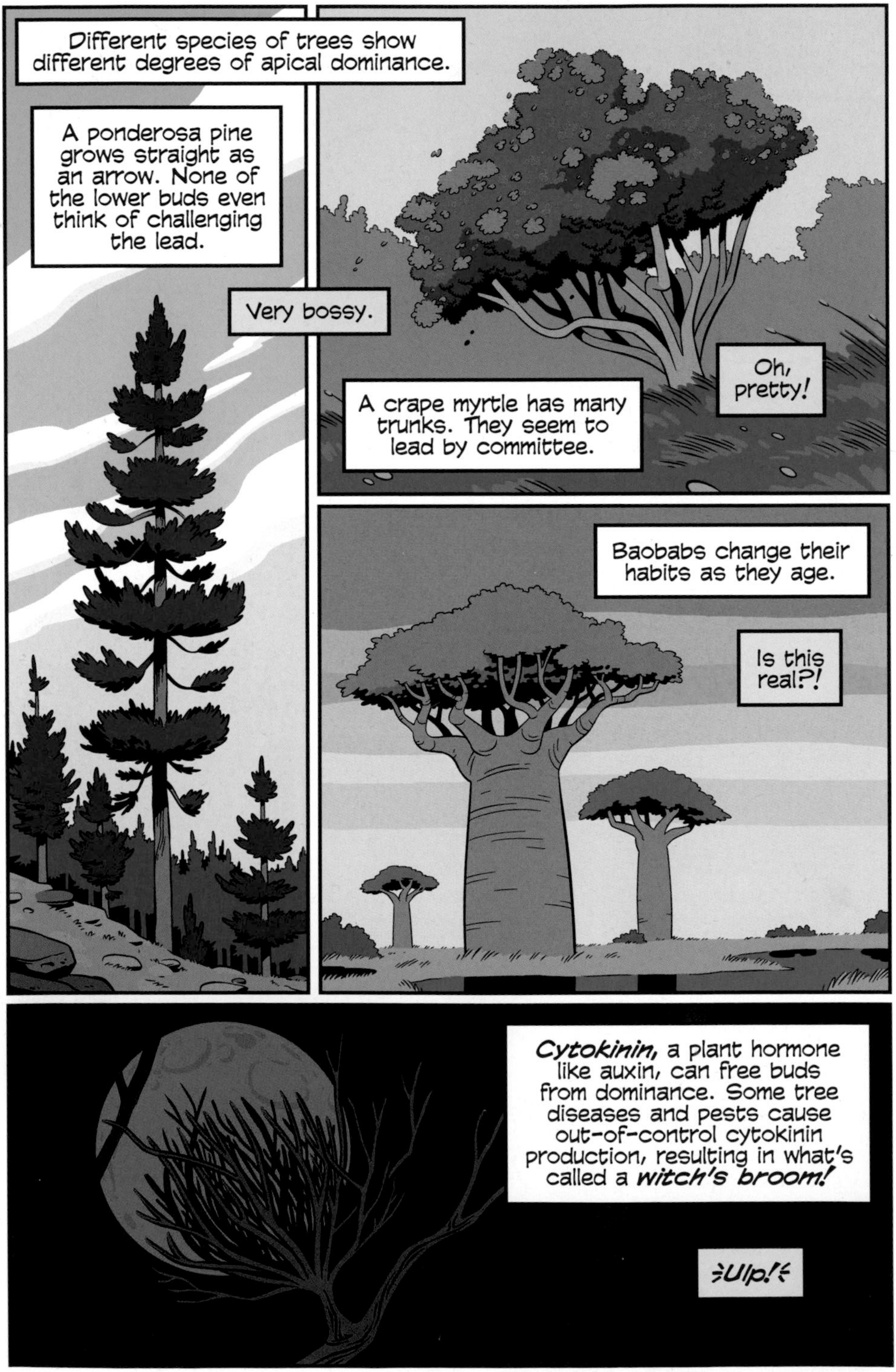
Different species of trees show different degrees of apical dominance.
A ponderosa pine grows straight as an arrow. None of the lower buds even think of challenging the lead.
Very bossy.
A crape myrtle has many trunks. They seem to lead by committee.
Oh, pretty!
Baobabs change their habits as they age.
Is this real?!
Cytokinin, a plant hormone like auxin, can free buds from dominance. Some tree diseases and pests cause out-of-control cytokinin production, resulting in what's called a *witch's broom!*
Ulp!

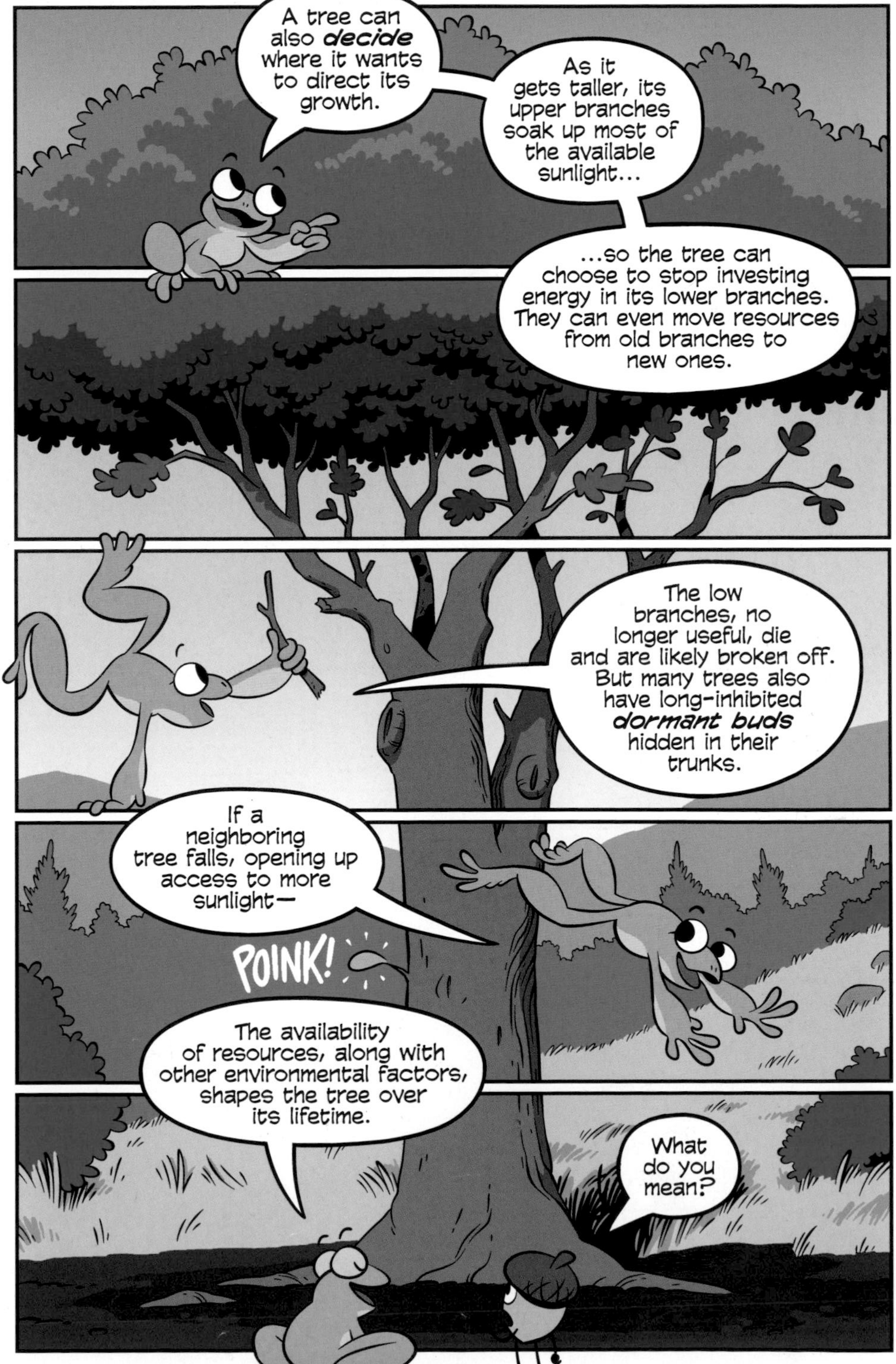

A tree can also ***decide*** where it wants to direct its growth.
As it gets taller, its upper branches soak up most of the available sunlight...
...so the tree can choose to stop investing energy in its lower branches. They can even move resources from old branches to new ones.
The low branches, no longer useful, die and are likely broken off. But many trees also have long-inhibited ***dormant buds*** hidden in their trunks.
If a neighboring tree falls, opening up access to more sunlight—
POINK!
The availability of resources, along with other environmental factors, shapes the tree over its lifetime.
What do you mean?

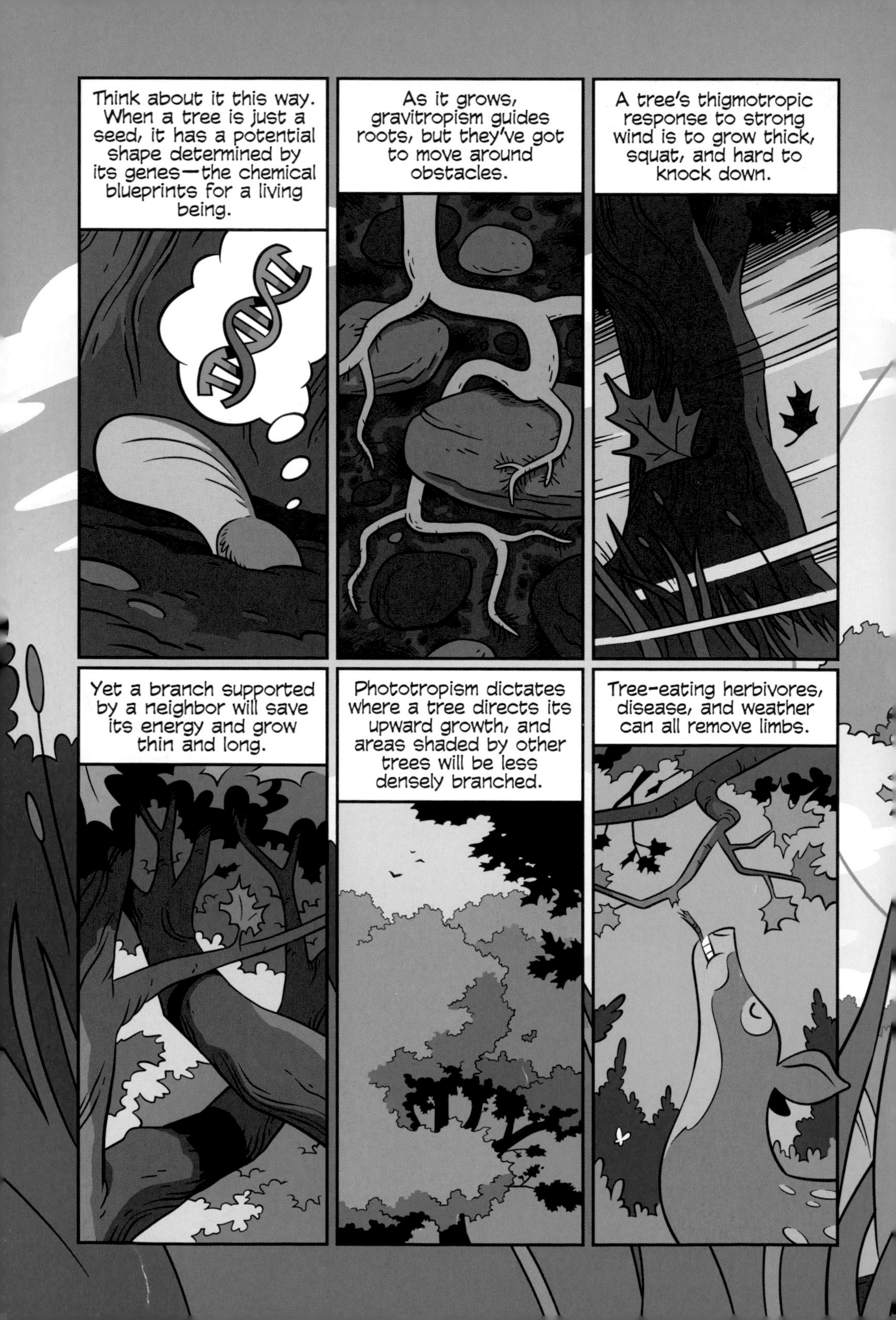
Think about it this way. When a tree is just a seed, it has a potential shape determined by its genes—the chemical blueprints for a living being.
As it grows, gravitropism guides roots, but they've got to move around obstacles.
A tree's thigmotropic response to strong wind is to grow thick, squat, and hard to knock down.
Yet a branch supported by a neighbor will save its energy and grow thin and long.
Phototropism dictates where a tree directs its upward growth, and areas shaded by other trees will be less densely branched.
Tree-eating herbivores, disease, and weather can all remove limbs.

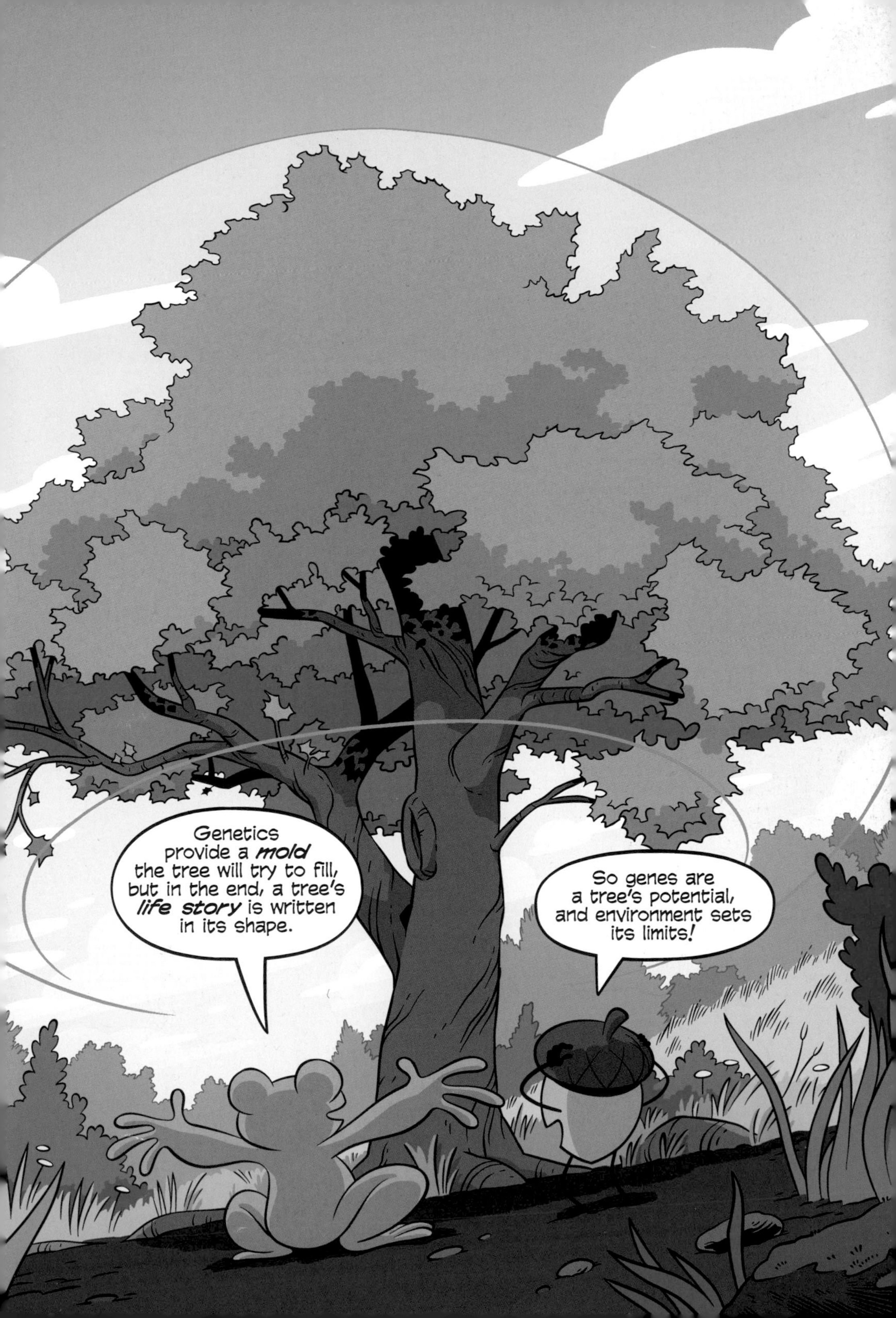
Genetics provide a *mold* the tree will try to fill, but in the end, a tree's *life story* is written in its shape.
So genes are a tree's potential, and environment sets its limits!

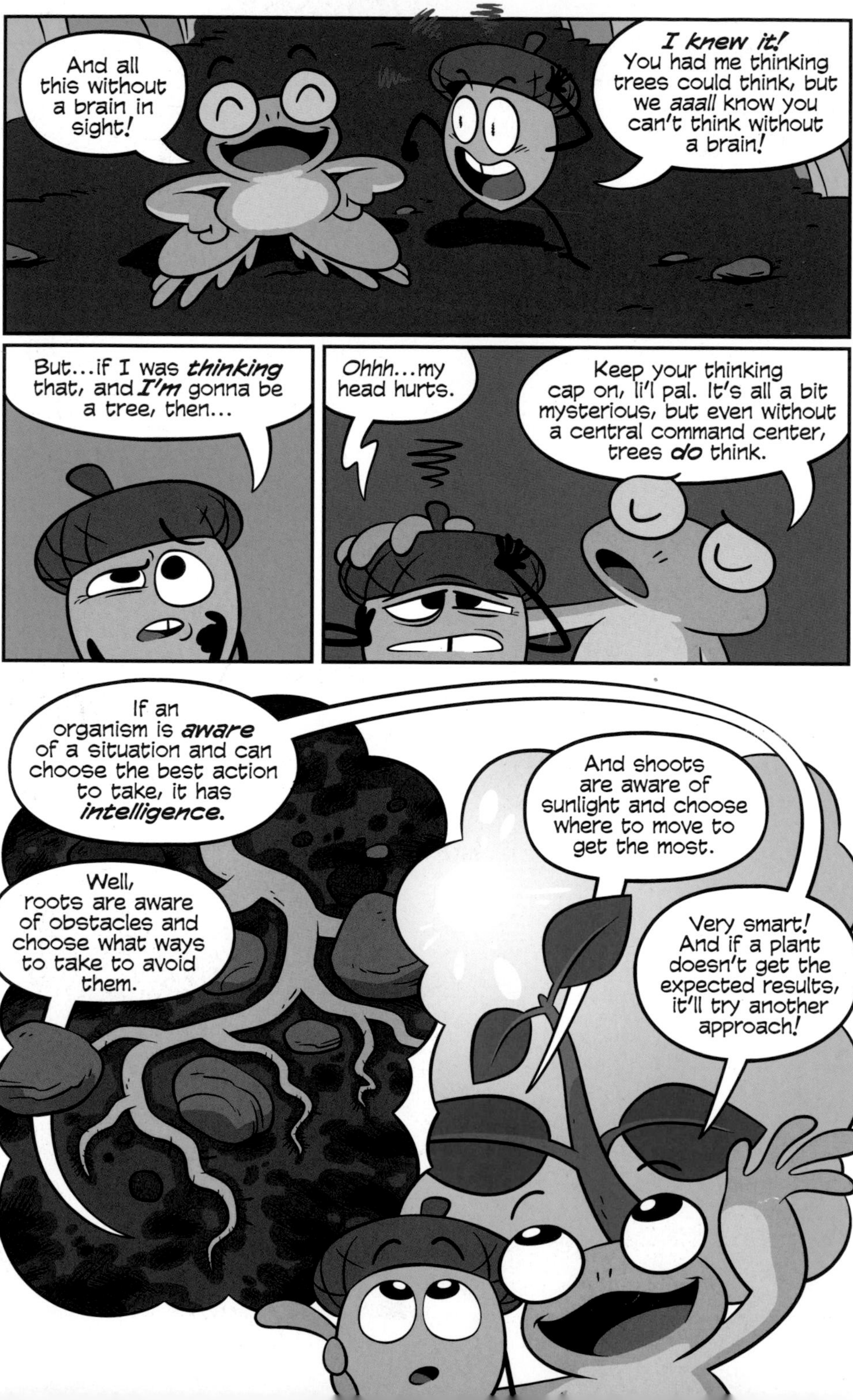
And all this without a brain in sight!
I knew it! You had me thinking trees could think, but we aaall know you can't think without a brain!
But...if I was thinking that, and I'm gonna be a tree, then...
Ohhh...my head hurts.
Keep your thinking cap on, li'l pal. It's all a bit mysterious, but even without a central command center, trees do think.
If an organism is aware of a situation and can choose the best action to take, it has intelligence.
Well, roots are aware of obstacles and choose what ways to take to avoid them.
And shoots are aware of sunlight and choose where to move to get the most.
Very smart! And if a plant doesn't get the expected results, it'll try another approach!

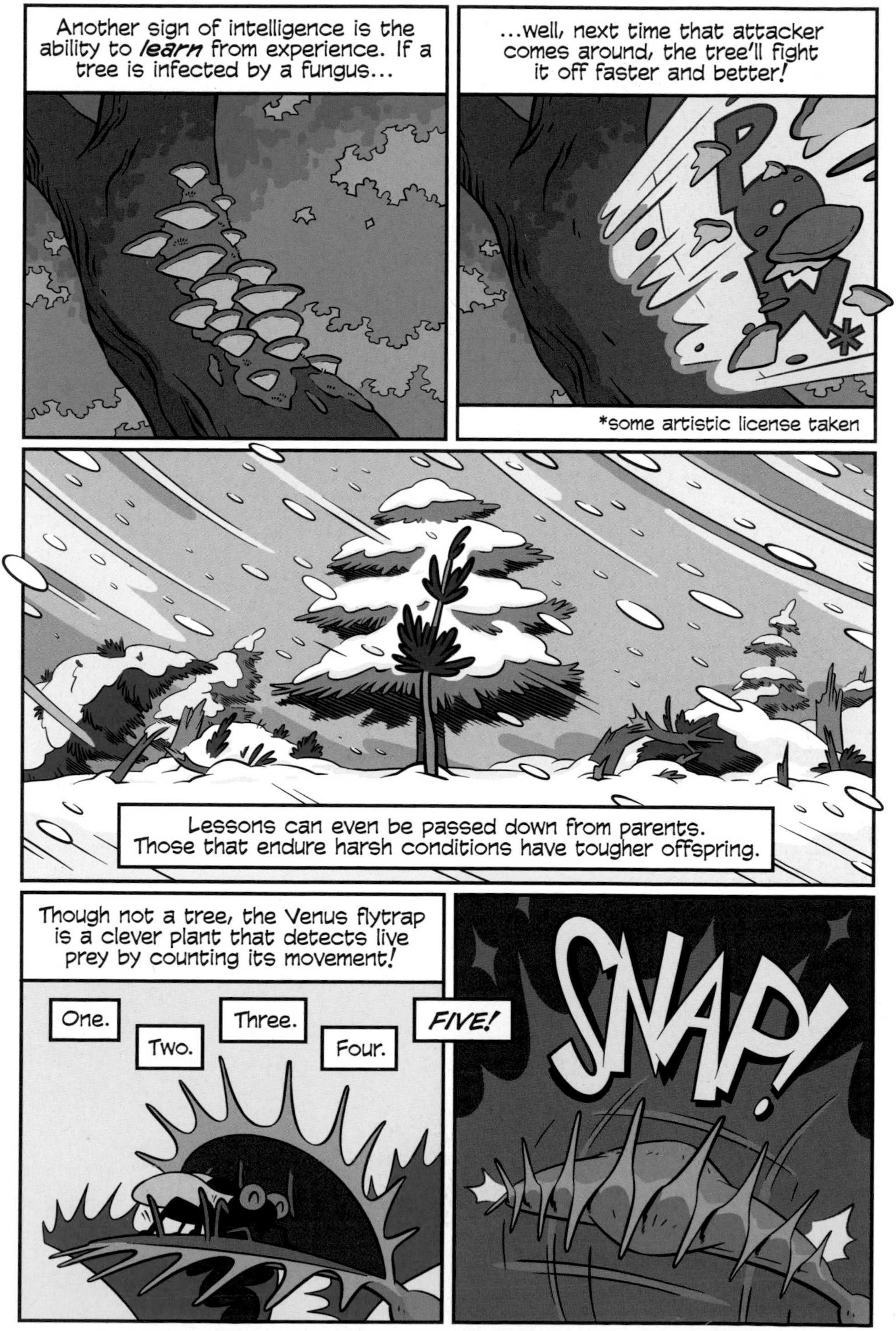
Another sign of intelligence is the ability to *learn* from experience. If a tree is infected by a fungus...
...well, next time that attacker comes around, the tree'll fight it off faster and better!
POW*
*some artistic license taken
Lessons can even be passed down from parents. Those that endure harsh conditions have tougher offspring.
Though not a tree, the Venus flytrap is a clever plant that detects live prey by counting its movement!
One.
Two.
Three.
Four.
FIVE!
SNAP!

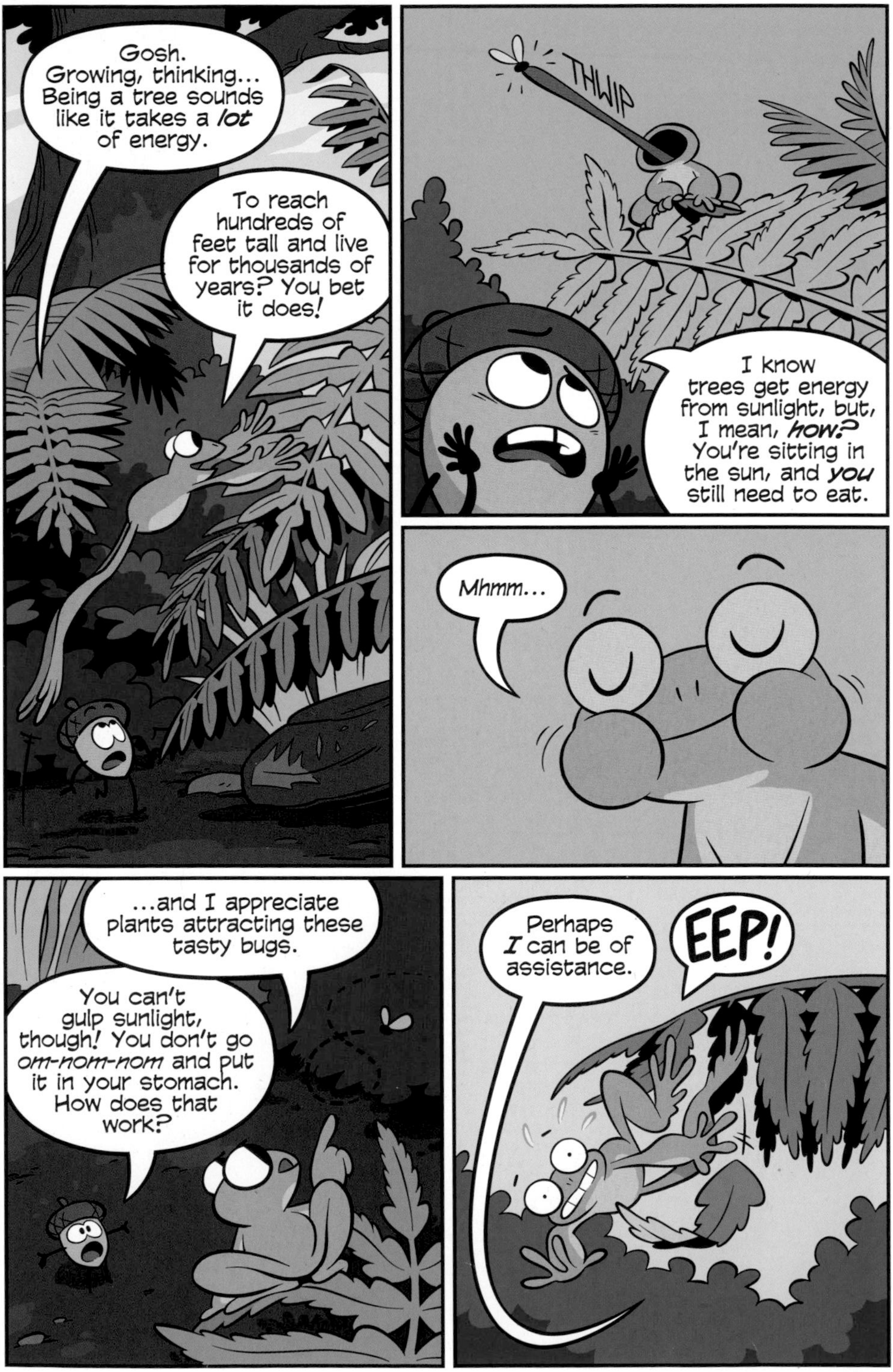
Gosh. Growing, thinking... Being a tree sounds like it takes a *lot* of energy.
To reach hundreds of feet tall and live for thousands of years? You bet it does!
THWIP
I know trees get energy from sunlight, but, I mean, ***how?*** You're sitting in the sun, and ***you*** still need to eat.
Mhmm...
...and I appreciate plants attracting these tasty bugs.
You can't gulp sunlight, though! You don't go *om-nom-nom* and put it in your stomach. How does that work?
Perhaps *I* can be of assistance.
EEP!

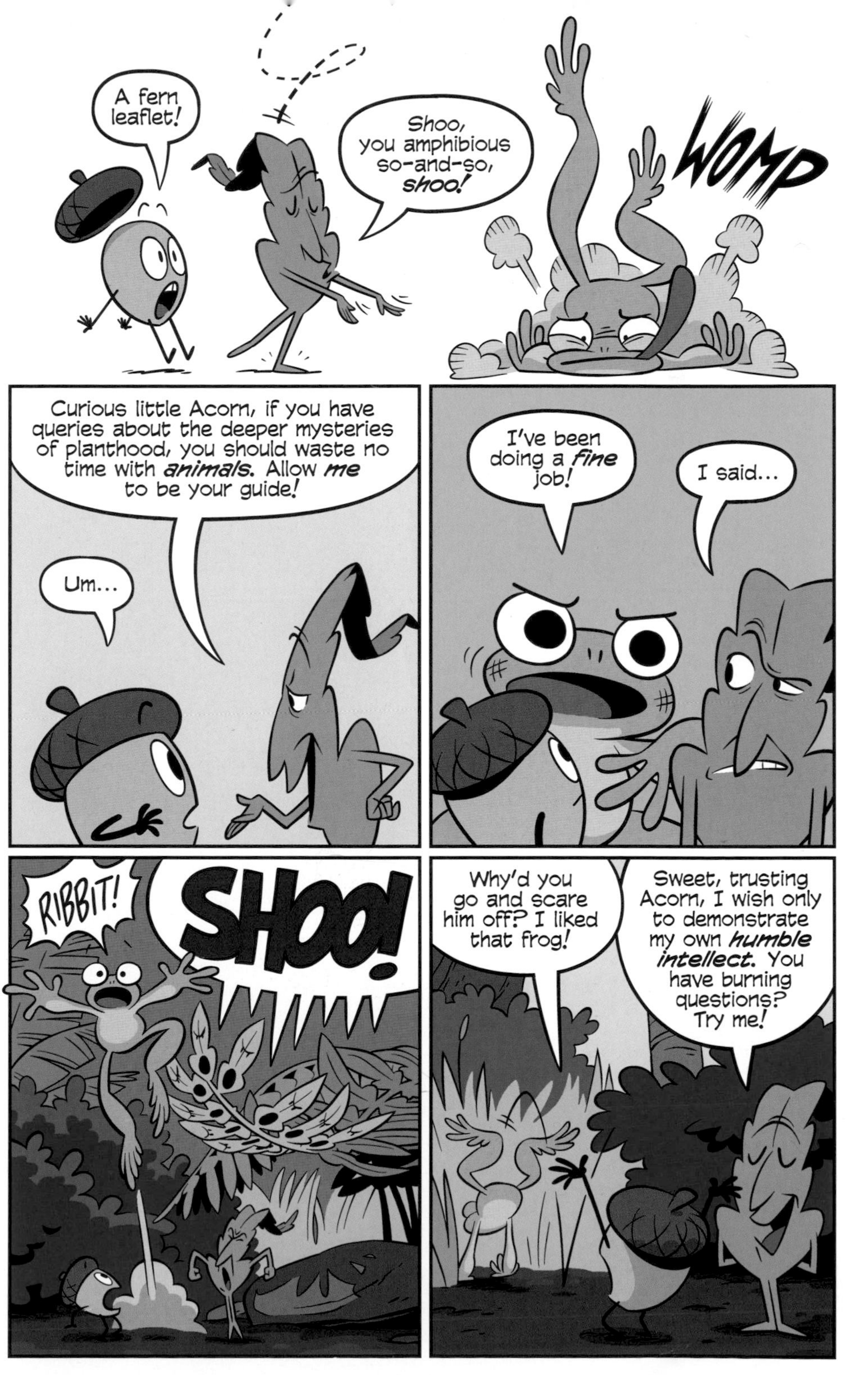

A fern leaflet!
Shoo, you amphibious so-and-so, *shoo!*
WOMP
Curious little Acorn, if you have queries about the deeper mysteries of planthood, you should waste no time with *animals.* Allow *me* to be your guide!
Um...
I've been doing a *fine* job!
I said...
RIBBIT!
SHOO!
Why'd you go and scare him off? I liked that frog!
Sweet, trusting Acorn, I wish only to demonstrate my own *humble intellect.* You have burning questions? Try me!

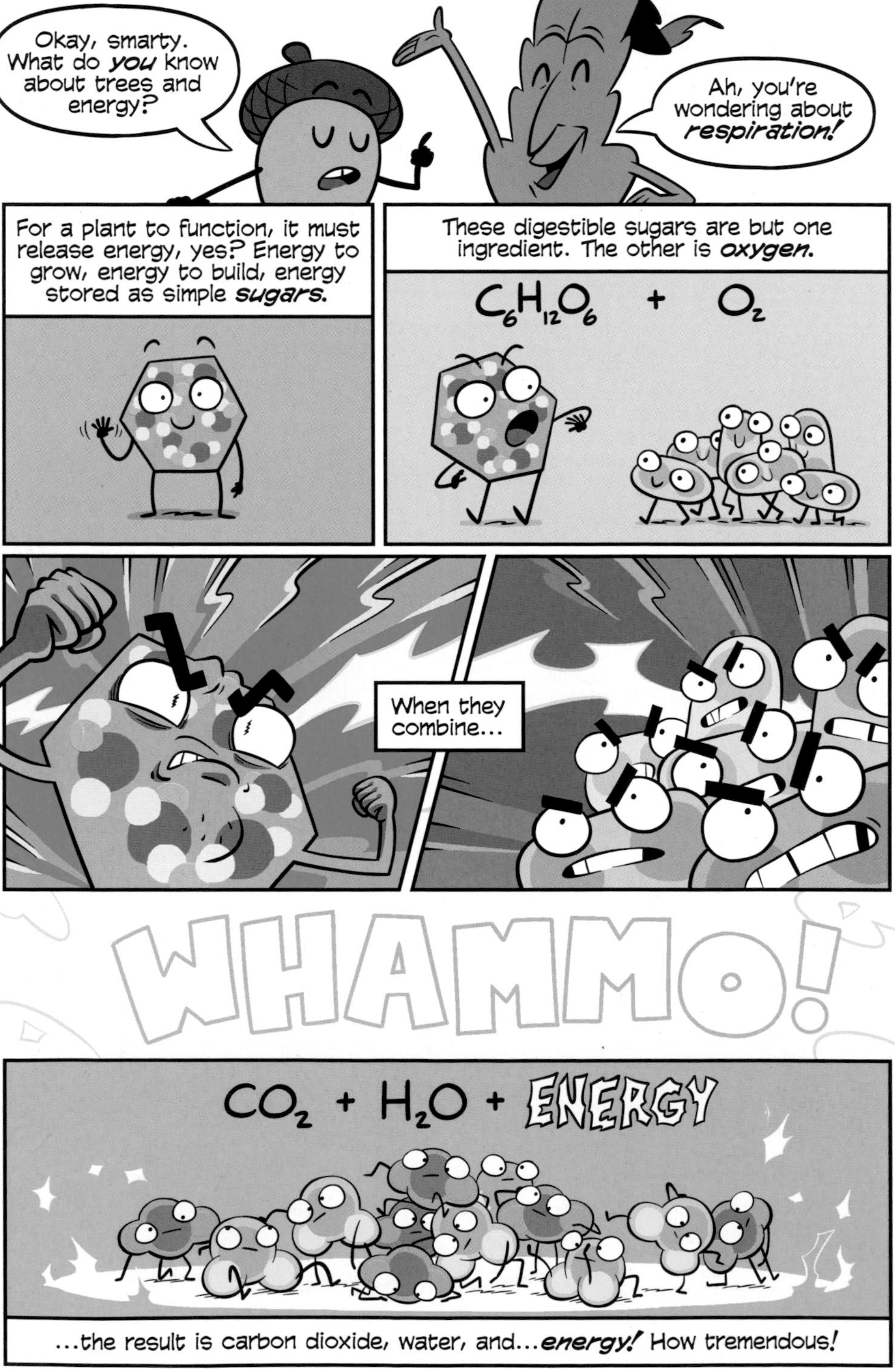

Okay, smarty. What do *you* know about trees and energy?
Ah, you're wondering about *respiration!*
For a plant to function, it must release energy, yes? Energy to grow, energy to build, energy stored as simple *sugars.*
These digestible sugars are but one ingredient. The other is *oxygen.*
$C_6H_{12}O_6$ + O_2
When they combine...
WHAMMO!
CO_2 + H_2O + ENERGY
...the result is carbon dioxide, water, and...*energy!* How tremendous!

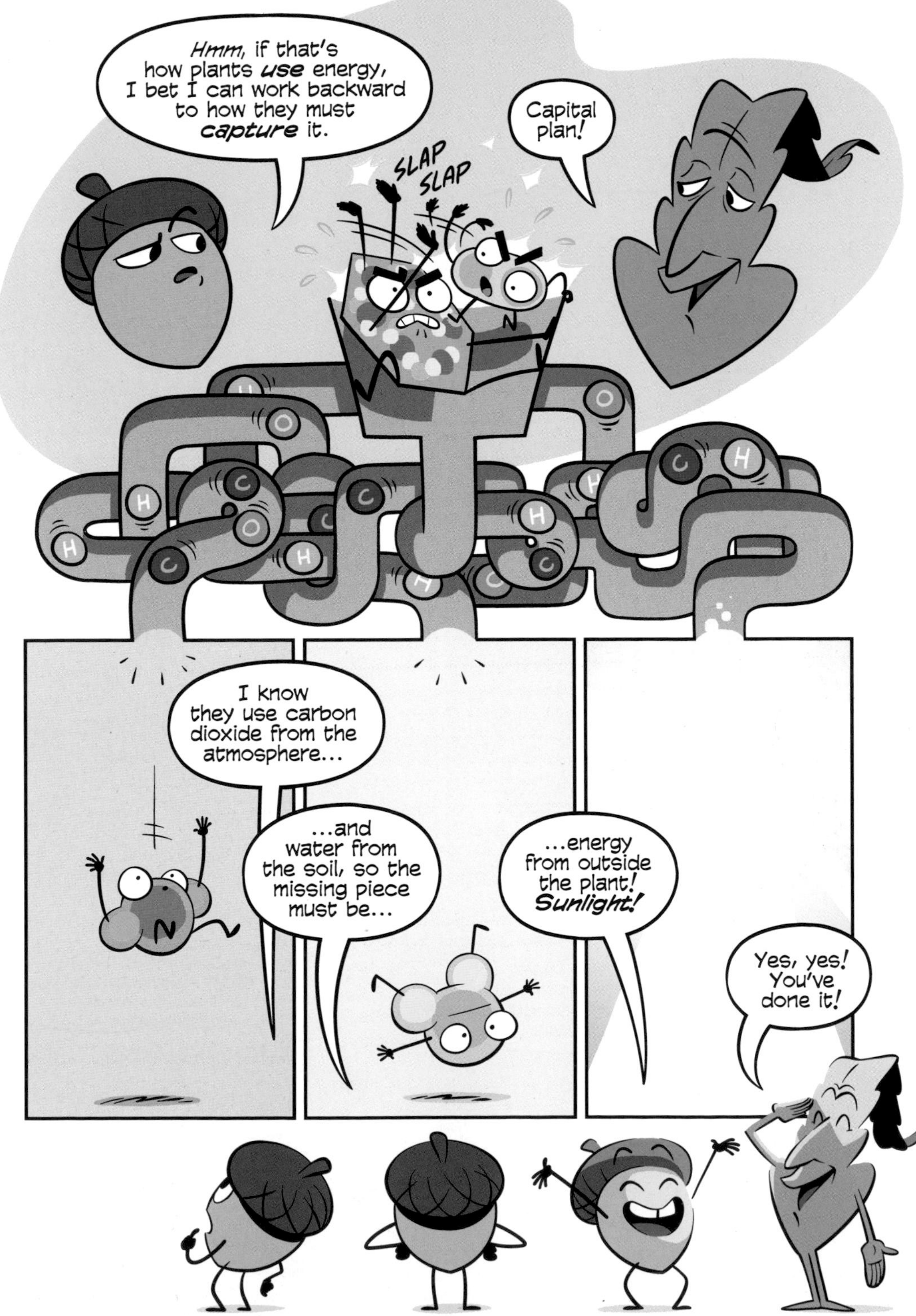

Hmm, if that's how plants ***use*** energy, I bet I can work backward to how they must ***capture*** it.
SLAP SLAP
Capital plan!
I know they use carbon dioxide from the atmosphere...
...and water from the soil, so the missing piece must be...
...energy from outside the plant! ***Sunlight!***
Yes, yes! You've done it!

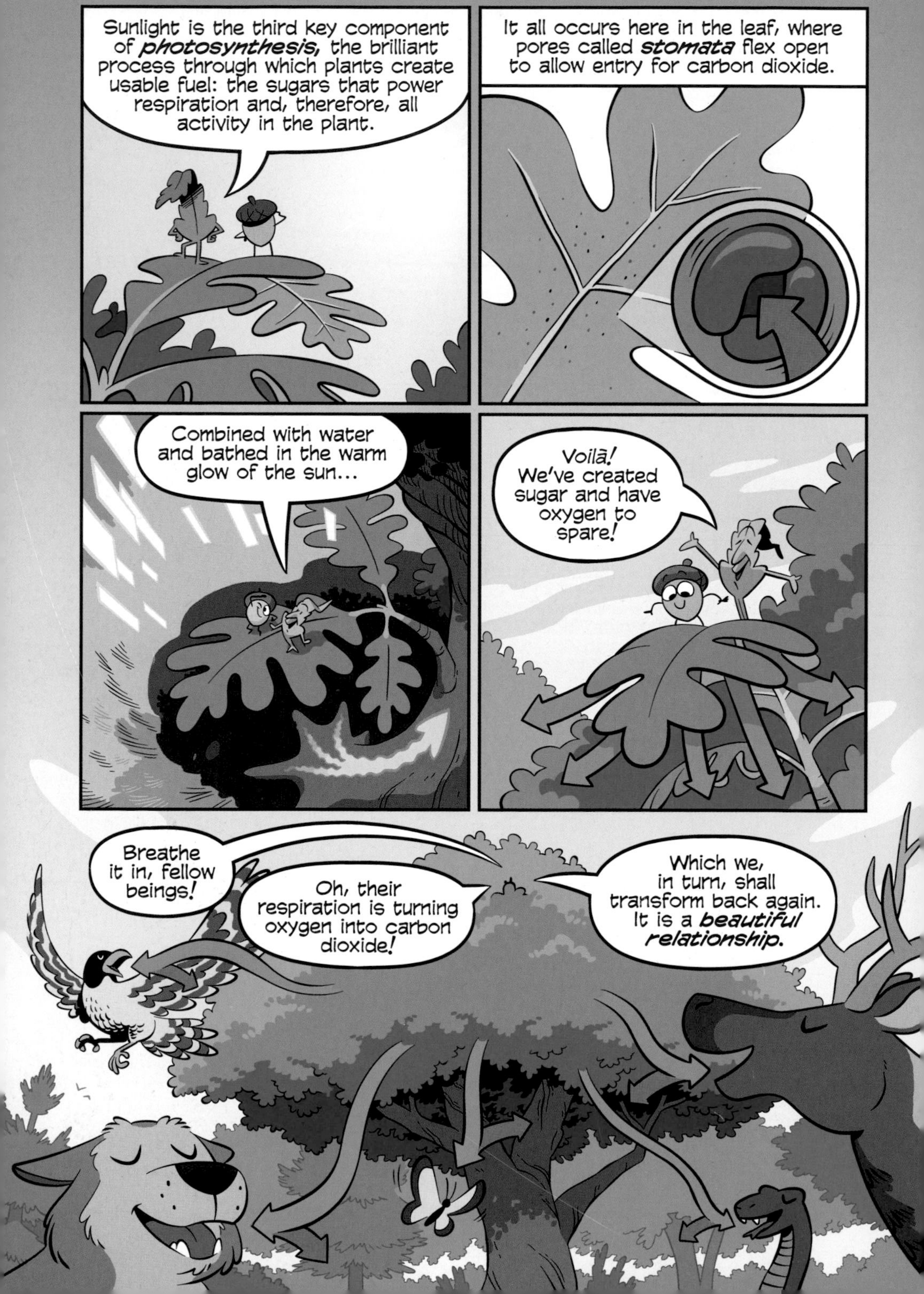
Sunlight is the third key component of ***photosynthesis,*** the brilliant process through which plants create usable fuel: the sugars that power respiration and, therefore, all activity in the plant.
It all occurs here in the leaf, where pores called ***stomata*** flex open to allow entry for carbon dioxide.
Combined with water and bathed in the warm glow of the sun...
Voilà! We've created sugar and have oxygen to spare*!*
Breathe it in, fellow beings*!*
Oh, their respiration is turning oxygen into carbon dioxide*!*
Which we, in turn, shall transform back again. It is a ***beautiful relationship.***

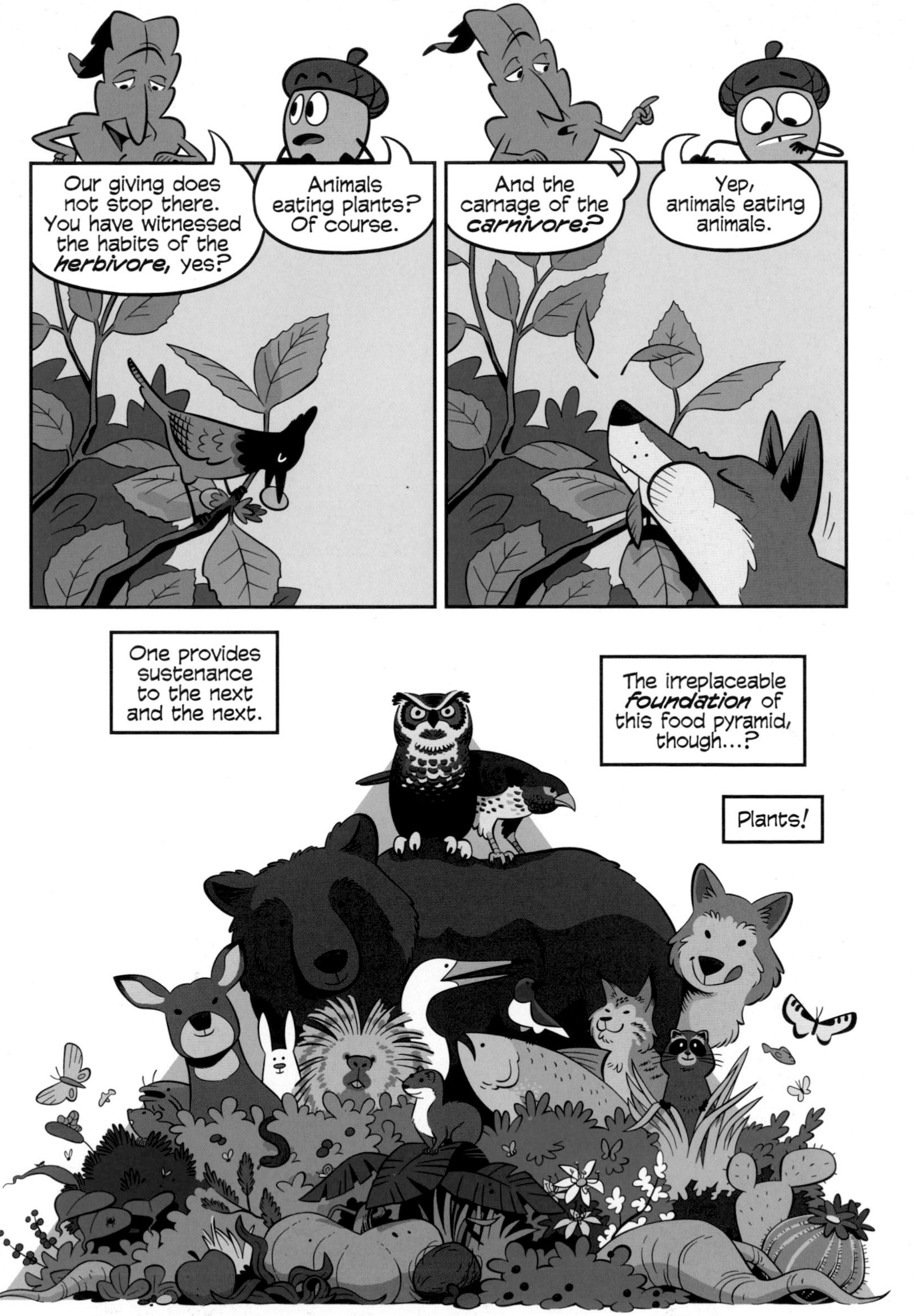
Our giving does not stop there. You have witnessed the habits of the *herbivore*, yes?
Animals eating plants? Of course.
And the carnage of the *carnivore*?
Yep, animals eating animals.
One provides sustenance to the next and the next.
The irreplaceable *foundation* of this food pyramid, though...?
Plants!

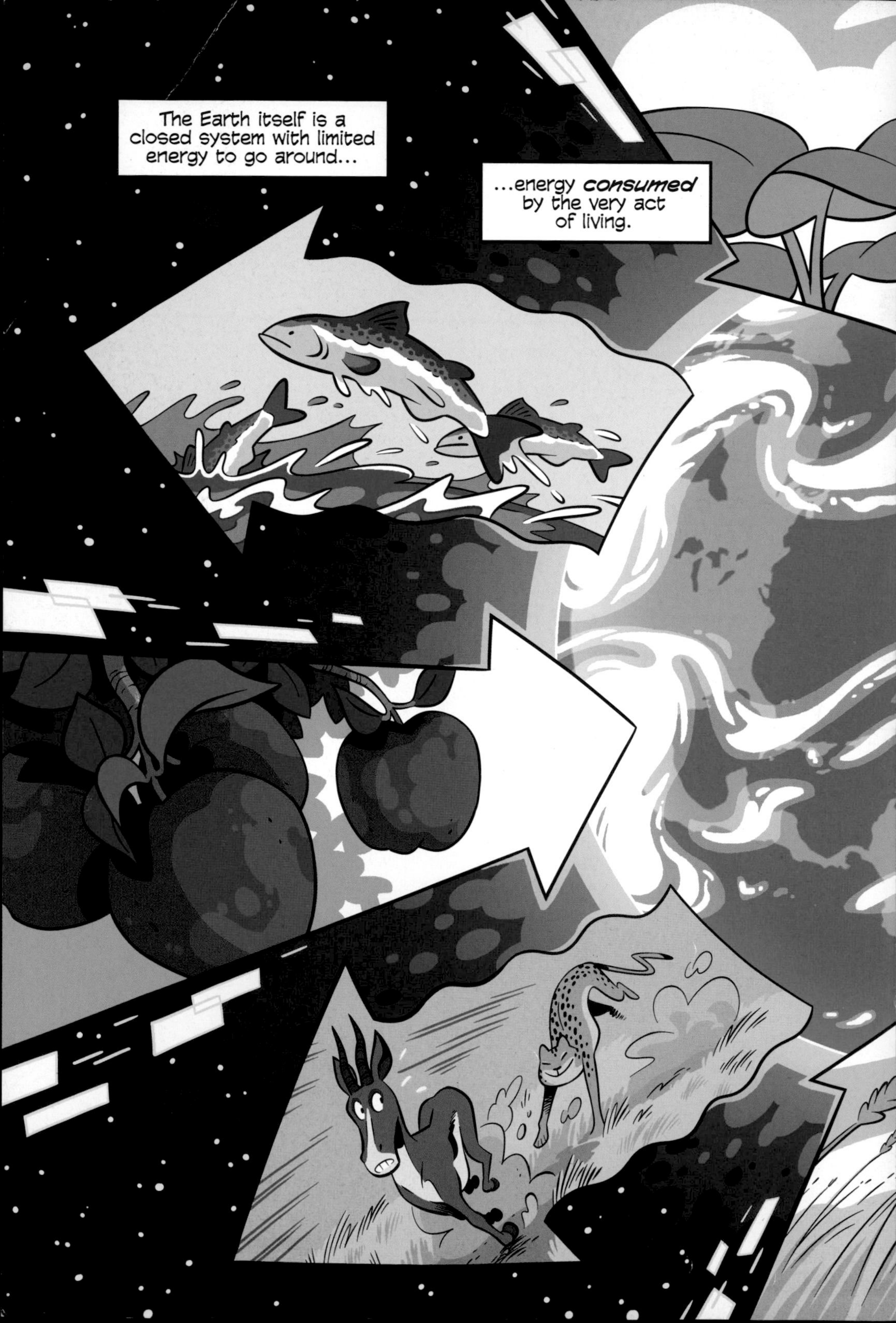
The Earth itself is a closed system with limited energy to go around...
...energy *consumed* by the very act of living.

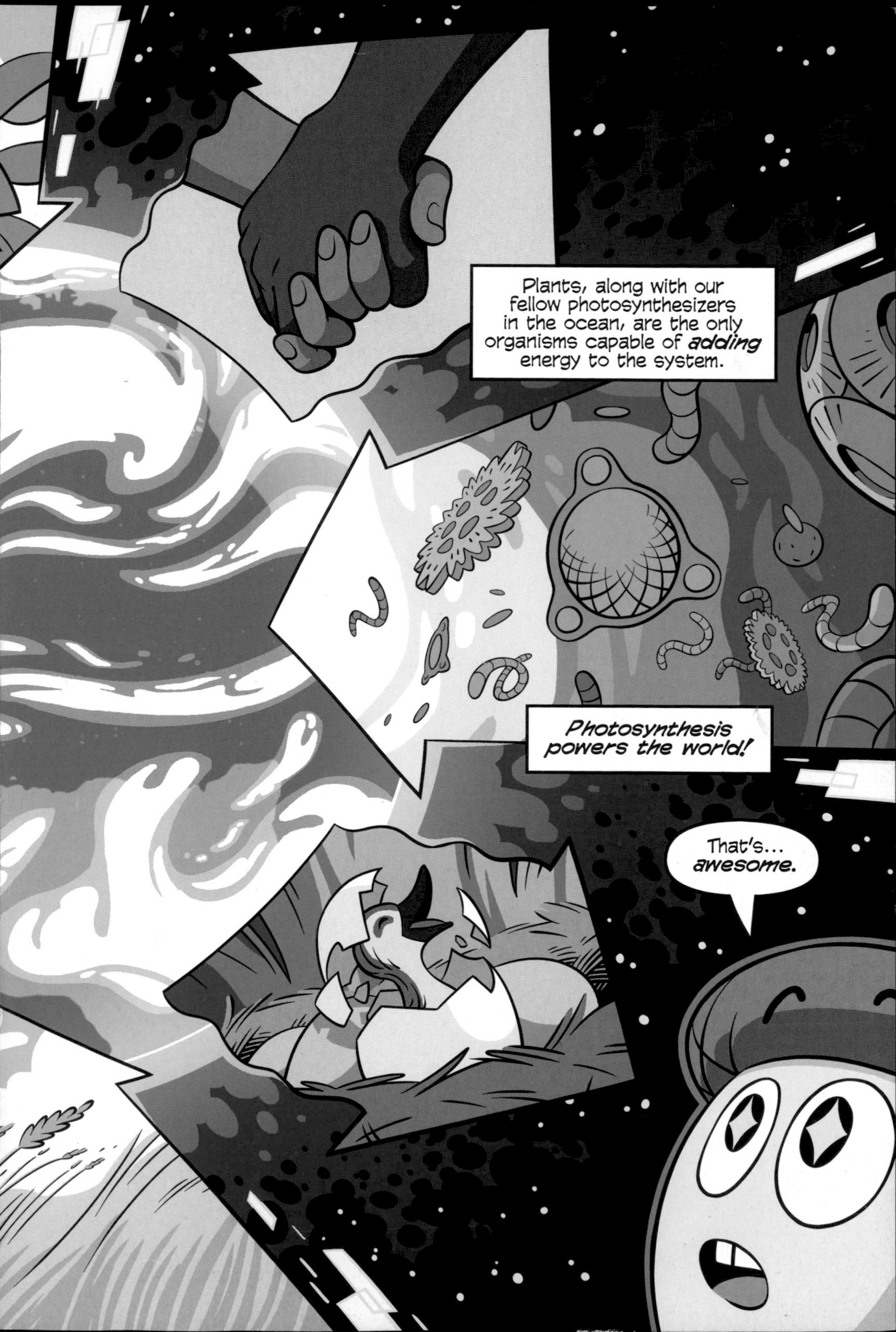
Plants, along with our fellow photosynthesizers in the ocean, are the only organisms capable of *adding* energy to the system.
Photosynthesis powers the world!
That's... *awesome.*

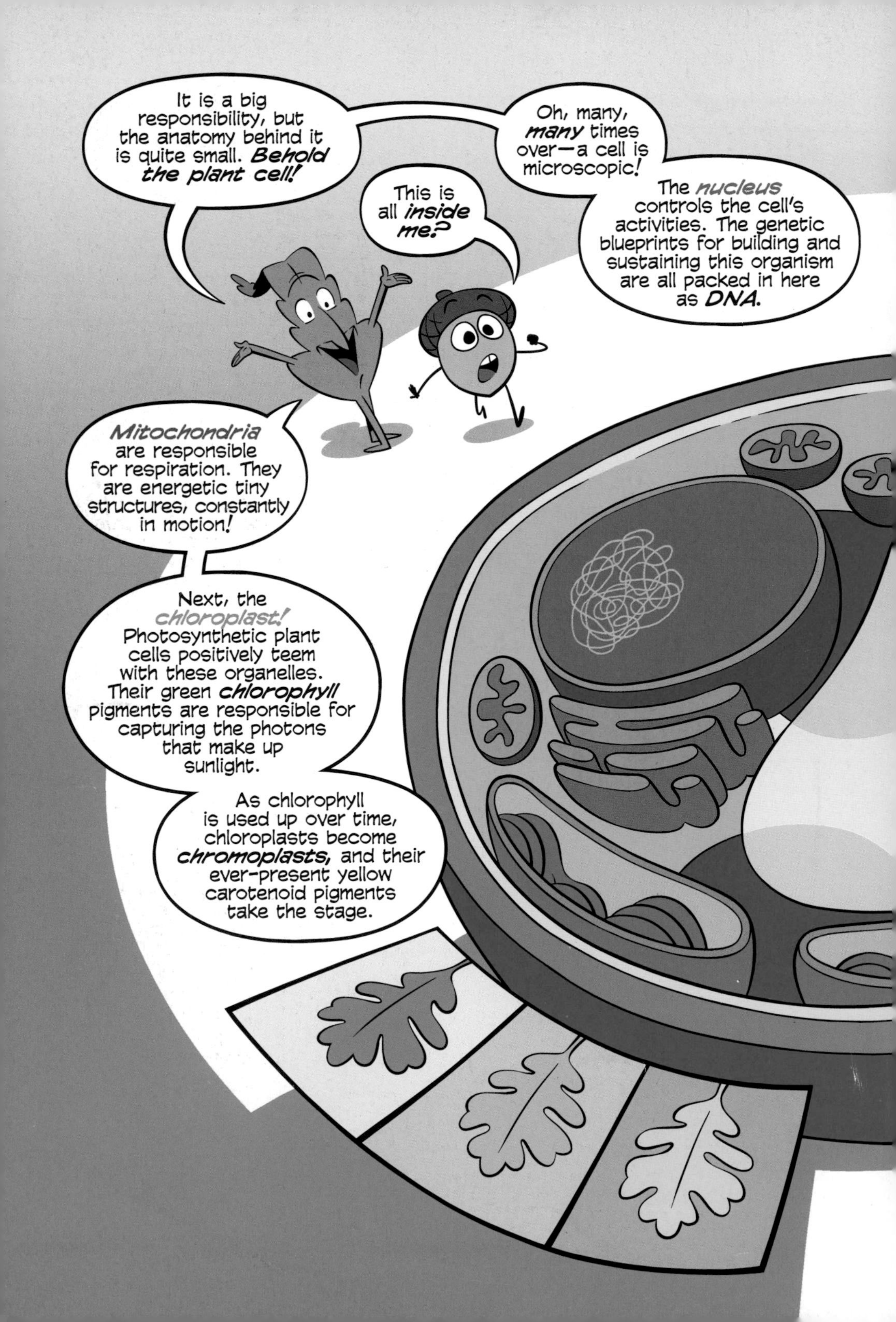

It is a big responsibility, but the anatomy behind it is quite small. *Behold the plant cell!*
This is all *inside me?*
Oh, many, *many* times over—a cell is microscopic!
The *nucleus* controls the cell's activities. The genetic blueprints for building and sustaining this organism are all packed in here as *DNA.*
Mitochondria are responsible for respiration. They are energetic tiny structures, constantly in motion!
Next, the *chloroplast!* Photosynthetic plant cells positively teem with these organelles. Their green *chlorophyll* pigments are responsible for capturing the photons that make up sunlight.
As chlorophyll is used up over time, chloroplasts become *chromoplasts,* and their ever-present yellow carotenoid pigments take the stage.

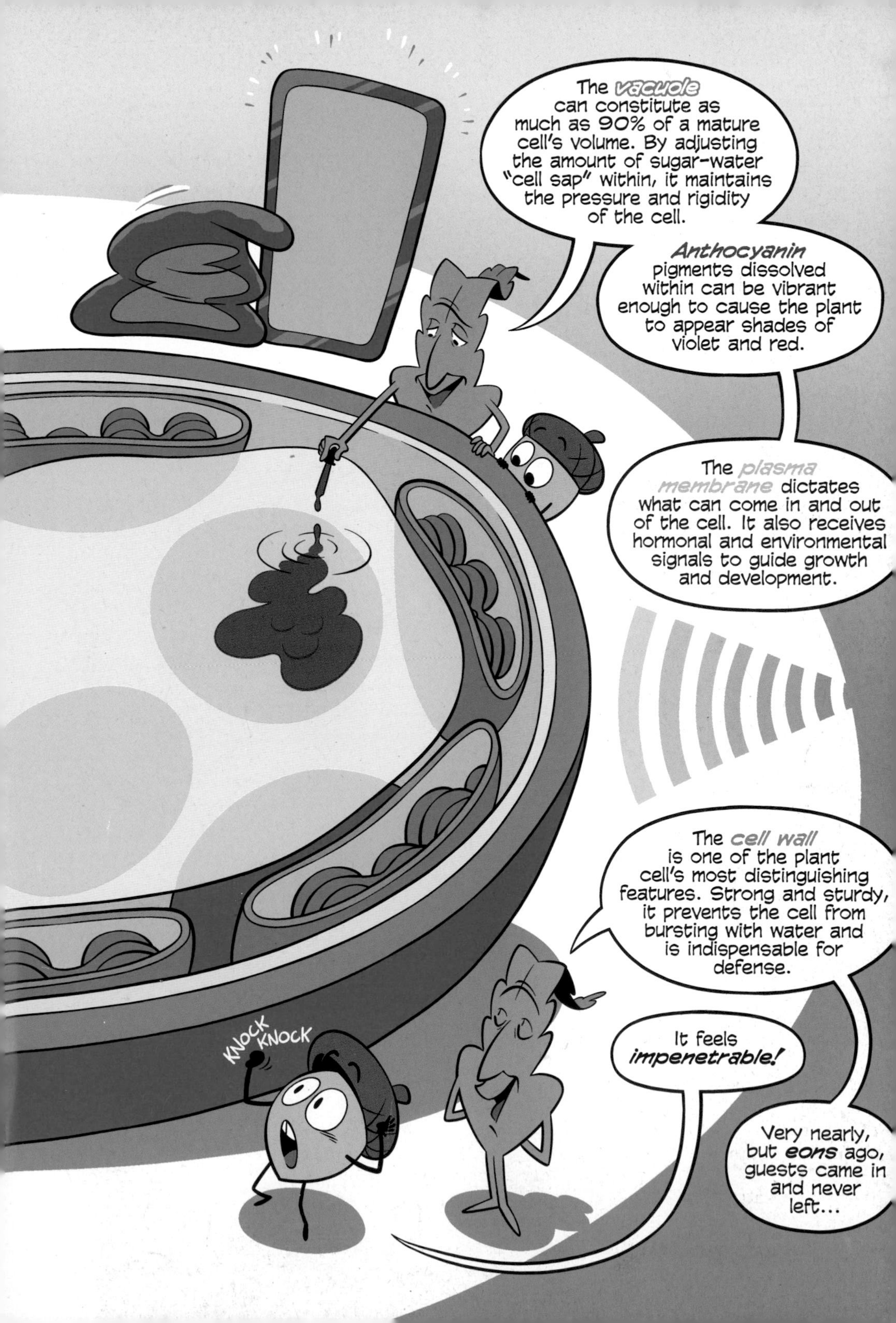
The vacuole can constitute as much as 90% of a mature cell's volume. By adjusting the amount of sugar-water "cell sap" within, it maintains the pressure and rigidity of the cell.
Anthocyanin pigments dissolved within can be vibrant enough to cause the plant to appear shades of violet and red.
The plasma membrane dictates what can come in and out of the cell. It also receives hormonal and environmental signals to guide growth and development.
The cell wall is one of the plant cell's most distinguishing features. Strong and sturdy, it prevents the cell from bursting with water and is indispensable for defense.
KNOCK KNOCK
It feels impenetrable!
Very nearly, but eons ago, guests came in and never left...

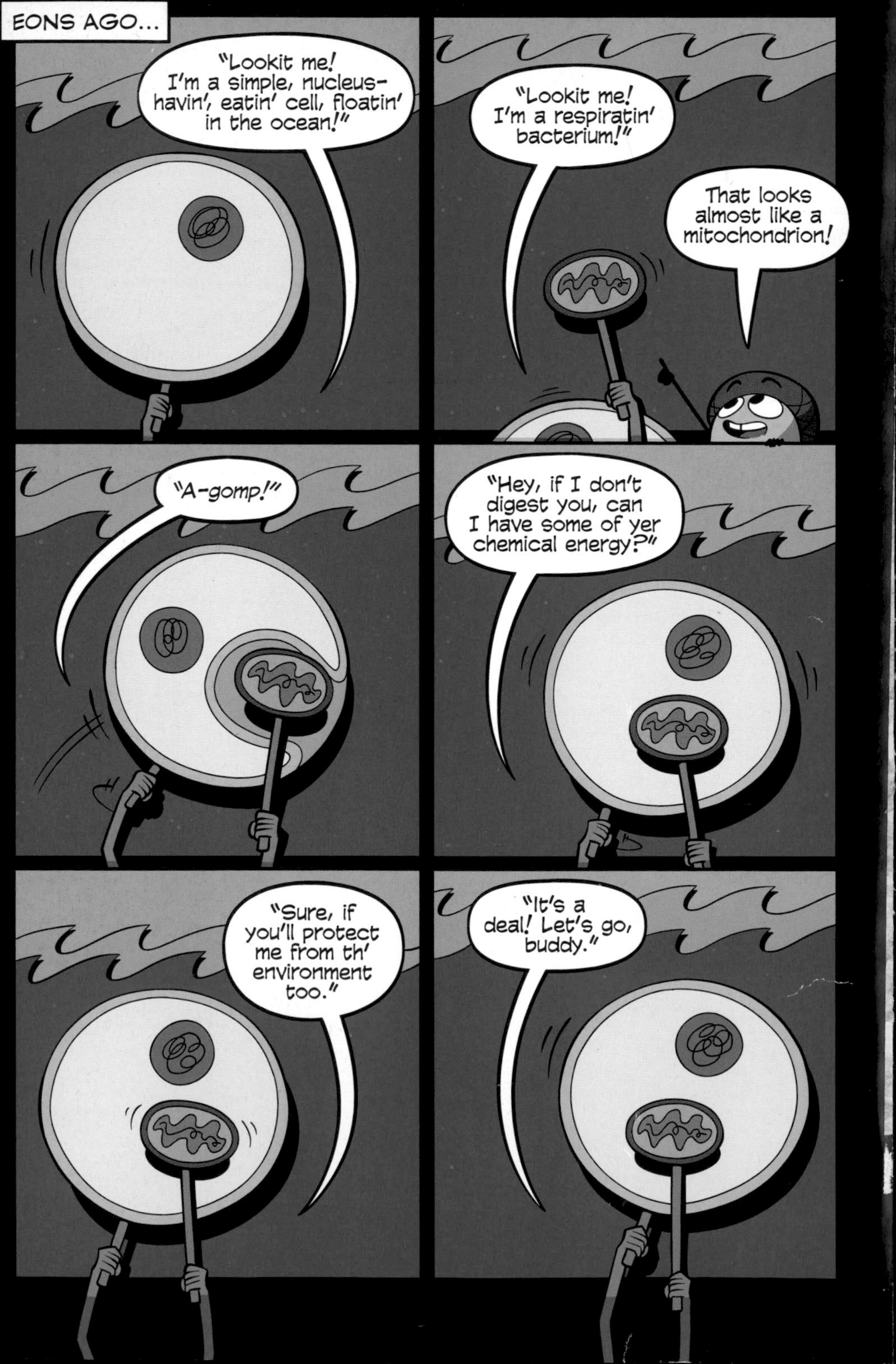
EONS AGO...
"Lookit me! I'm a simple, nucleus-havin', eatin' cell, floatin' in the ocean!"
"Lookit me! I'm a respiratin' bacterium!"
That looks almost like a mitochondrion!
"A-gomp!"
"Hey, if I don't digest you, can I have some of yer chemical energy?"
"Sure, if you'll protect me from th' environment too."
"It's a deal! Let's go, buddy."

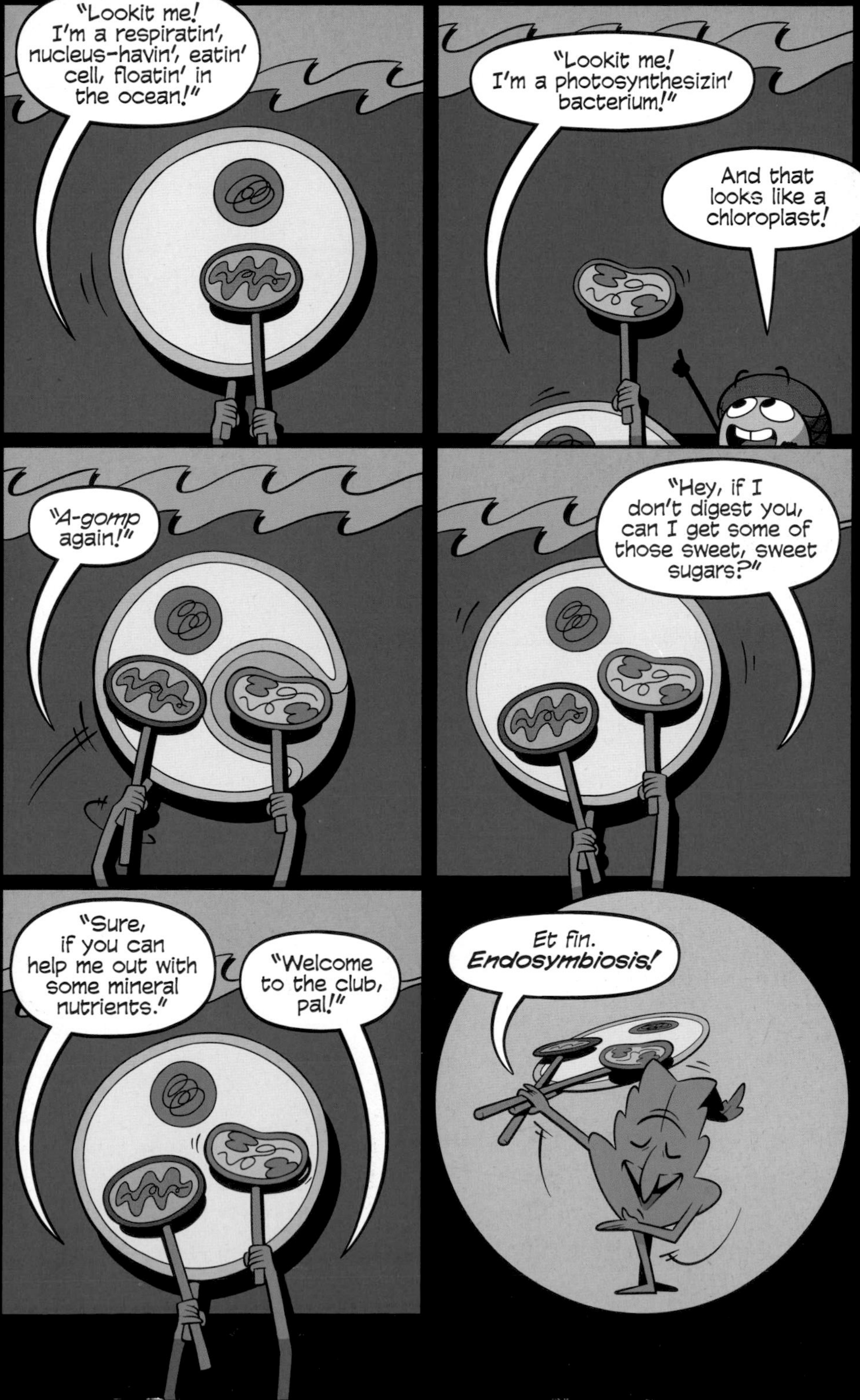
"Lookit me! I'm a respiratin', nucleus-havin', eatin' cell, floatin' in the ocean!"
"Lookit me! I'm a photosynthesizin' bacterium!"
And that looks like a chloroplast!
"A-gomp again!"
"Hey, if I don't digest you, can I get some of those sweet, sweet sugars?"
"Sure, if you can help me out with some mineral nutrients."
"Welcome to the club, pal!"
Et fin. *Endosymbiosis!*

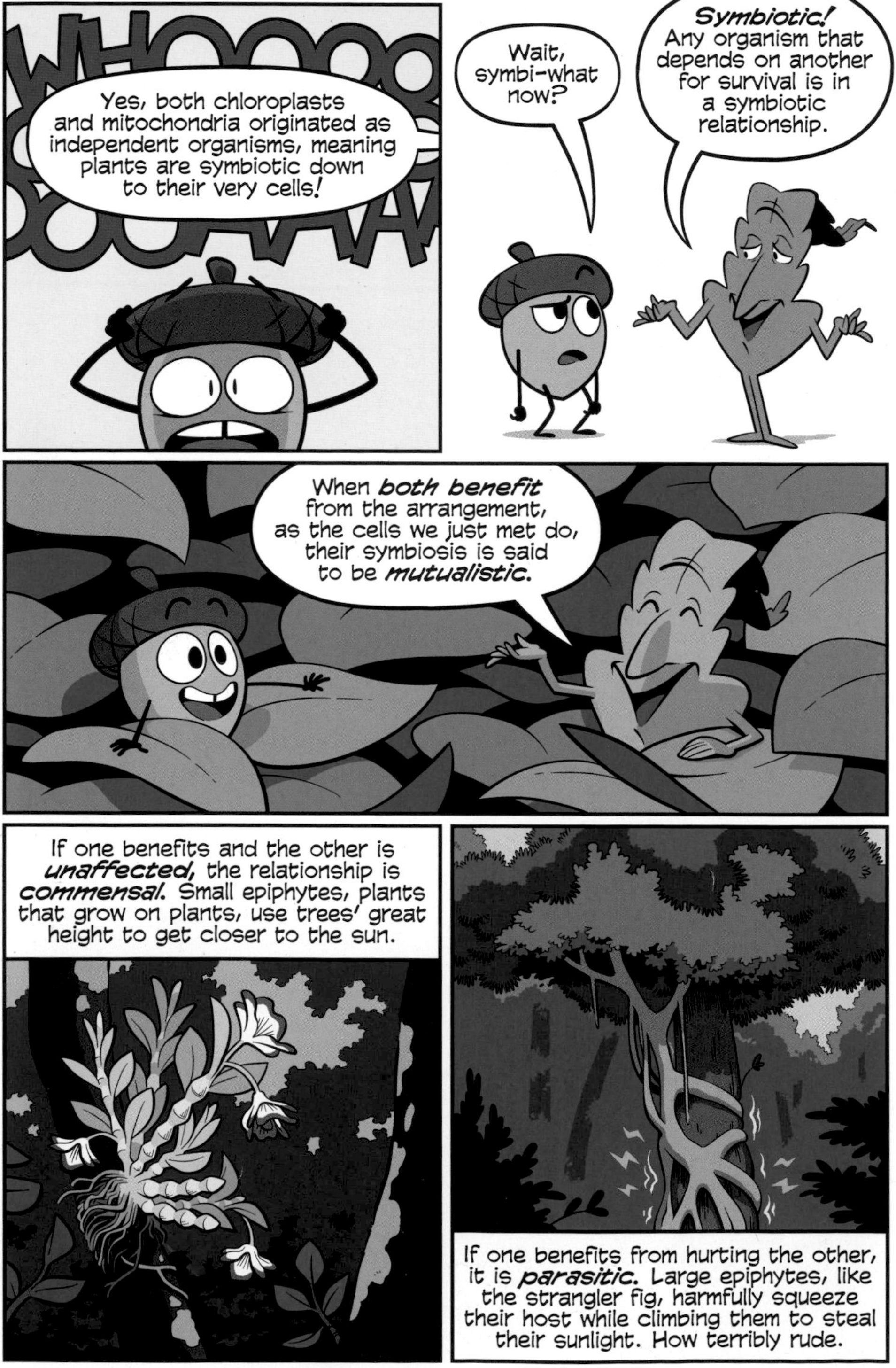
Yes, both chloroplasts and mitochondria originated as independent organisms, meaning plants are symbiotic down to their very cells!
Wait, symbi-what now?
Symbiotic! Any organism that depends on another for survival is in a symbiotic relationship.
When both benefit from the arrangement, as the cells we just met do, their symbiosis is said to be mutualistic.
If one benefits and the other is unaffected, the relationship is commensal. Small epiphytes, plants that grow on plants, use trees' great height to get closer to the sun.
If one benefits from hurting the other, it is parasitic. Large epiphytes, like the strangler fig, harmfully squeeze their host while climbing them to steal their sunlight. How terribly rude.

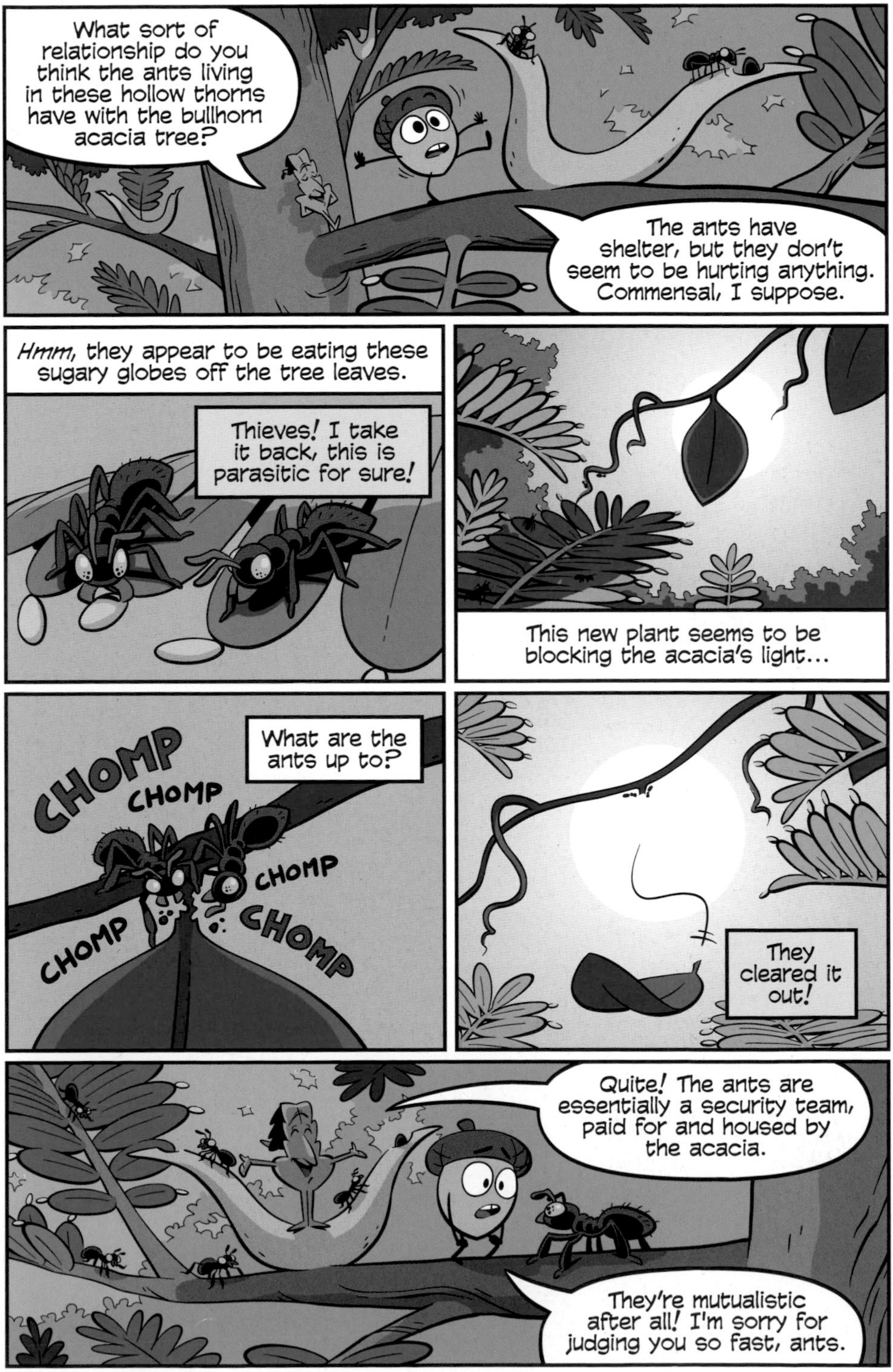
What sort of relationship do you think the ants living in these hollow thorns have with the bullhorn acacia tree?
The ants have shelter, but they don't seem to be hurting anything. Commensal, I suppose.
Hmm, they appear to be eating these sugary globes off the tree leaves.
Thieves! I take it back, this is parasitic for sure!
This new plant seems to be blocking the acacia's light...
What are the ants up to?
CHOMP
CHOMP
CHOMP
CHOMP
CHOMP
They cleared it out!
Quite! The ants are essentially a security team, paid for and housed by the acacia.
They're mutualistic after all! I'm sorry for judging you so fast, ants.

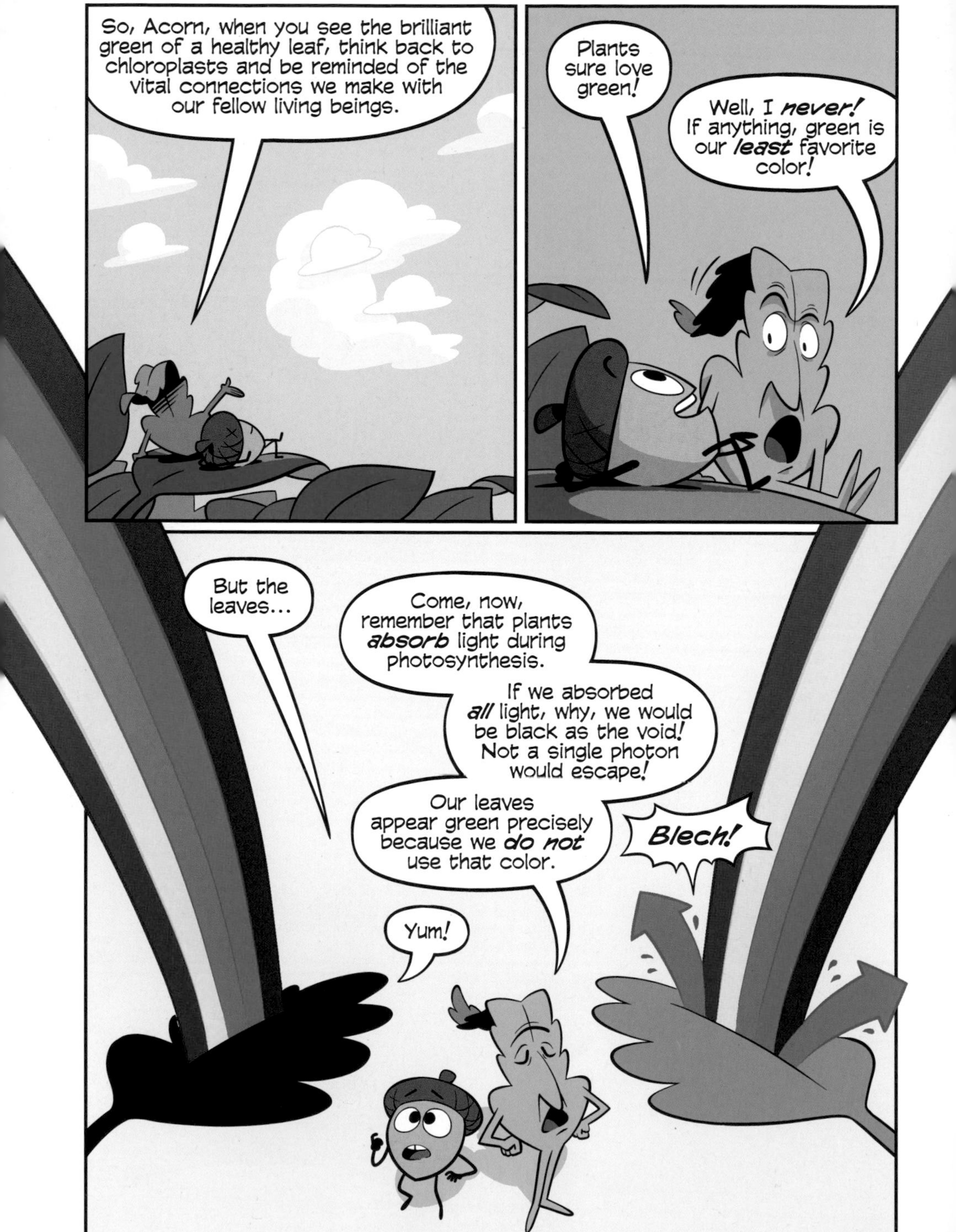
So, Acorn, when you see the brilliant green of a healthy leaf, think back to chloroplasts and be reminded of the vital connections we make with our fellow living beings.
Plants sure love green!
Well, I *never!* If anything, green is our *least* favorite color!
But the leaves...
Come, now, remember that plants *absorb* light during photosynthesis.
If we absorbed *all* light, why, we would be black as the void! Not a single photon would escape!
Our leaves appear green precisely because we *do not* use that color.
Blech!
Yum!

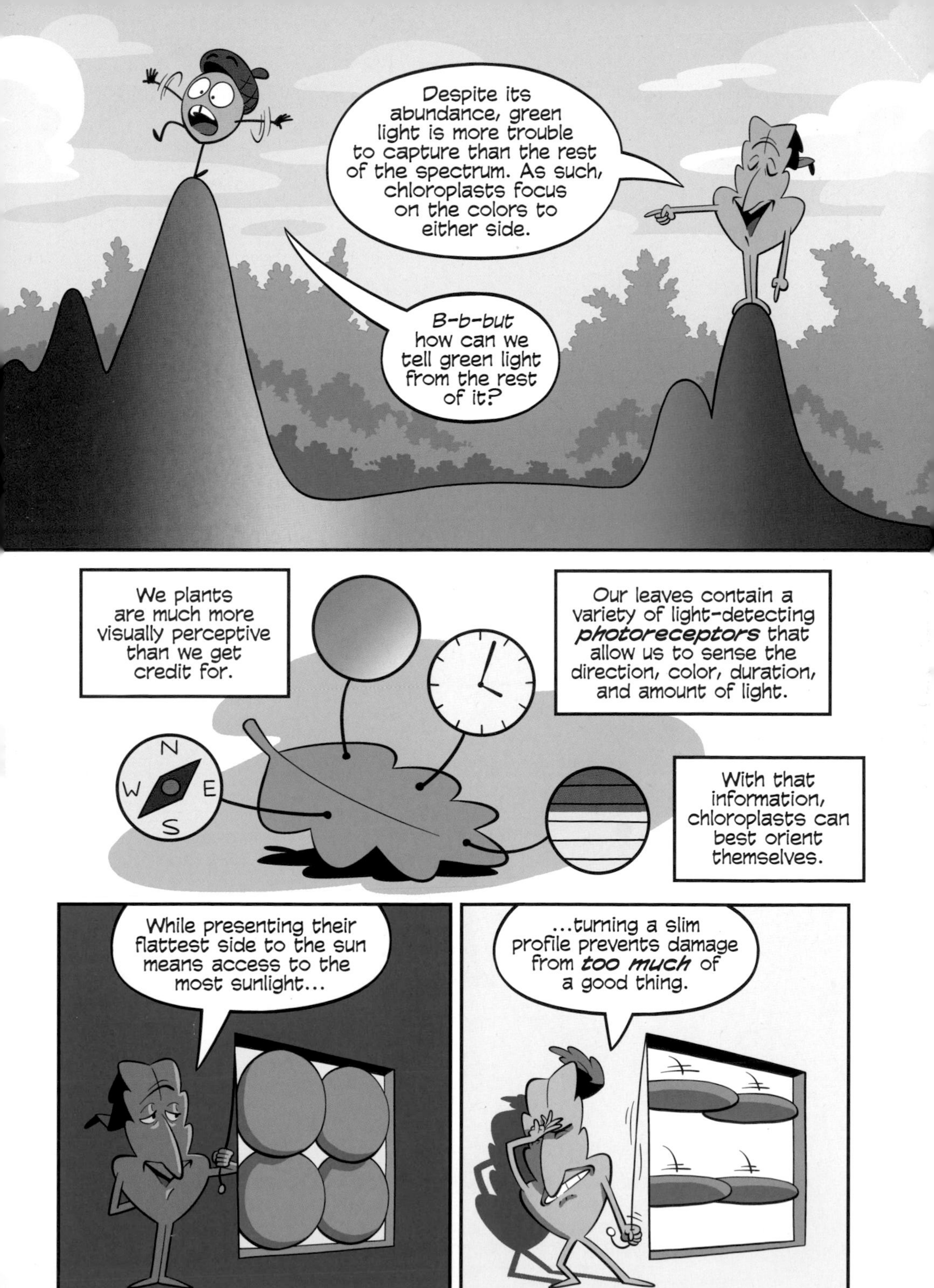

Despite its abundance, green light is more trouble to capture than the rest of the spectrum. As such, chloroplasts focus on the colors to either side.
B-b-but how can we tell green light from the rest of it?
We plants are much more visually perceptive than we get credit for.
Our leaves contain a variety of light-detecting ***photoreceptors*** that allow us to sense the direction, color, duration, and amount of light.
N
W
E
S
With that information, chloroplasts can best orient themselves.
While presenting their flattest side to the sun means access to the most sunlight...
...turning a slim profile prevents damage from ***too much*** of a good thing.

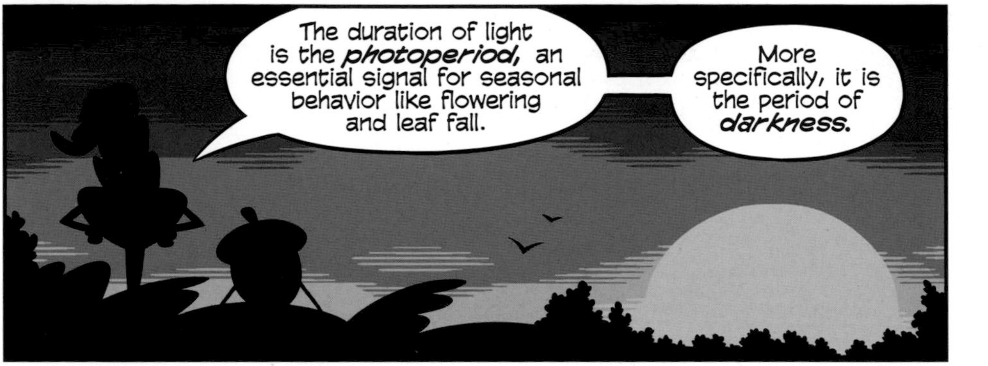
The duration of light is the *photoperiod,* an essential signal for seasonal behavior like flowering and leaf fall.
More specifically, it is the period of *darkness.*

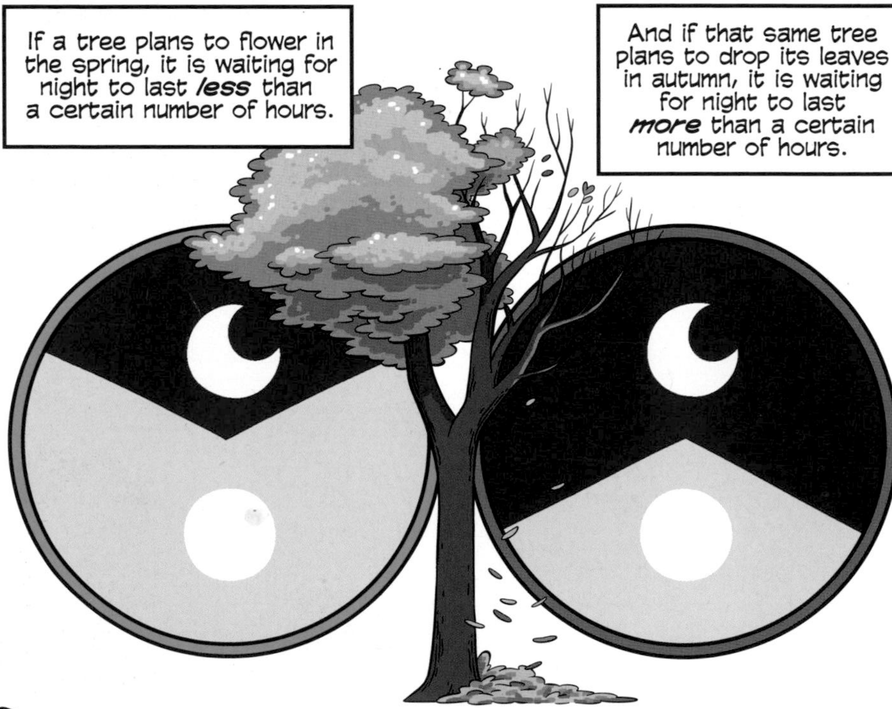
If a tree plans to flower in the spring, it is waiting for night to last *less* than a certain number of hours.
And if that same tree plans to drop its leaves in autumn, it is waiting for night to last *more* than a certain number of hours.

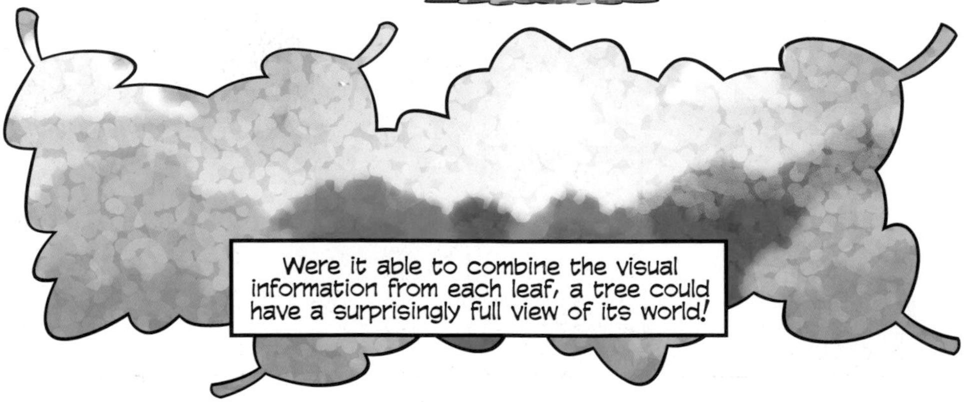
Were it able to combine the visual information from each leaf, a tree could have a surprisingly full view of its world!

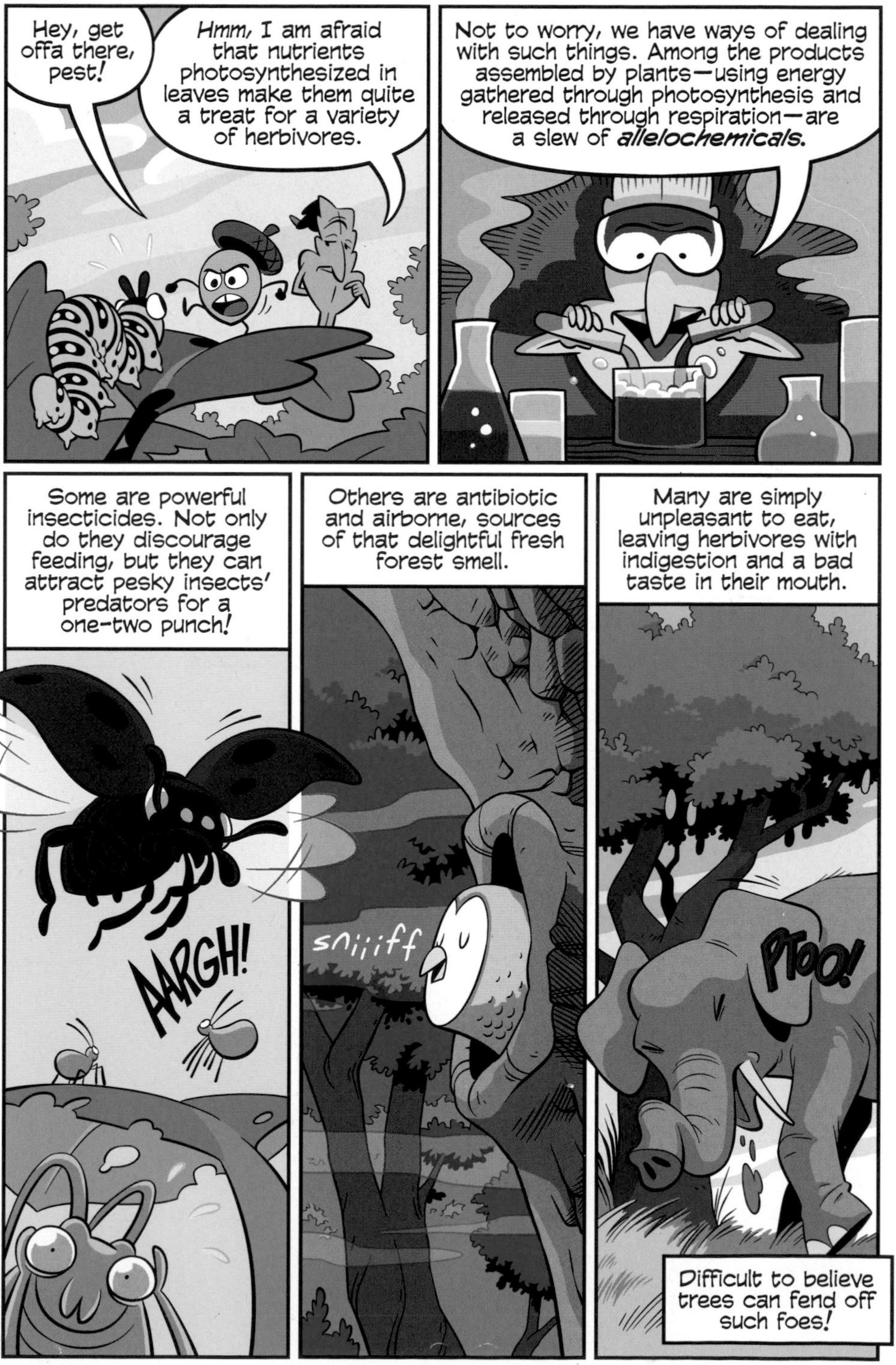
Hey, get offa there, pest!
Hmm, I am afraid that nutrients photosynthesized in leaves make them quite a treat for a variety of herbivores.
Not to worry, we have ways of dealing with such things. Among the products assembled by plants—using energy gathered through photosynthesis and released through respiration—are a slew of allelochemicals.
Some are powerful insecticides. Not only do they discourage feeding, but they can attract pesky insects' predators for a one-two punch!
AARGH!
Others are antibiotic and airborne, sources of that delightful fresh forest smell.
sniiiff
Many are simply unpleasant to eat, leaving herbivores with indigestion and a bad taste in their mouth.
PTOO!
Difficult to believe trees can fend off such foes!

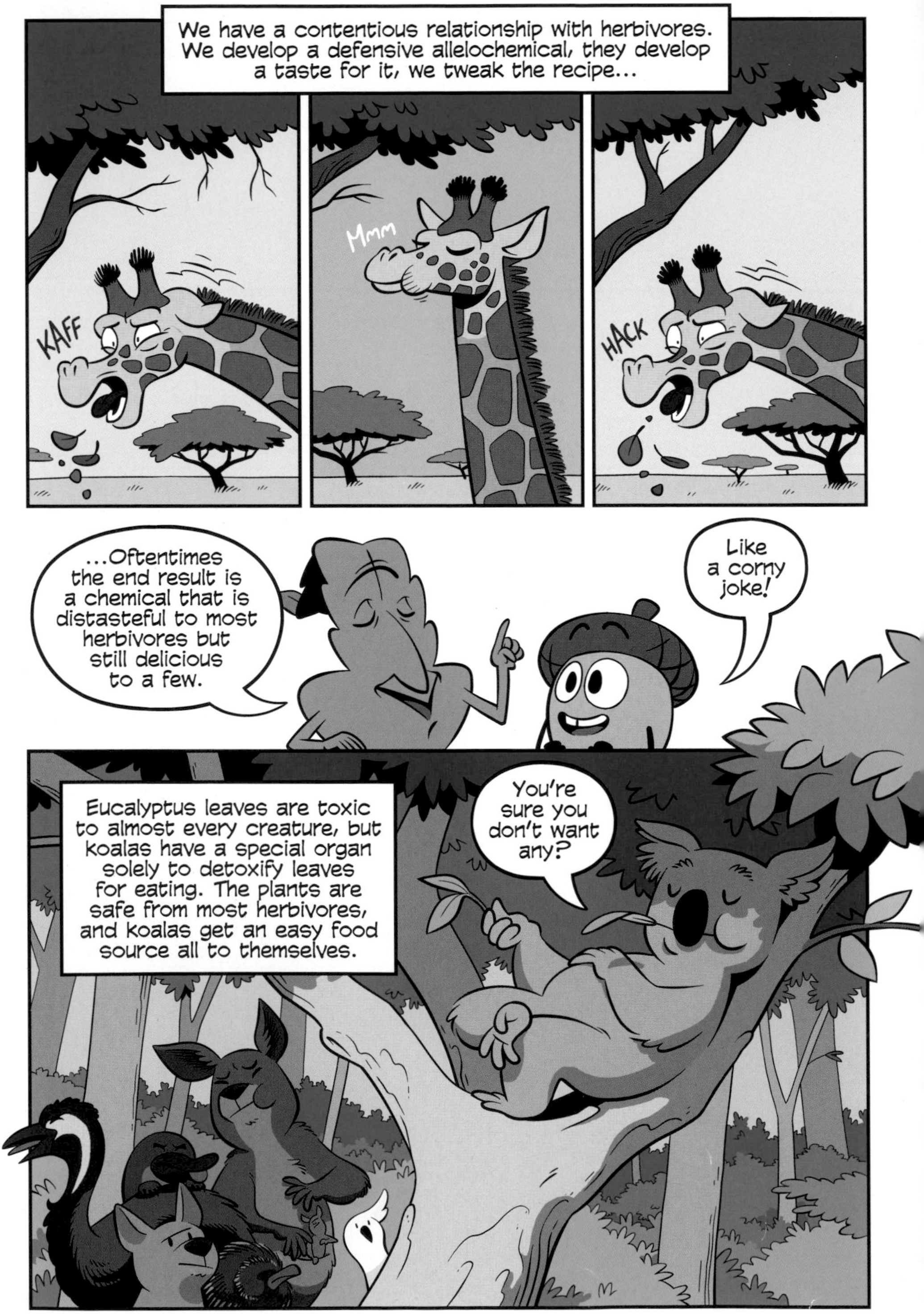

We have a contentious relationship with herbivores. We develop a defensive allelochemical, they develop a taste for it, we tweak the recipe...
KAFF
Mmm
HACK
...Oftentimes the end result is a chemical that is distasteful to most herbivores but still delicious to a few.
Like a corny joke!
Eucalyptus leaves are toxic to almost every creature, but koalas have a special organ solely to detoxify leaves for eating. The plants are safe from most herbivores, and koalas get an easy food source all to themselves.
You're sure you don't want any?

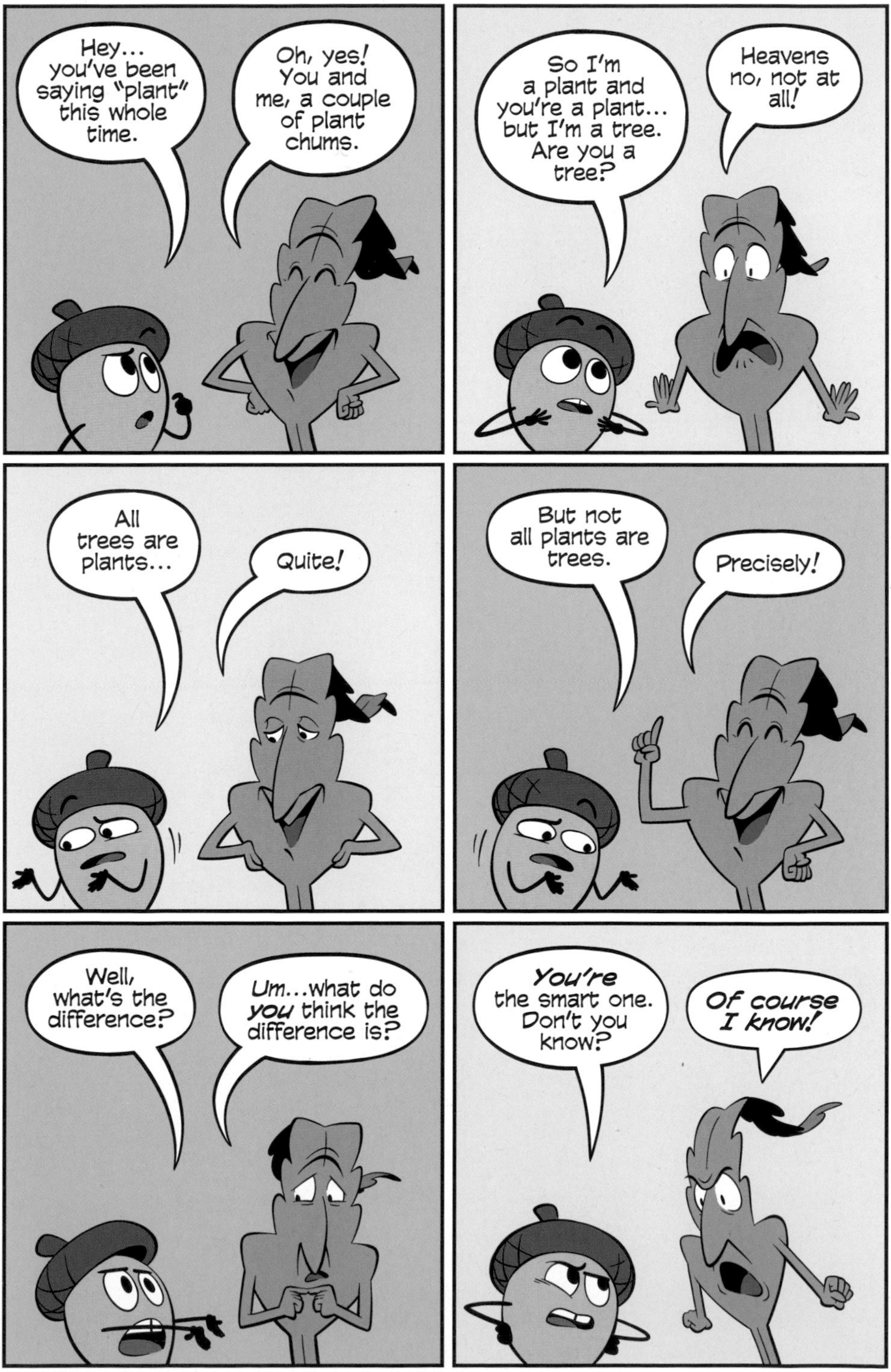
Hey... you've been saying "plant" this whole time.
Oh, yes! You and me, a couple of plant chums.
So I'm a plant and you're a plant... but I'm a tree. Are you a tree?
Heavens no, not at all!
All trees are plants...
Quite!
But not all plants are trees.
Precisely!
Well, what's the difference?
*Um...what do **you** think the difference is?*
You're the smart one. Don't you know?
Of course I know!

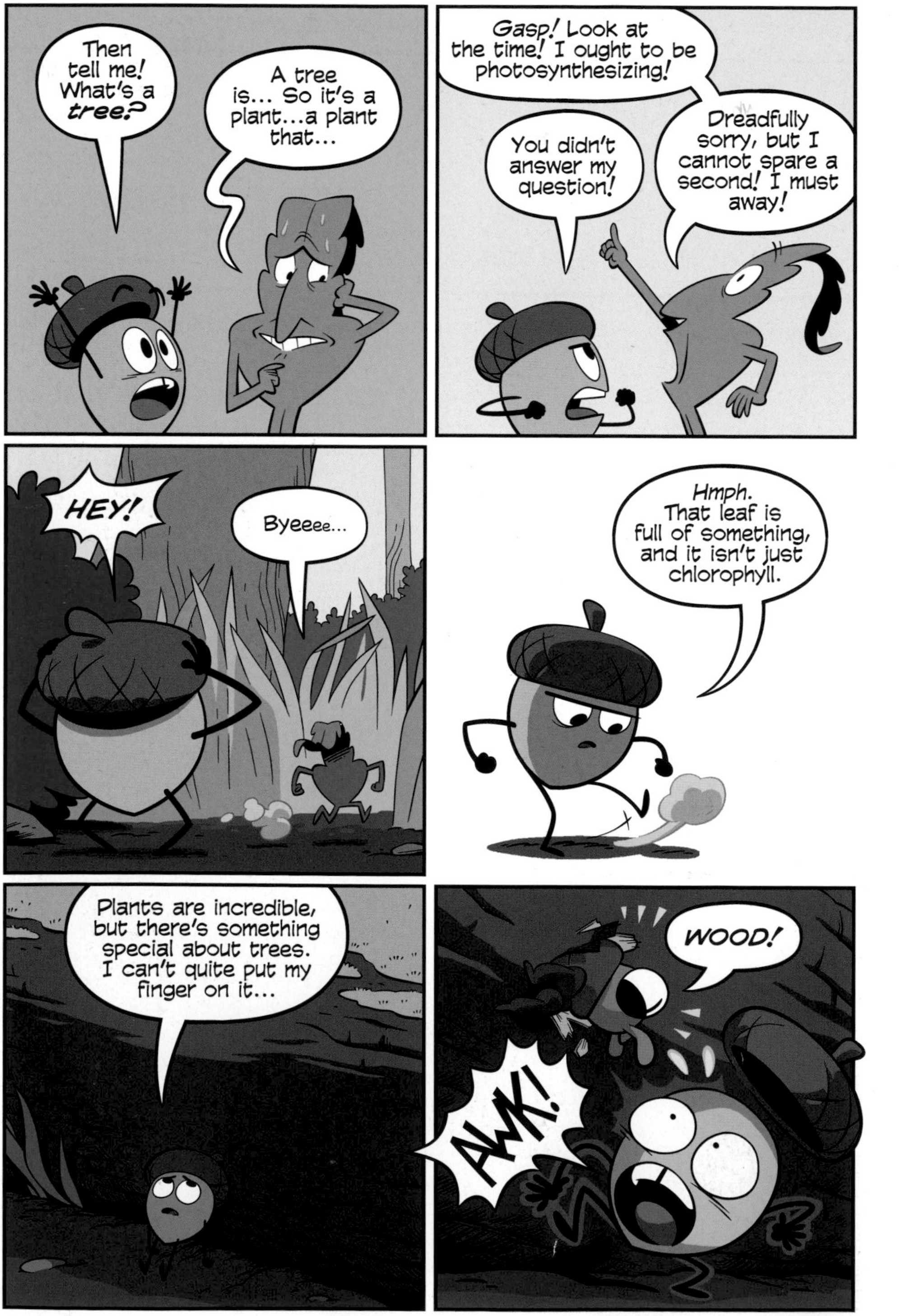
Then tell me! What's a *tree?*
A tree is... So it's a plant...a plant that...
Gasp! Look at the time! I ought to be photosynthesizing!
You didn't answer my question!
Dreadfully sorry, but I cannot spare a second! I must away!
HEY!
Byeeee...
Hmph. That leaf is full of something, and it isn't just chlorophyll.
Plants are incredible, but there's something special about trees. I can't quite put my finger on it...
WOOD!
AWK!

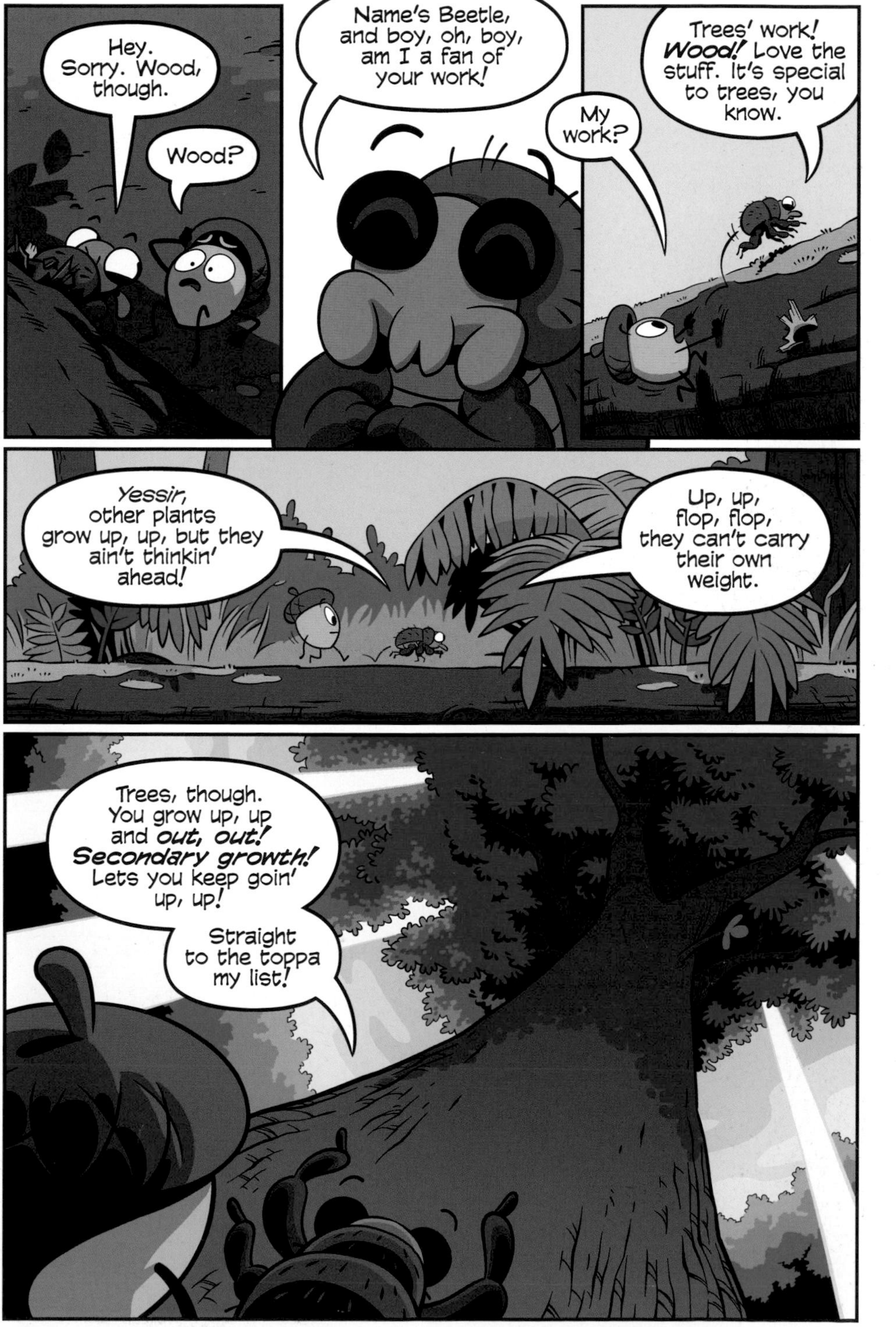

Hey. Sorry. Wood, though.
Wood?
Name's Beetle, and boy, oh, boy, am I a fan of your work!
My work?
Trees' work! *Wood!* Love the stuff. It's special to trees, you know.
Yessir, other plants grow up, up, but they ain't thinkin' ahead!
Up, up, flop, flop, they can't carry their own weight.
Trees, though. You grow up, up and ***out, out! Secondary growth!*** Lets you keep goin' up, up!
Straight to the toppa my list!

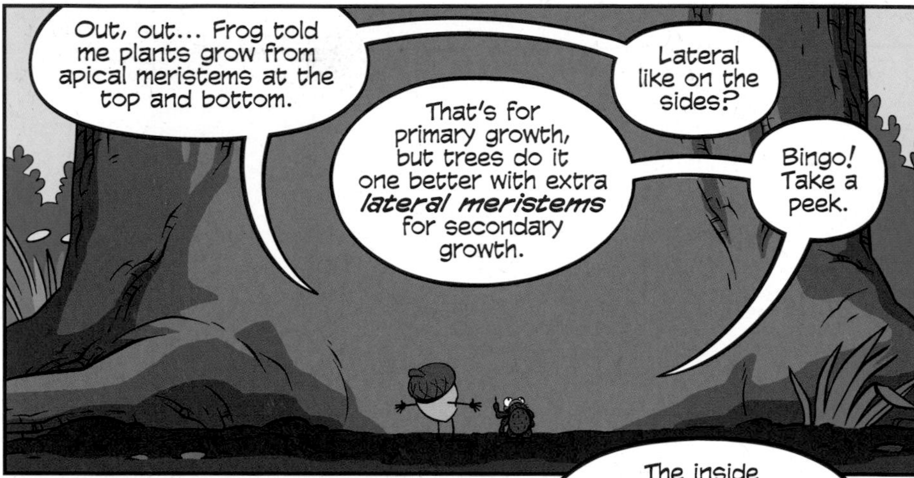

Out, out... Frog told me plants grow from apical meristems at the top and bottom.
That's for primary growth, but trees do it one better with extra *lateral meristems* for secondary growth.
Lateral like on the sides?
Bingo! Take a peek.

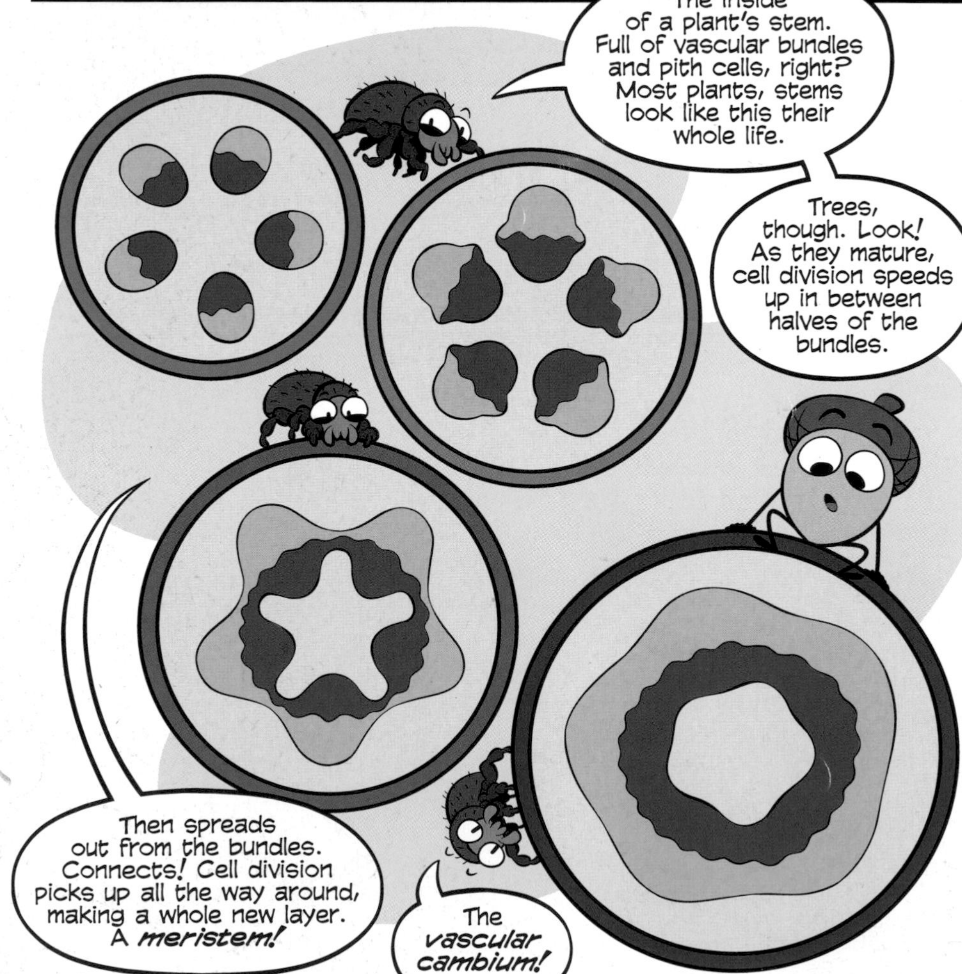

The inside of a plant's stem. Full of vascular bundles and pith cells, right? Most plants, stems look like this their whole life.
Trees, though. Look! As they mature, cell division speeds up in between halves of the bundles.
Then spreads out from the bundles. Connects! Cell division picks up all the way around, making a whole new layer. A *meristem!*
The *vascular cambium!*

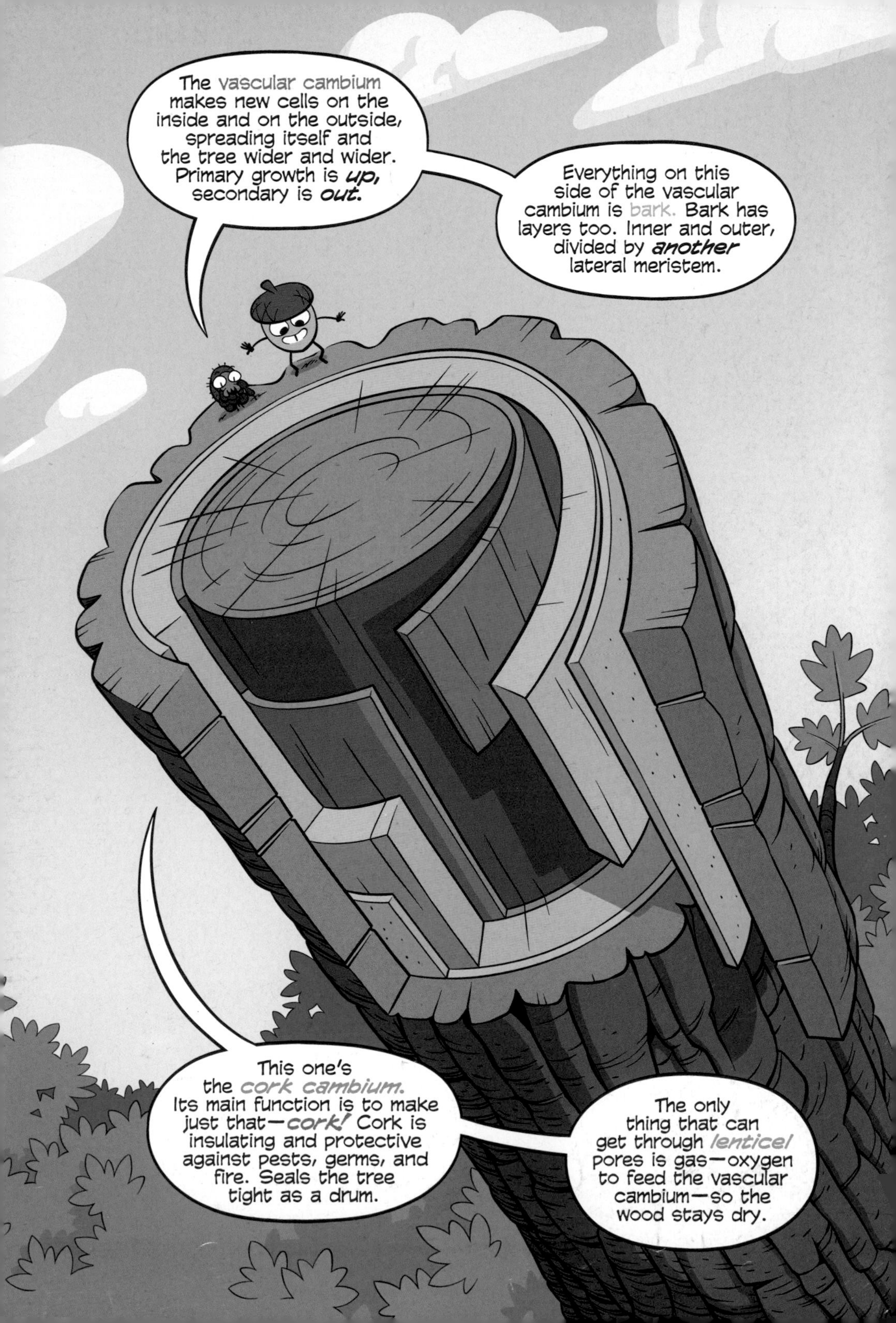
The vascular cambium makes new cells on the inside and on the outside, spreading itself and the tree wider and wider. Primary growth is *up*, secondary is *out*.
Everything on this side of the vascular cambium is bark. Bark has layers too. Inner and outer, divided by *another* lateral meristem.
This one's the *cork cambium*. Its main function is to make just that—*cork!* Cork is insulating and protective against pests, germs, and fire. Seals the tree tight as a drum.
The only thing that can get through *lenticel* pores is gas—oxygen to feed the vascular cambium—so the wood stays dry.

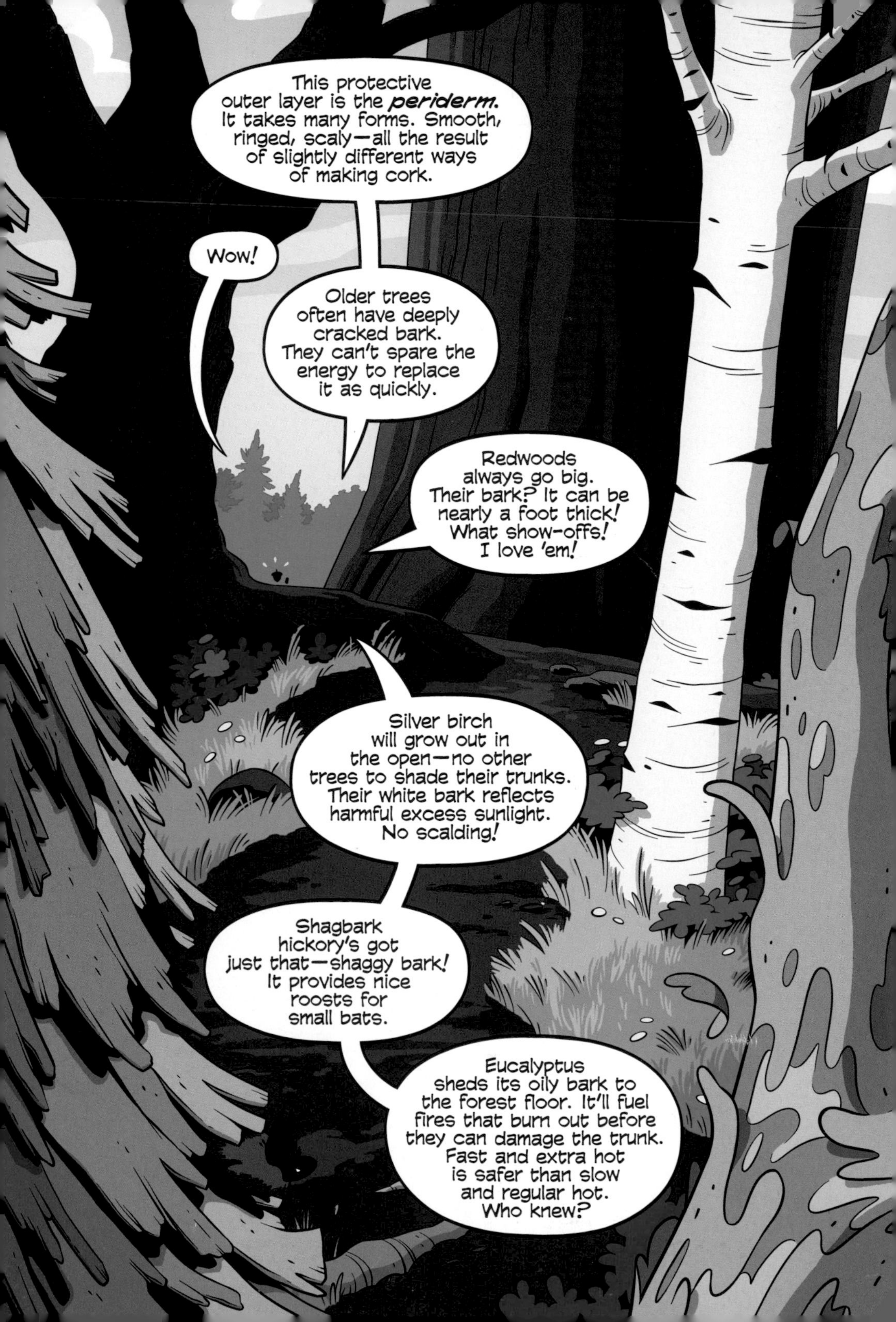
This protective outer layer is the ***periderm.*** It takes many forms. Smooth, ringed, scaly—all the result of slightly different ways of making cork.
Wow!
Older trees often have deeply cracked bark. They can't spare the energy to replace it as quickly.
Redwoods always go big. Their bark? It can be nearly a foot thick! What show-offs! I love 'em!
Silver birch will grow out in the open—no other trees to shade their trunks. Their white bark reflects harmful excess sunlight. No scalding!
Shagbark hickory's got just that—shaggy bark! It provides nice roosts for small bats.
Eucalyptus sheds its oily bark to the forest floor. It'll fuel fires that burn out before they can damage the trunk. Fast and extra hot is safer than slow and regular hot. Who knew?

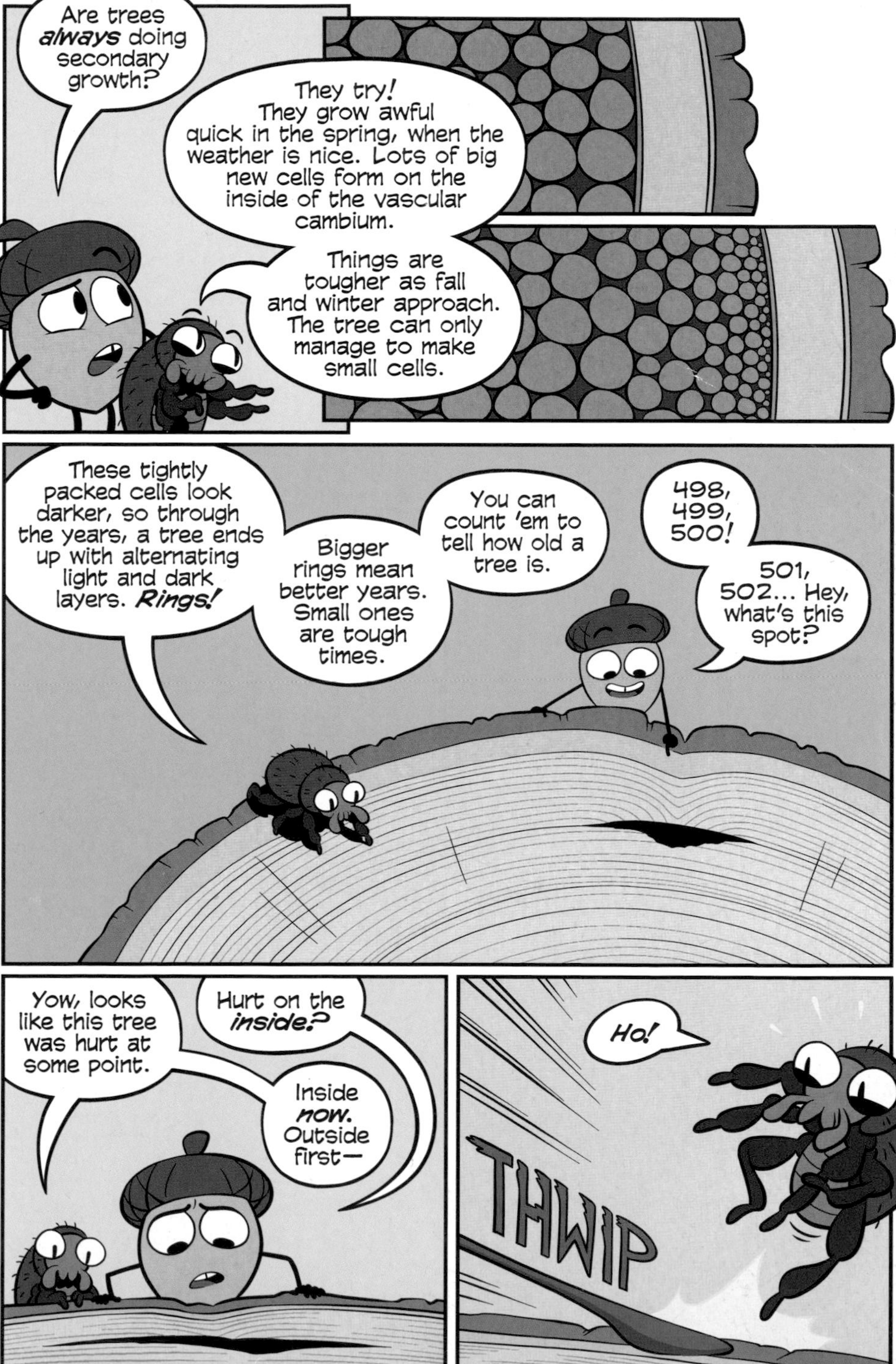
Are trees *always* doing secondary growth?
They try! They grow awful quick in the spring, when the weather is nice. Lots of big new cells form on the inside of the vascular cambium.
Things are tougher as fall and winter approach. The tree can only manage to make small cells.
These tightly packed cells look darker, so through the years, a tree ends up with alternating light and dark layers. *Rings!*
Bigger rings mean better years. Small ones are tough times.
You can count 'em to tell how old a tree is.
498, 499, 500!
501, 502... Hey, what's this spot?
Yow, looks like this tree was hurt at some point.
Hurt on the *inside?*
Inside *now.* Outside first—
Ho!
THWIP

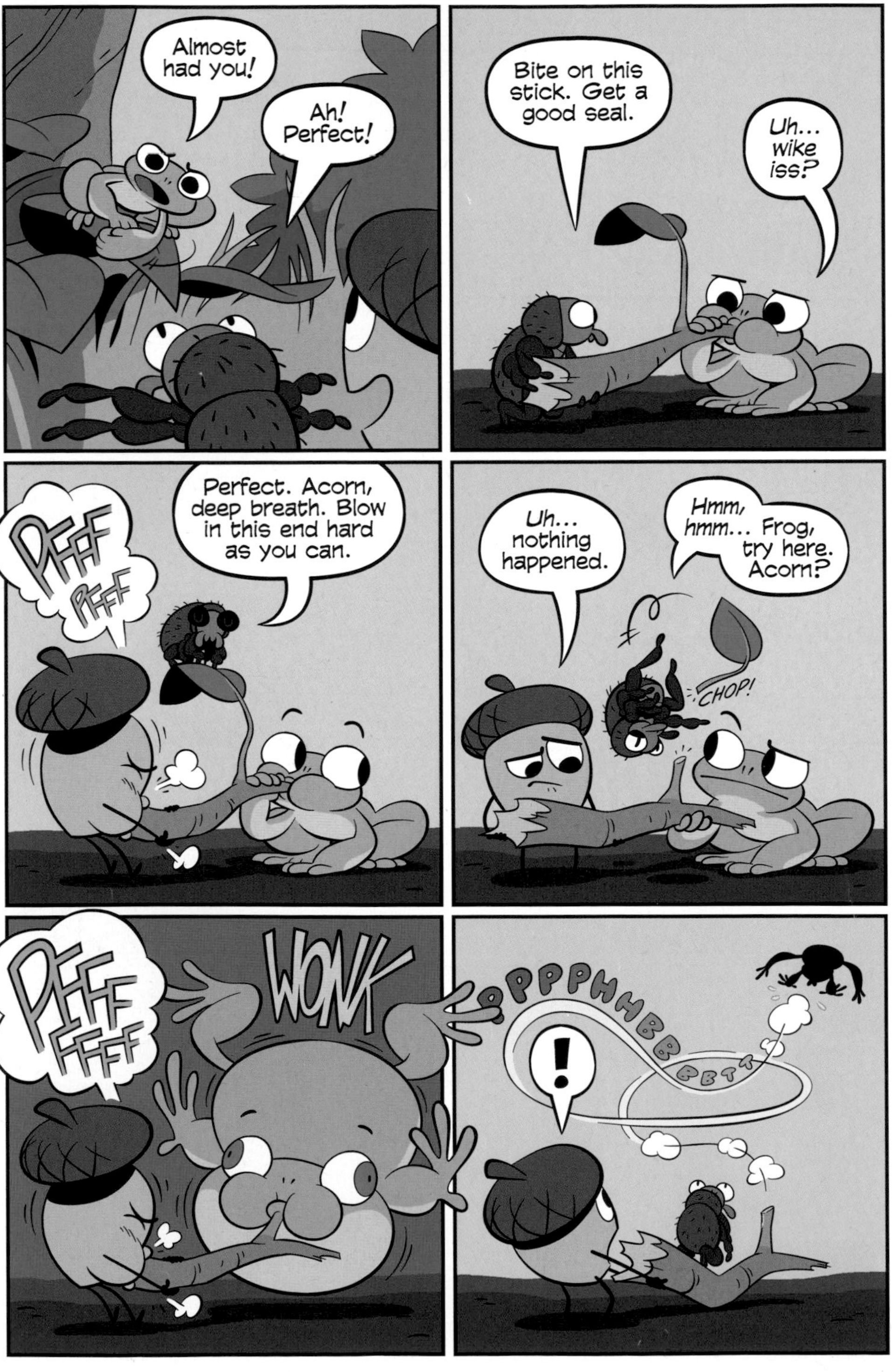
Almost had you!
Ah! Perfect!
Bite on this stick. Get a good seal.
Uh... wike iss?
PFFF PFFF
Perfect. Acorn, deep breath. Blow in this end hard as you can.
Uh... nothing happened.
Hmm, hmm... Frog, try here. Acorn?
CHOP!
PFFFFFFFF
WONK
PPPPPHHBBBBTT
!

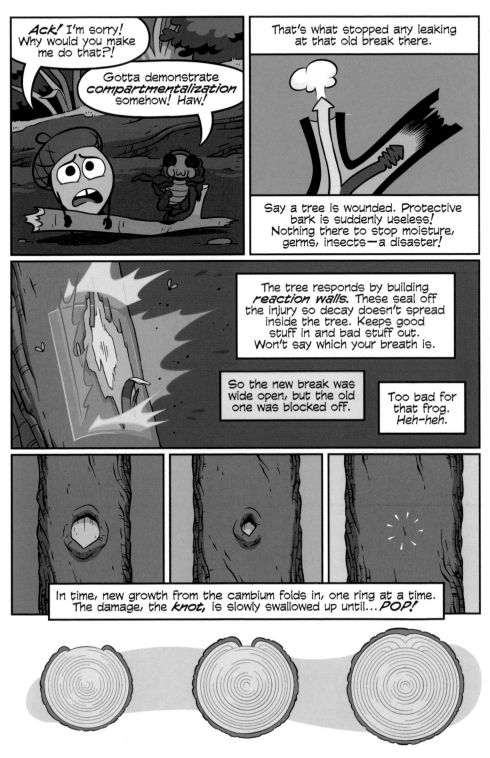

Ack! I'm sorry! Why would you make me do that?!

Gotta demonstrate *compartmentalization* somehow! Haw!

That's what stopped any leaking at that old break there.

Say a tree is wounded. Protective bark is suddenly useless! Nothing there to stop moisture, germs, insects—a disaster!

The tree responds by building *reaction walls*. These seal off the injury so decay doesn't spread inside the tree. Keeps good stuff in and bad stuff out. Won't say which your breath is.

So the new break was wide open, but the old one was blocked off.

Too bad for that frog. Heh-heh.

In time, new growth from the cambium folds in, one ring at a time. The damage, the *knot*, is slowly swallowed up until... *POP!*

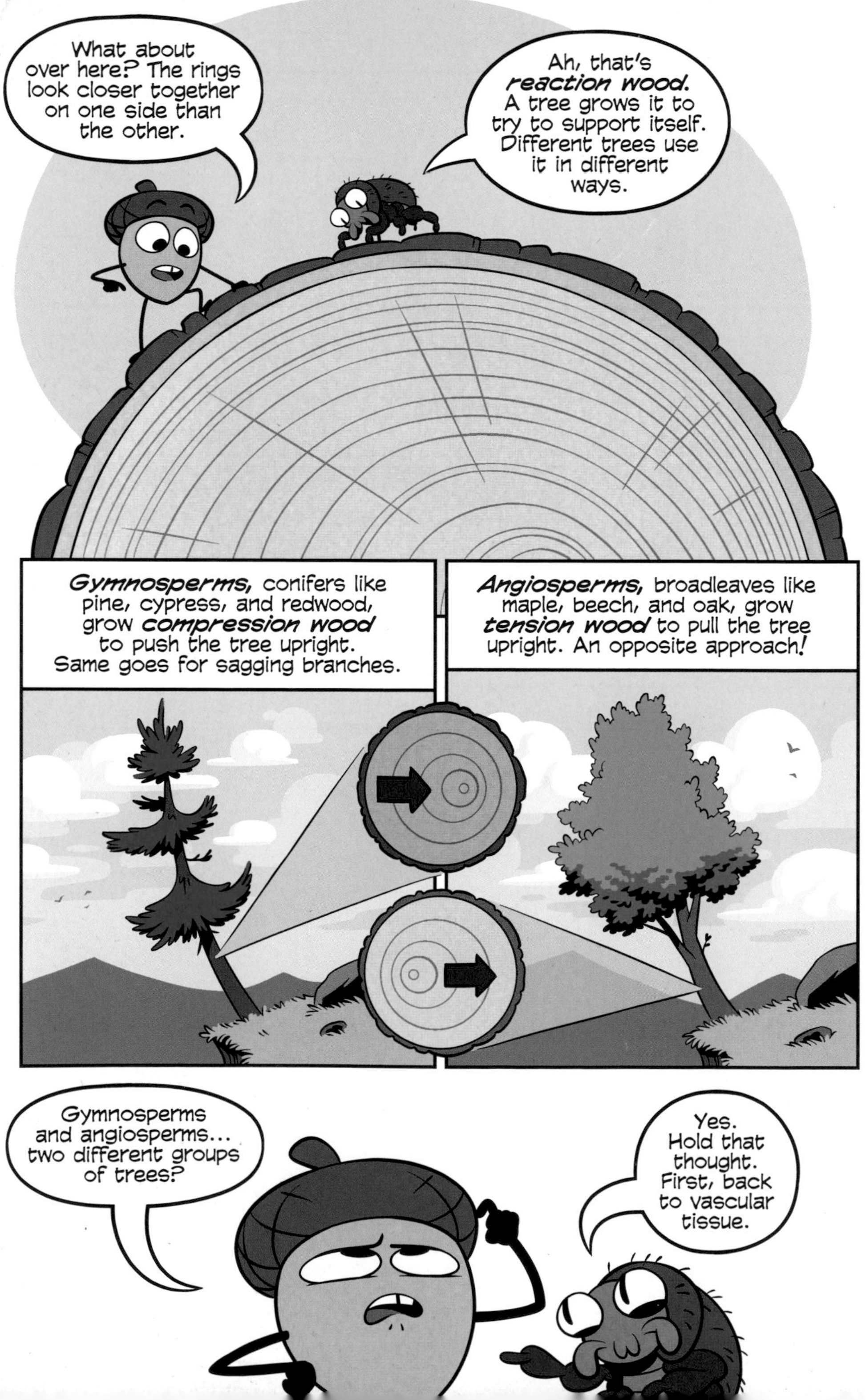
What about over here? The rings look closer together on one side than the other.
Ah, that's *reaction wood.* A tree grows it to try to support itself. Different trees use it in different ways.
Gymnosperms, conifers like pine, cypress, and redwood, grow *compression wood* to push the tree upright. Same goes for sagging branches.
Angiosperms, broadleaves like maple, beech, and oak, grow *tension wood* to pull the tree upright. An opposite approach!
Gymnosperms and angiosperms... two different groups of trees?
Yes. Hold that thought. First, back to vascular tissue.

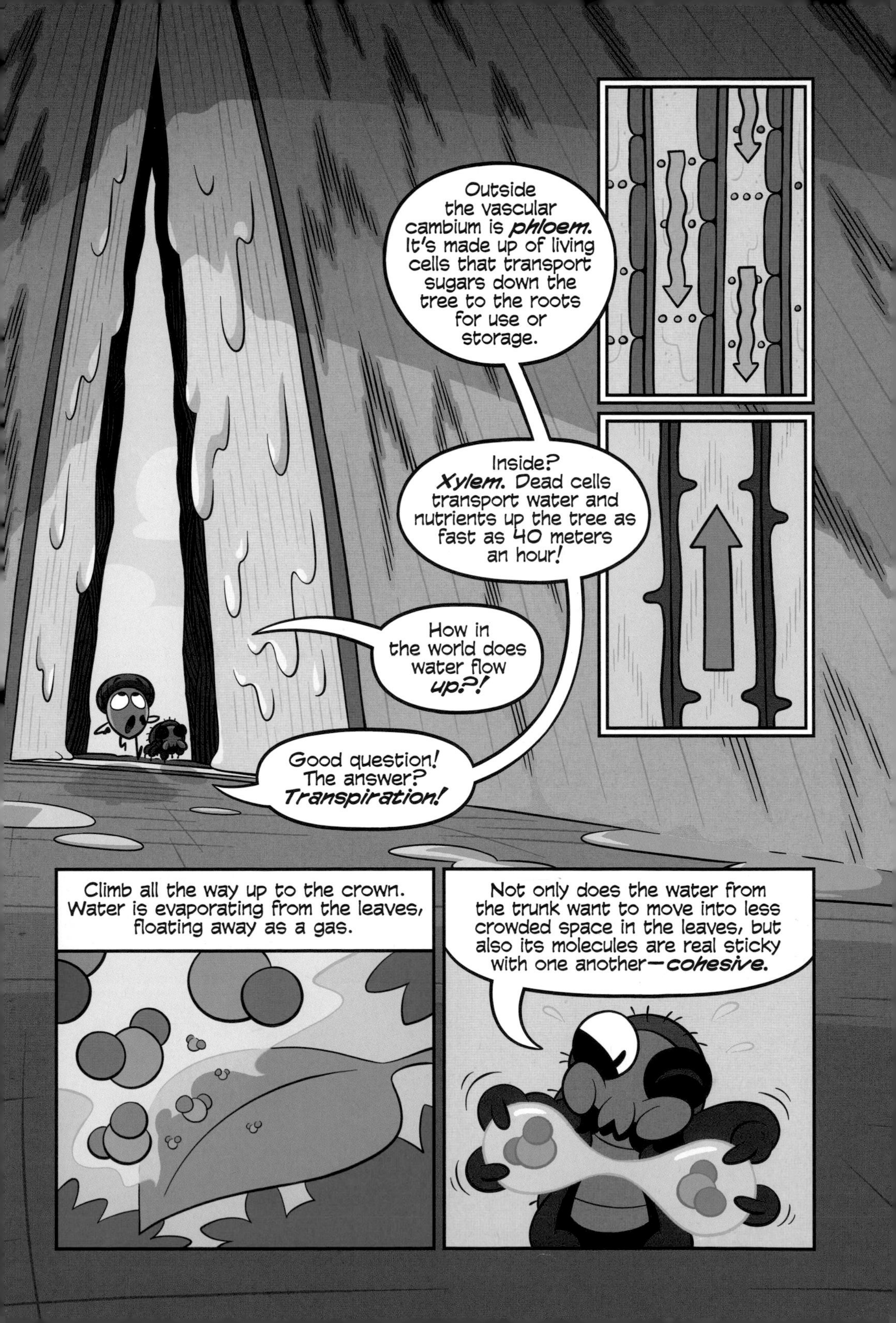
Outside the vascular cambium is *phloem*. It's made up of living cells that transport sugars down the tree to the roots for use or storage.
Inside? *Xylem*. Dead cells transport water and nutrients up the tree as fast as 40 meters an hour!
How in the world does water flow *up?!*
Good question! The answer? *Transpiration!*
Climb all the way up to the crown. Water is evaporating from the leaves, floating away as a gas.
Not only does the water from the trunk want to move into less crowded space in the leaves, but also its molecules are real sticky with one another—*cohesive*.

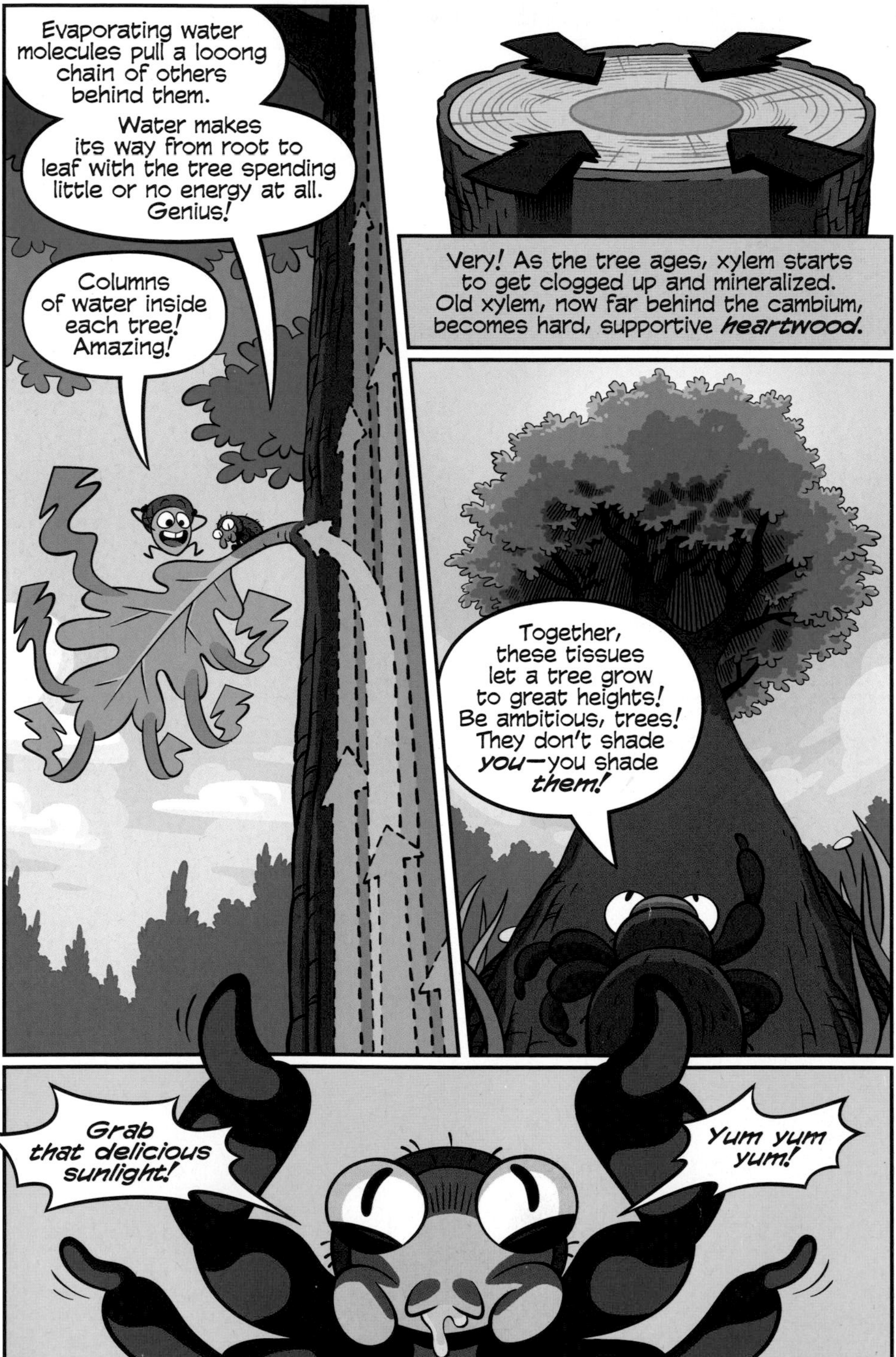
Evaporating water molecules pull a looong chain of others behind them.
Water makes its way from root to leaf with the tree spending little or no energy at all. Genius!
Columns of water inside each tree! Amazing!
Very! As the tree ages, xylem starts to get clogged up and mineralized. Old xylem, now far behind the cambium, becomes hard, supportive *heartwood.*
Together, these tissues let a tree grow to great heights! Be ambitious, trees! They don't shade *you*—you shade *them!*
Grab that delicious sunlight!
Yum yum yum!

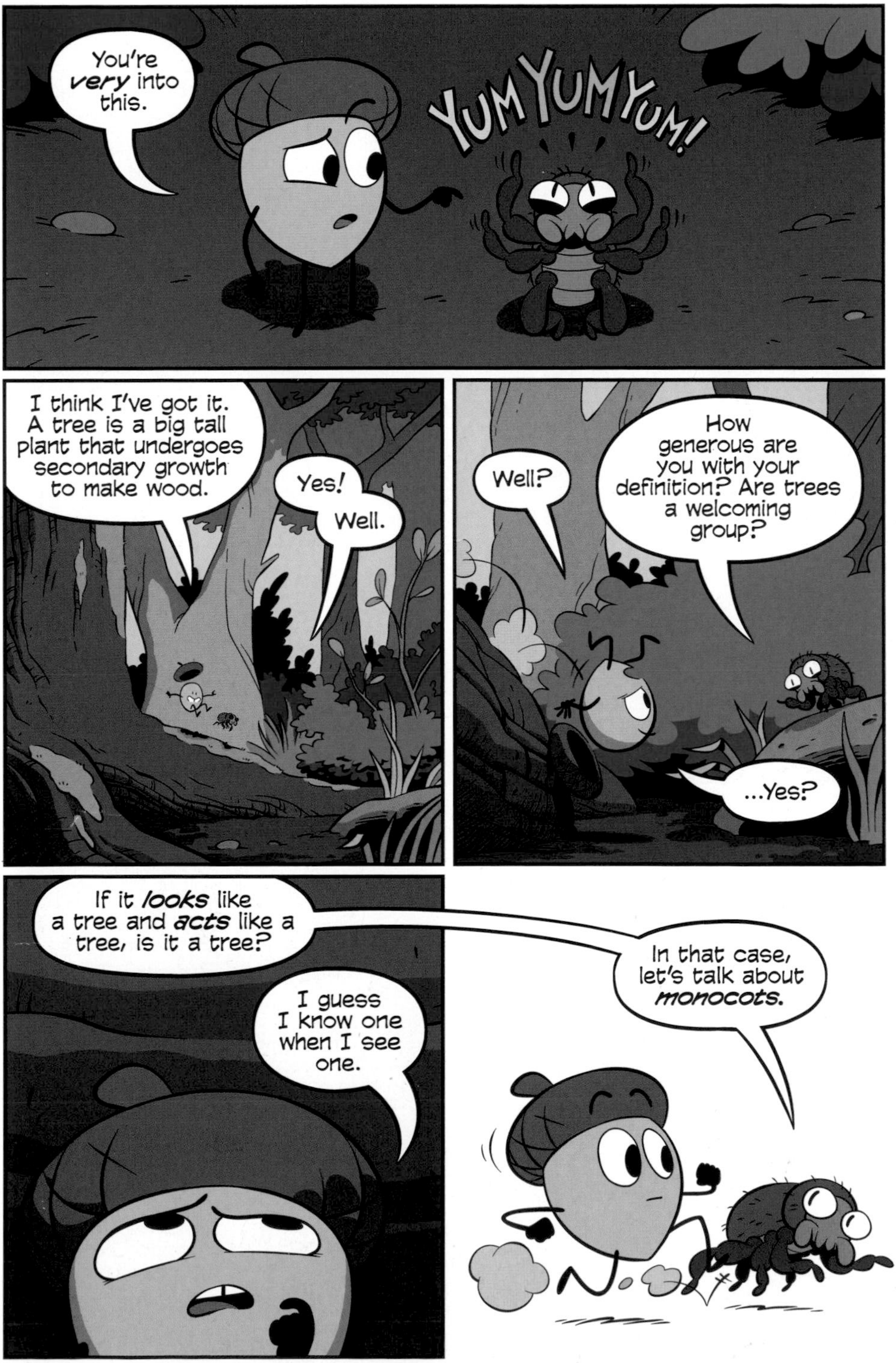
You're *very* into this.
YUM YUM YUM!
I think I've got it. A tree is a big tall plant that undergoes secondary growth to make wood.
Yes!
Well.
Well?
How generous are you with your definition? Are trees a welcoming group?
...Yes?
If it *looks* like a tree and *acts* like a tree, is it a tree?
I guess I know one when I see one.
In that case, let's talk about *monocots*.

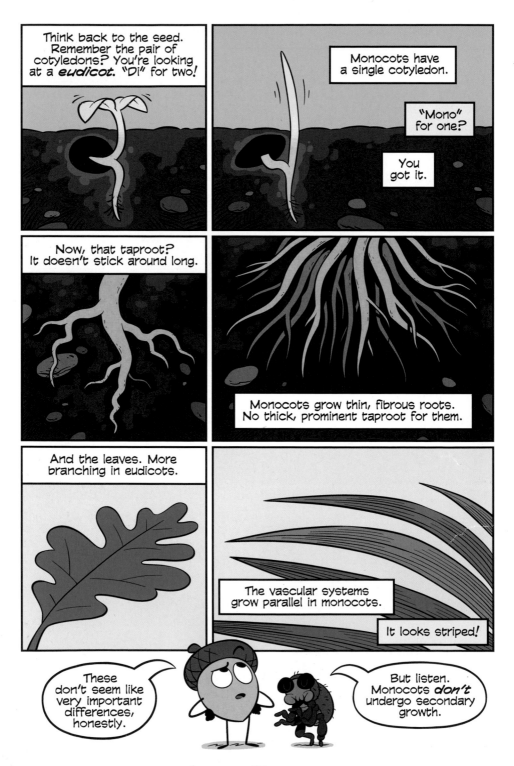

Think back to the seed. Remember the pair of cotyledons? You're looking at a *eudicot*. "Di" for two!

Monocots have a single cotyledon.

"Mono" for one?

You got it.

Now, that taproot? It doesn't stick around long.

Monocots grow thin, fibrous roots. No thick, prominent taproot for them.

And the leaves. More branching in eudicots.

The vascular systems grow parallel in monocots.

It looks striped!

These don't seem like very important differences, honestly.

But listen. Monocots *don't* undergo secondary growth.

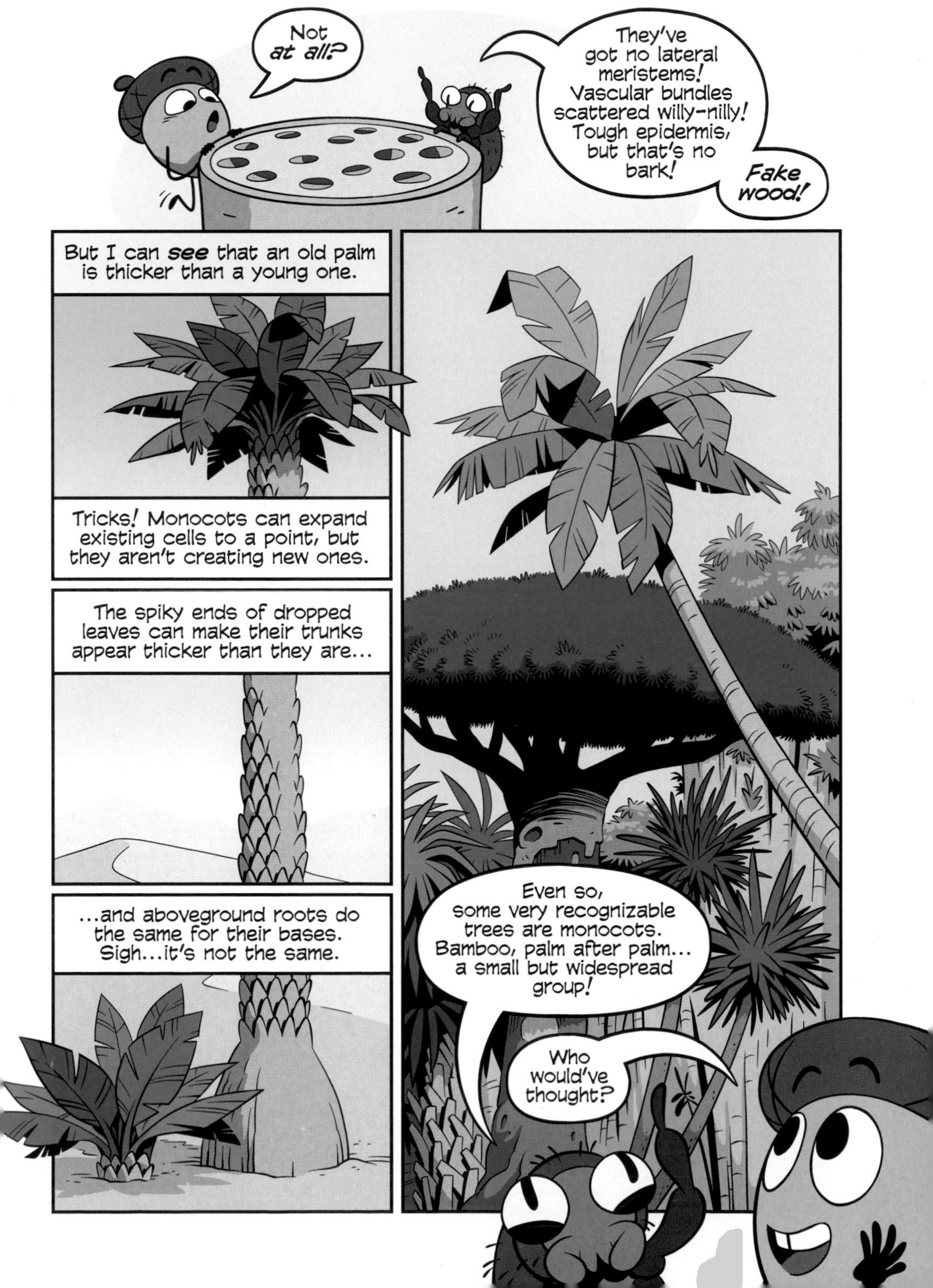
Not at all?
They've got no lateral meristems! Vascular bundles scattered willy-nilly! Tough epidermis, but that's no bark!
Fake wood!
But I can see that an old palm is thicker than a young one.
Tricks! Monocots can expand existing cells to a point, but they aren't creating new ones.
The spiky ends of dropped leaves can make their trunks appear thicker than they are...
...and aboveground roots do the same for their bases. Sigh...it's not the same.
Even so, some very recognizable trees are monocots. Bamboo, palm after palm... a small but widespread group!
Who would've thought?

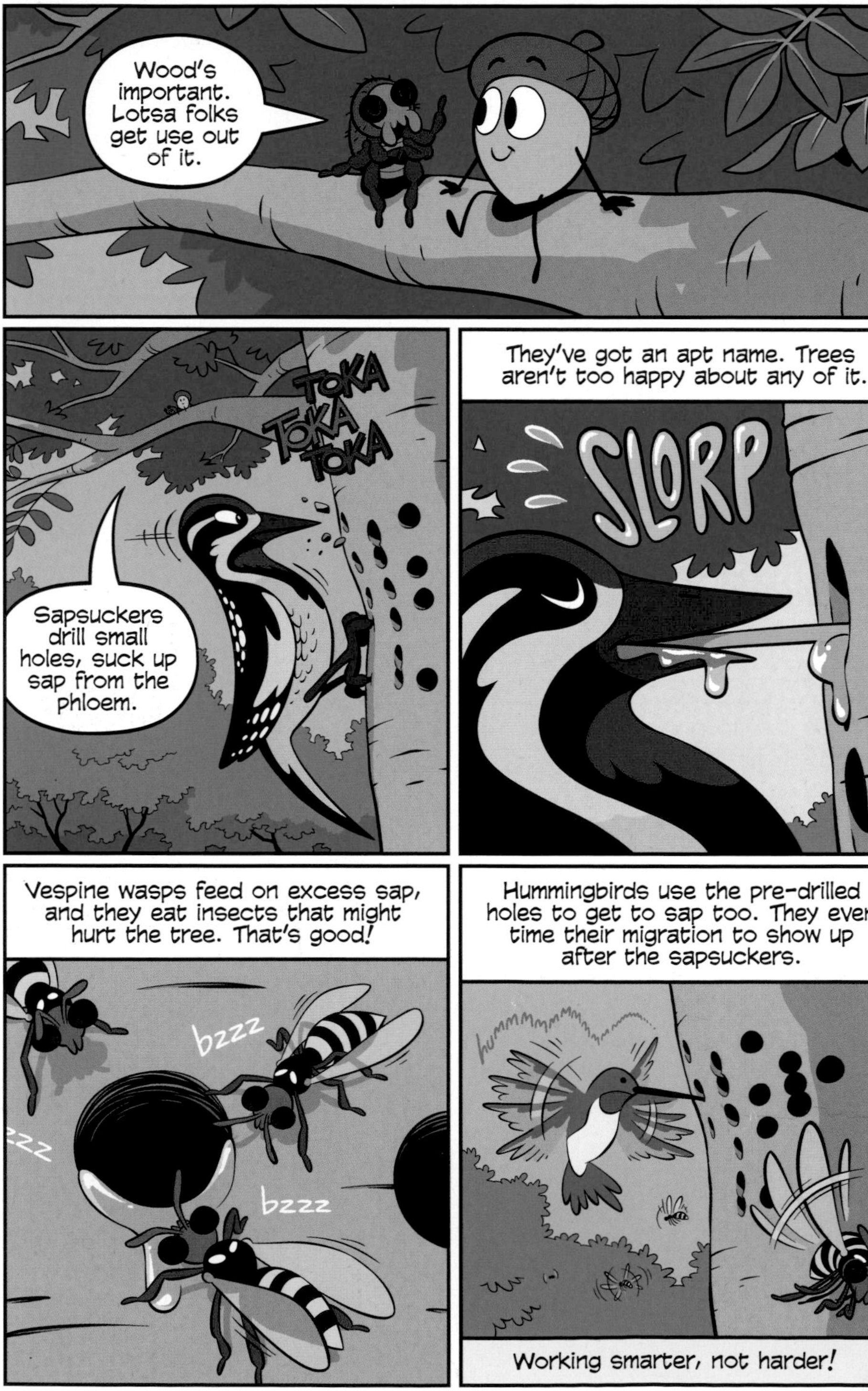
Wood's important. Lotsa folks get use out of it.
TOKA TOKA TOKA
Sapsuckers drill small holes, suck up sap from the phloem.
They've got an apt name. Trees aren't too happy about any of it.
SLORP
Vespine wasps feed on excess sap, and they eat insects that might hurt the tree. That's good!
bzzz
bzzz
Hummingbirds use the pre-drilled holes to get to sap too. They even time their migration to show up after the sapsuckers.
hummmmmmmmmmmm
Working smarter, not harder!

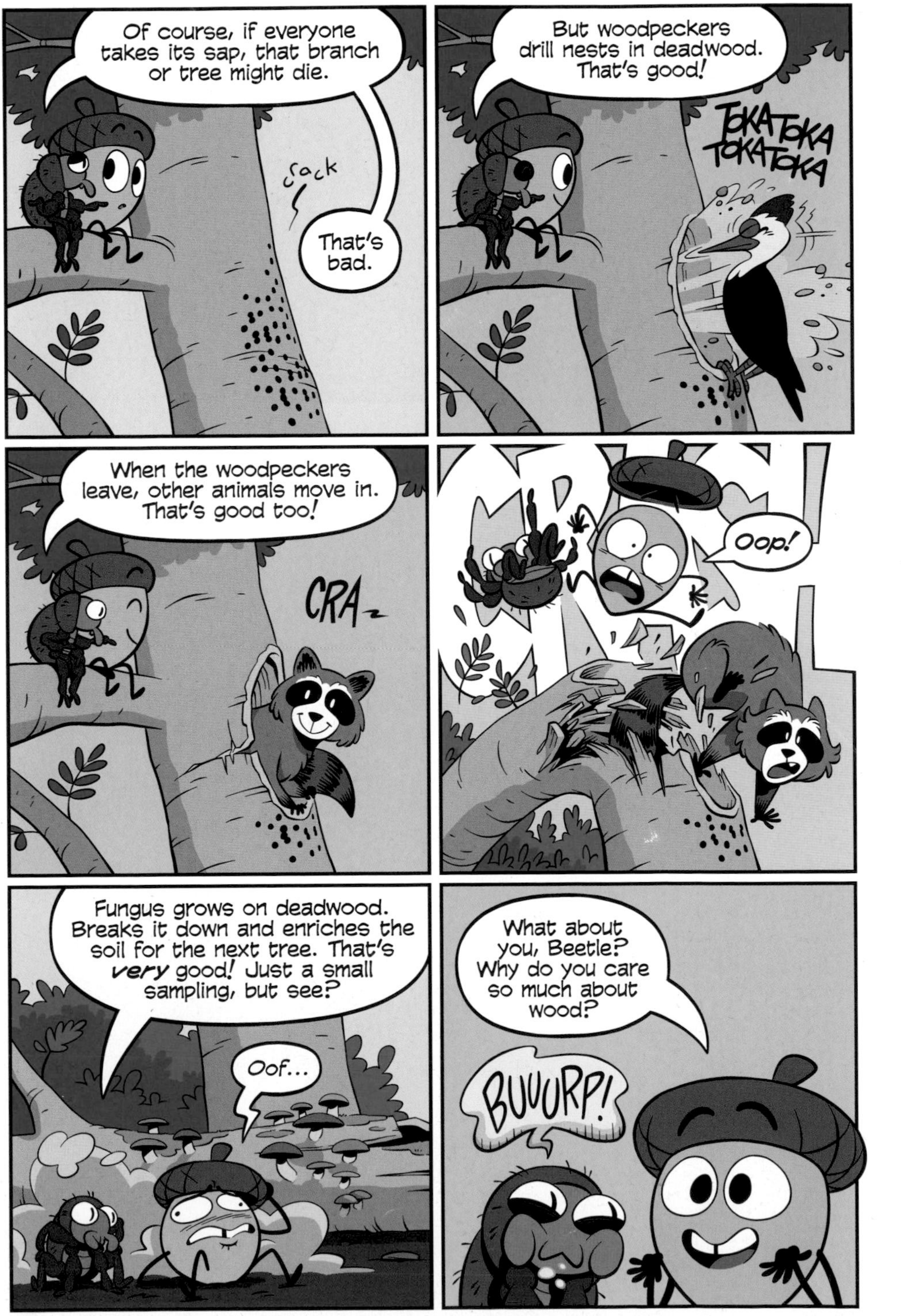
Of course, if everyone takes its sap, that branch or tree might die.
crack
That's bad.
But woodpeckers drill nests in deadwood. That's good!
TOKATOKA TOKATOKA
When the woodpeckers leave, other animals move in. That's good too!
CRA
Oop!
Fungus grows on deadwood. Breaks it down and enriches the soil for the next tree. That's *very* good! Just a small sampling, but see?
Oof...
What about you, Beetle? Why do you care so much about wood?
BUUURP!

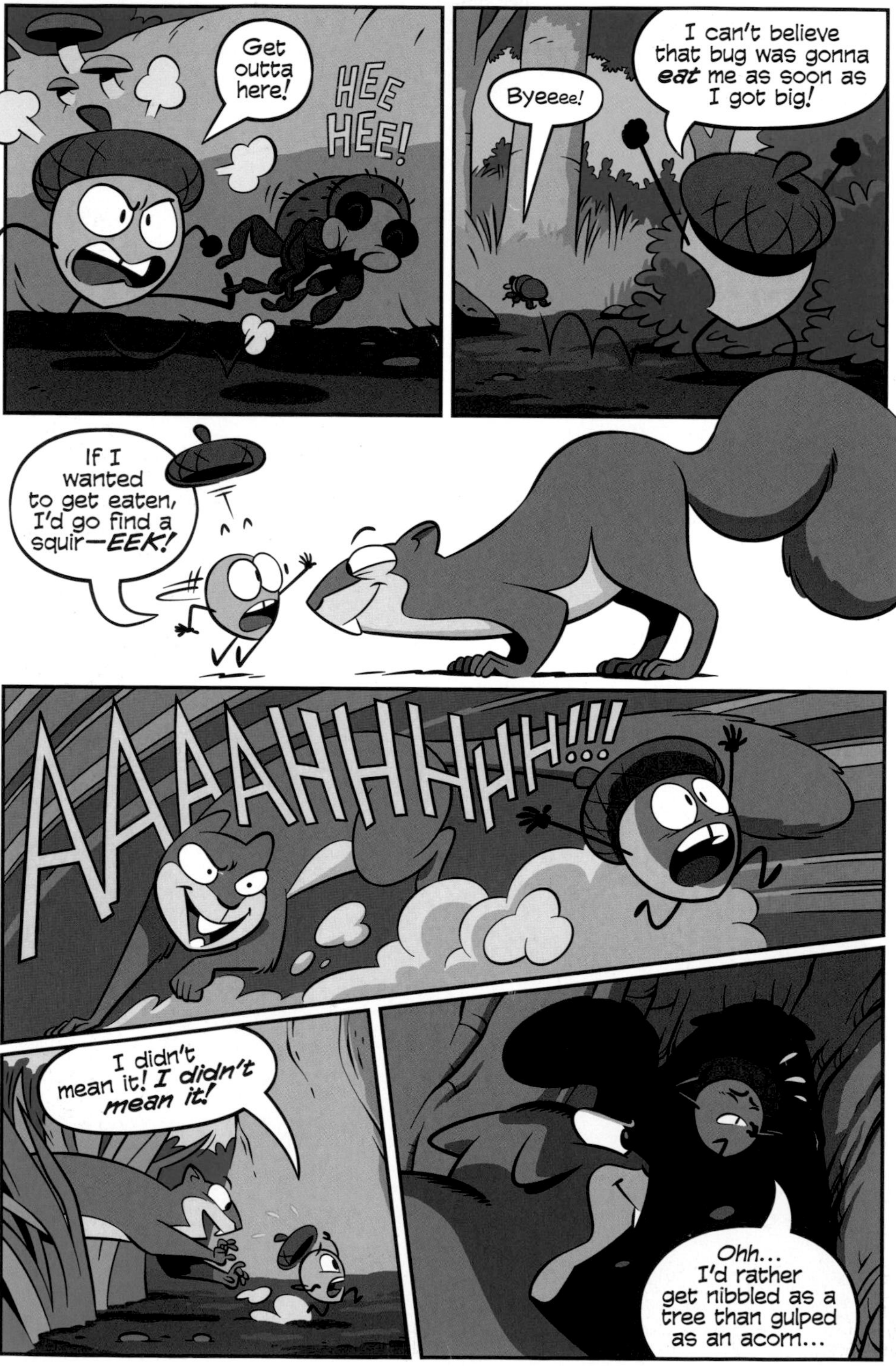
Get outta here!
HEE HEE!
Byeeee!
I can't believe that bug was gonna **eat** me as soon as I got big!
If I wanted to get eaten, I'd go find a squir—**EEK!**
AAAAHHHHHH!!!
I didn't mean it! ***I didn't mean it!***
Ohh... I'd rather get nibbled as a tree than gulped as an acorn...

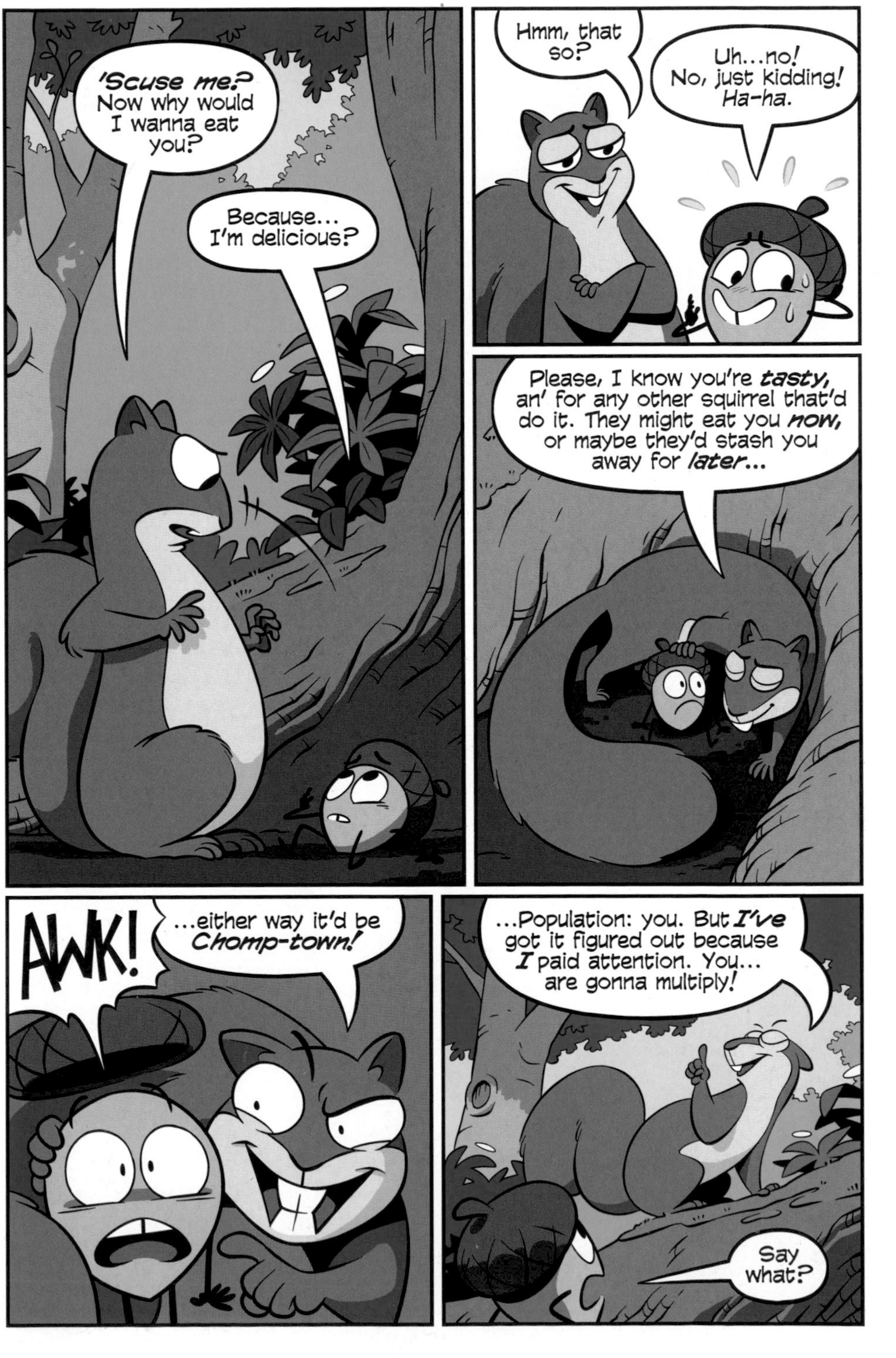
'Scuse me? Now why would I wanna eat you?
Because... I'm delicious?
Hmm, that so?
Uh...no! No, just kidding! Ha-ha.
Please, I know you're tasty, an' for any other squirrel that'd do it. They might eat you now, or maybe they'd stash you away for later...
AWK!
...either way it'd be Chomp-town!
...Population: you. But I've got it figured out because I paid attention. You... are gonna multiply!
Say what?

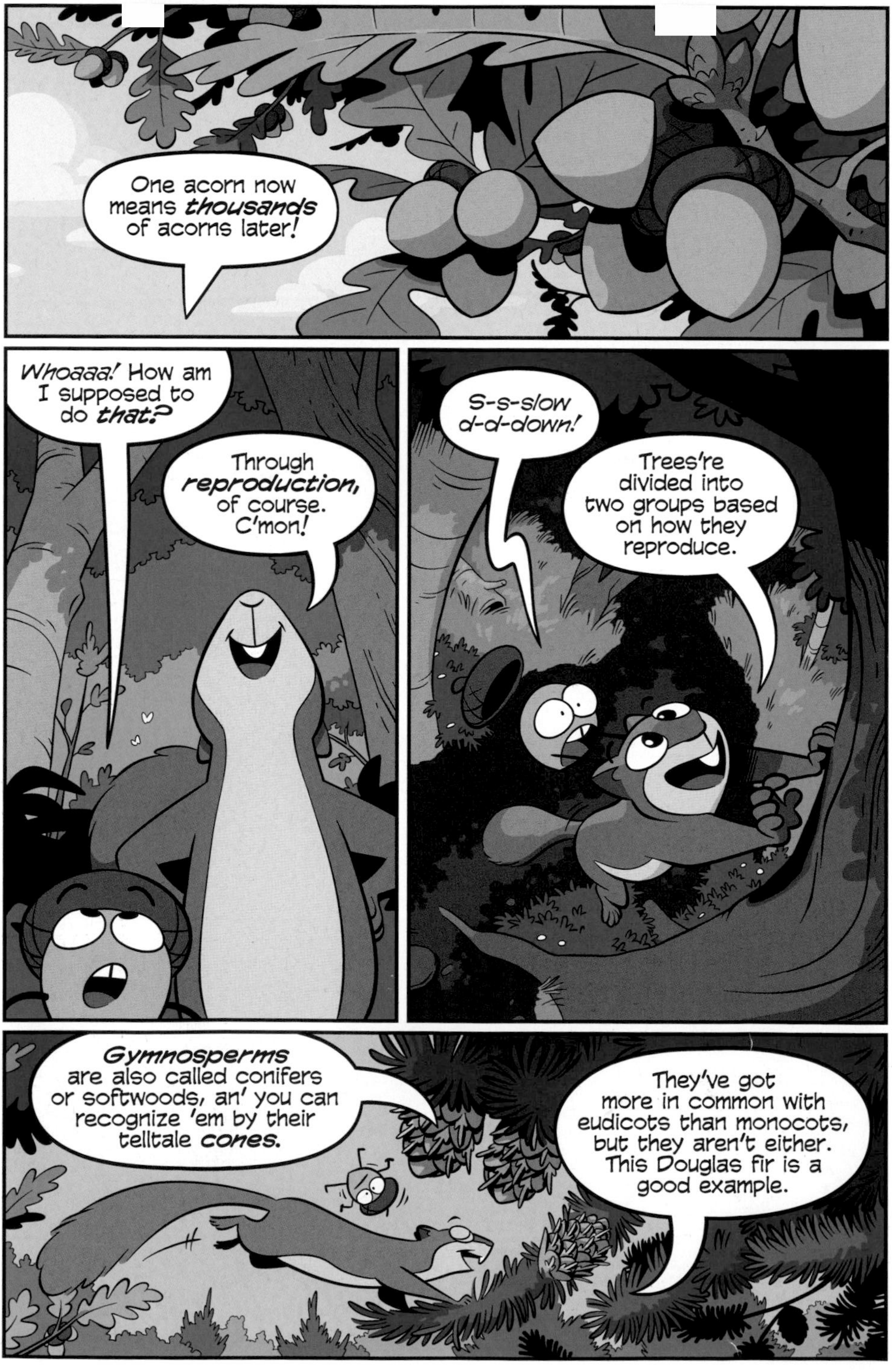
One acorn now means *thousands* of acorns later!
Whoaaa! How am I supposed to do *that?*
Through *reproduction,* of course. C'mon!
S-s-slow d-d-down!
Trees're divided into two groups based on how they reproduce.
Gymnosperms are also called conifers or softwoods, an' you can recognize 'em by their telltale *cones.*
They've got more in common with eudicots than monocots, but they aren't either. This Douglas fir is a good example.

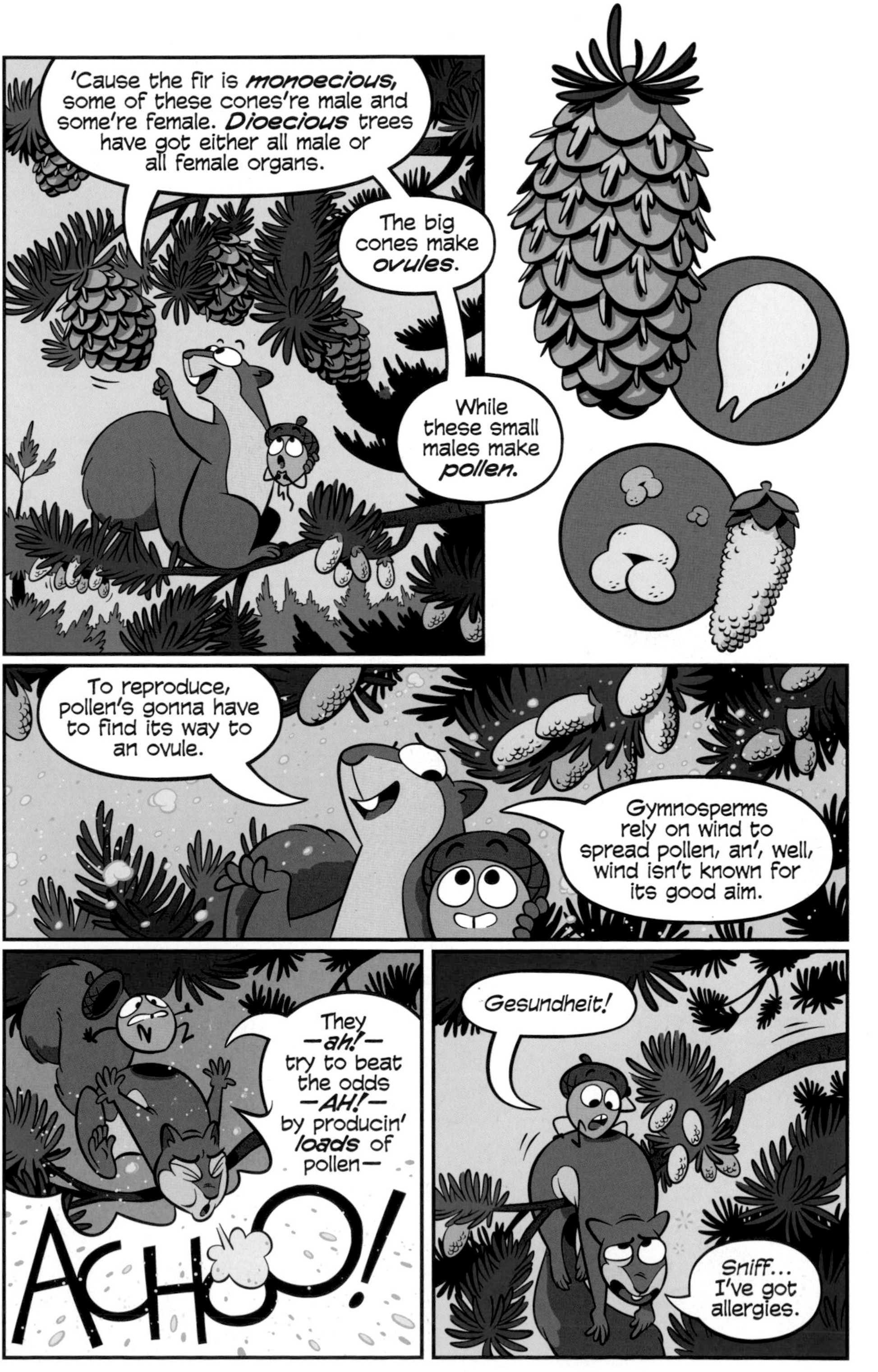
'Cause the fir is *monoecious*, some of these cones're male and some're female. *Dioecious* trees have got either all male or all female organs.
The big cones make *ovules*.
While these small males make *pollen*.
To reproduce, pollen's gonna have to find its way to an ovule.
Gymnosperms rely on wind to spread pollen, an', well, wind isn't known for its good aim.
They —*ah!*— try to beat the odds —*AH!*— by producin' *loads* of pollen—
ACHOO!
Gesundheit!
Sniff... I've got allergies.

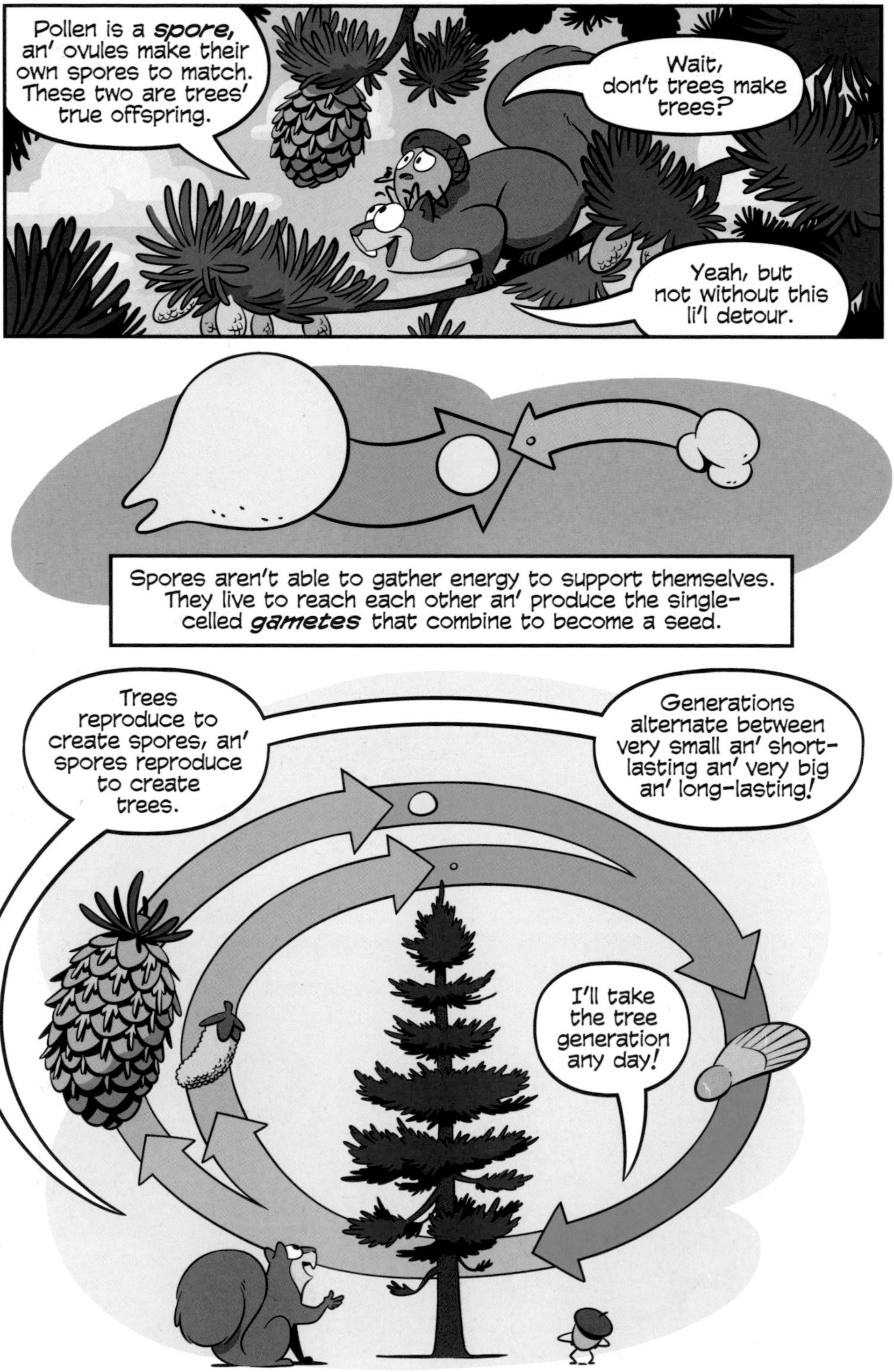
Pollen is a *spore,* an' ovules make their own spores to match. These two are trees' true offspring.
Wait, don't trees make trees?
Yeah, but not without this li'l detour.
Spores aren't able to gather energy to support themselves. They live to reach each other an' produce the single-celled ***gametes*** that combine to become a seed.
Trees reproduce to create spores, an' spores reproduce to create trees.
Generations alternate between very small an' short-lasting an' very big an' long-lasting!
I'll take the tree generation any day!

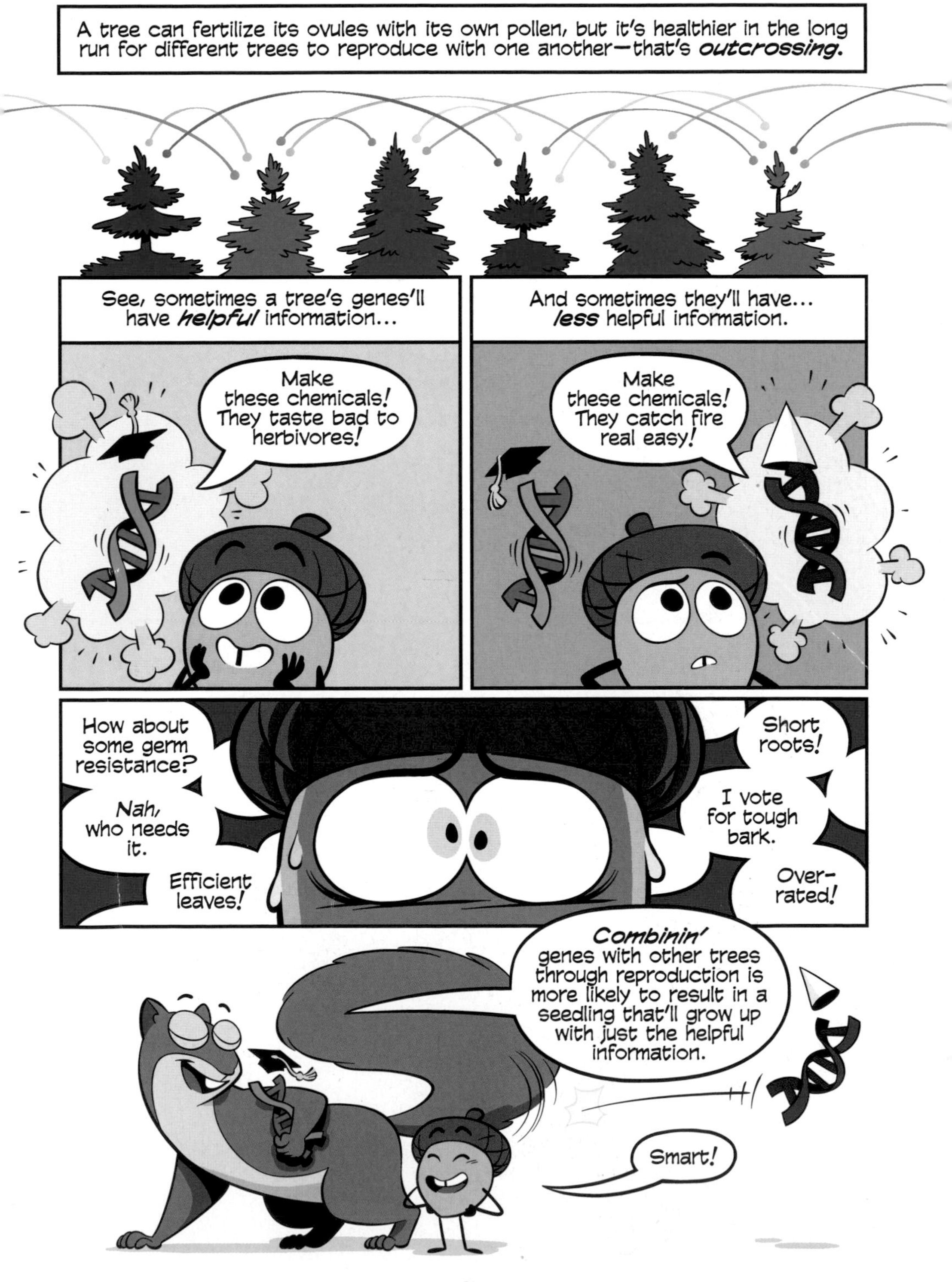
A tree can fertilize its ovules with its own pollen, but it's healthier in the long run for different trees to reproduce with one another—that's *outcrossing.*
See, sometimes a tree's genes'll have *helpful* information...
Make these chemicals! They taste bad to herbivores!
And sometimes they'll have... *less* helpful information.
Make these chemicals! They catch fire real easy!
How about some germ resistance?
Nah, who needs it.
Efficient leaves!
Short roots!
I vote for tough bark.
Over-rated!
Combinin' genes with other trees through reproduction is more likely to result in a seedling that'll grow up with just the helpful information.
Smart!

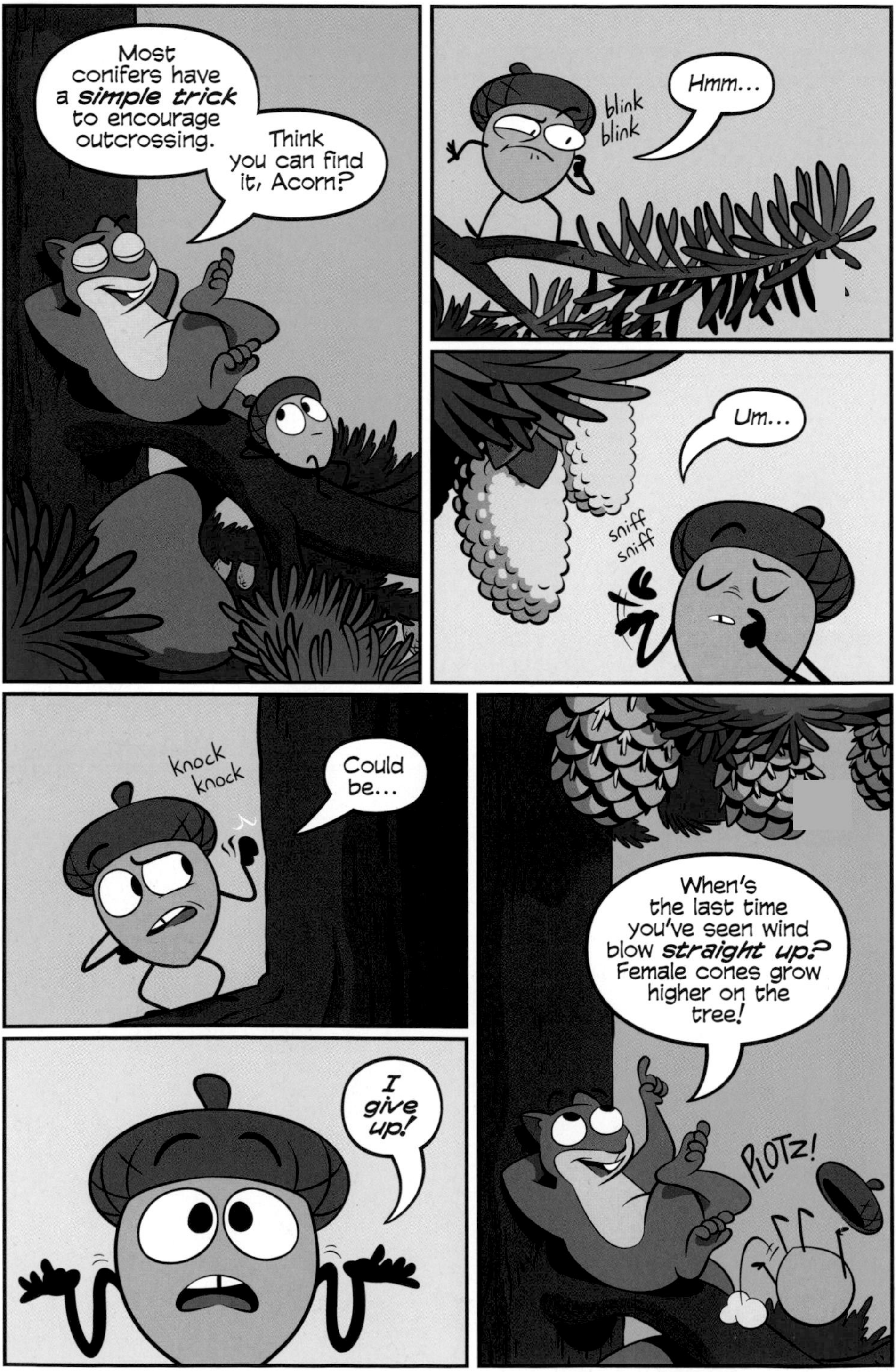
Most conifers have a ***simple trick*** to encourage outcrossing.
Think you can find it, Acorn?
blink blink
Hmm...
Um...
sniff sniff
knock knock
Could be...
I give up!
When's the last time you've seen wind blow ***straight up?*** Female cones grow higher on the tree!
PLOTZ!

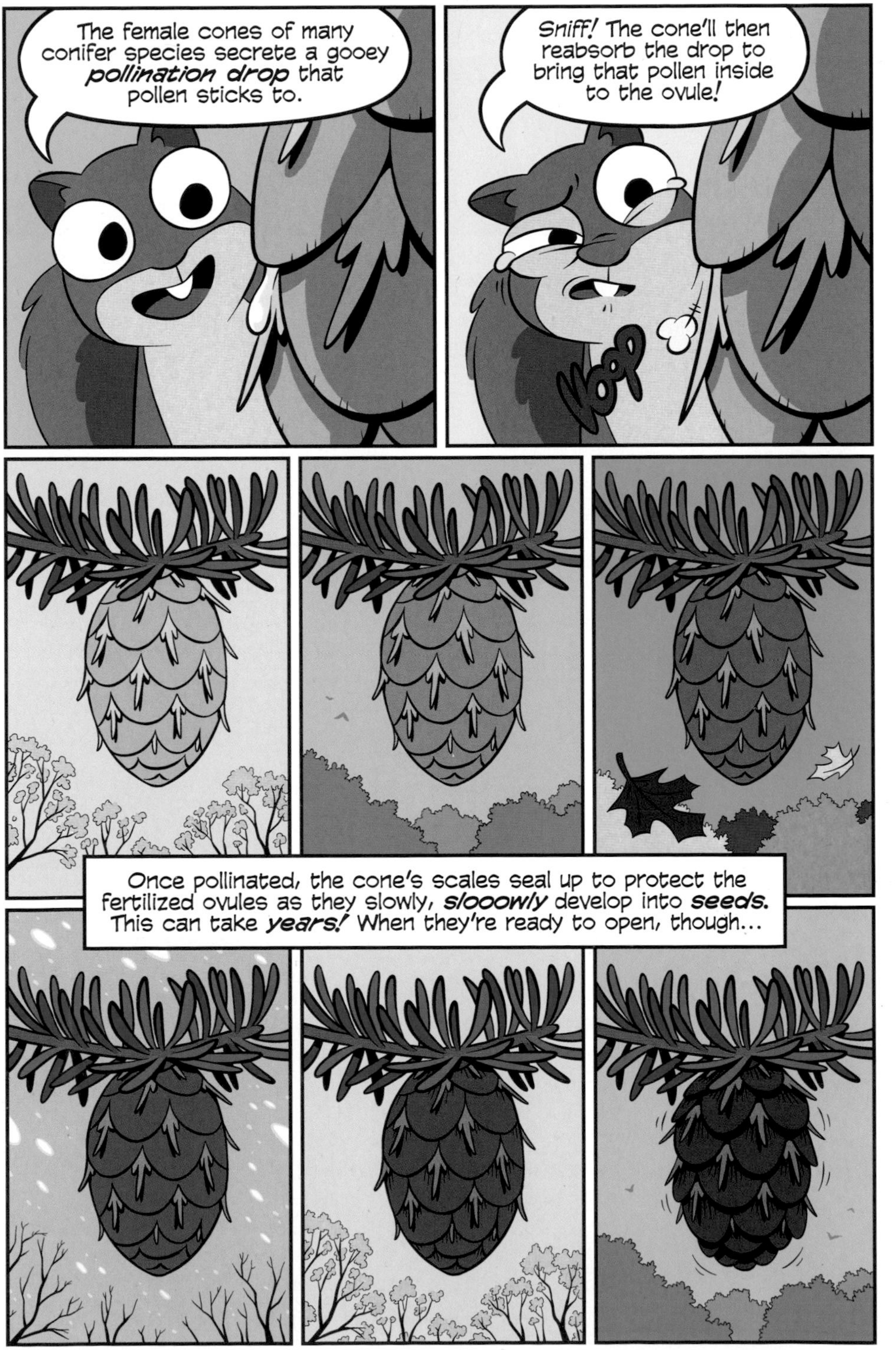
The female cones of many conifer species secrete a gooey *pollination drop* that pollen sticks to.
Sniff! The cone'll then reabsorb the drop to bring that pollen inside to the ovule!
Woop
Once pollinated, the cone's scales seal up to protect the fertilized ovules as they slowly, *slooowly* develop into *seeds.* This can take *years!* When they're ready to open, though...

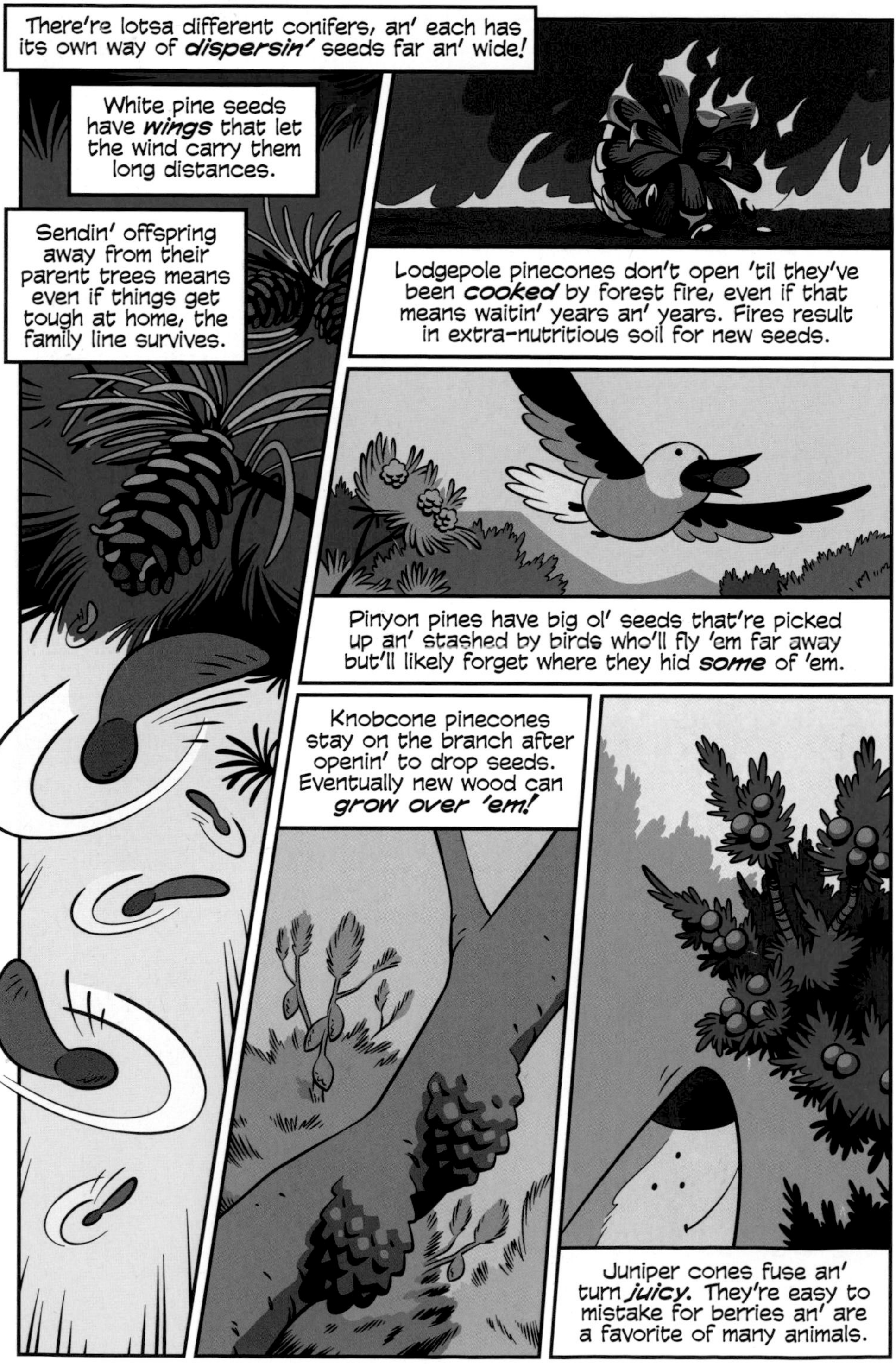

There're lotsa different conifers, an' each has its own way of *dispersin'* seeds far an' wide!
White pine seeds have *wings* that let the wind carry them long distances.
Sendin' offspring away from their parent trees means even if things get tough at home, the family line survives.
Lodgepole pinecones don't open 'til they've been *cooked* by forest fire, even if that means waitin' years an' years. Fires result in extra-nutritious soil for new seeds.
Pinyon pines have big ol' seeds that're picked up an' stashed by birds who'll fly 'em far away but'll likely forget where they hid *some* of 'em.
Knobcone pinecones stay on the branch after openin' to drop seeds. Eventually new wood can *grow over 'em!*
Juniper cones fuse an' turn *juicy*. They're easy to mistake for berries an' are a favorite of many animals.

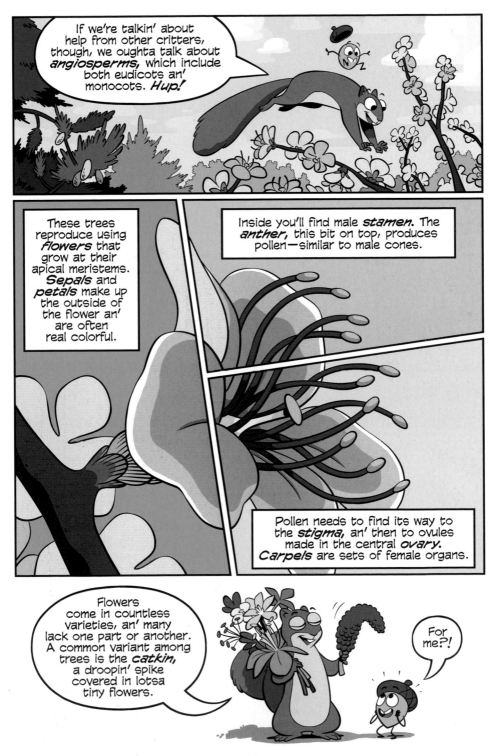

If we're talkin' about help from other critters, though, we oughta talk about *angiosperms*, which include both eudicots an' monocots. *Hup!*

These trees reproduce using *flowers* that grow at their apical meristems. *Sepals* and *petals* make up the outside of the flower an' are often real colorful.

Inside you'll find male *stamen*. The *anther*, this bit on top, produces pollen—similar to male cones.

Pollen needs to find its way to the *stigma*, an' then to ovules made in the central *ovary*. *Carpels* are sets of female organs.

Flowers come in countless varieties, an' many lack one part or another. A common variant among trees is the *catkin*, a droopin' spike covered in lotsa tiny flowers.

For me?!

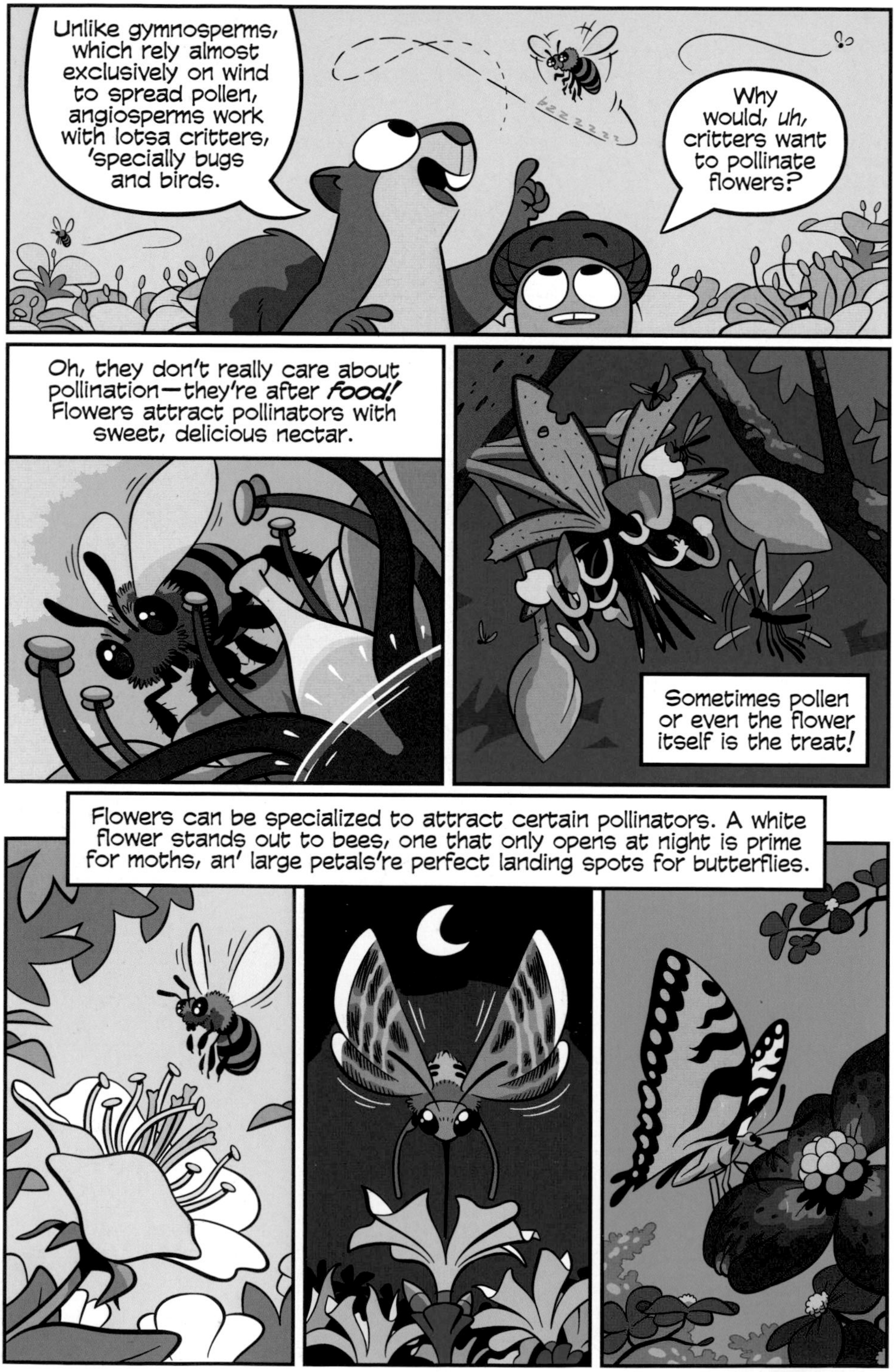

Unlike gymnosperms, which rely almost exclusively on wind to spread pollen, angiosperms work with lotsa critters, 'specially bugs and birds.
bzzzzzz
Why would, *uh*, critters want to pollinate flowers?
Oh, they don't really care about pollination—they're after *food!* Flowers attract pollinators with sweet, delicious nectar.
Sometimes pollen or even the flower itself is the treat!
Flowers can be specialized to attract certain pollinators. A white flower stands out to bees, one that only opens at night is prime for moths, an' large petals're perfect landing spots for butterflies.

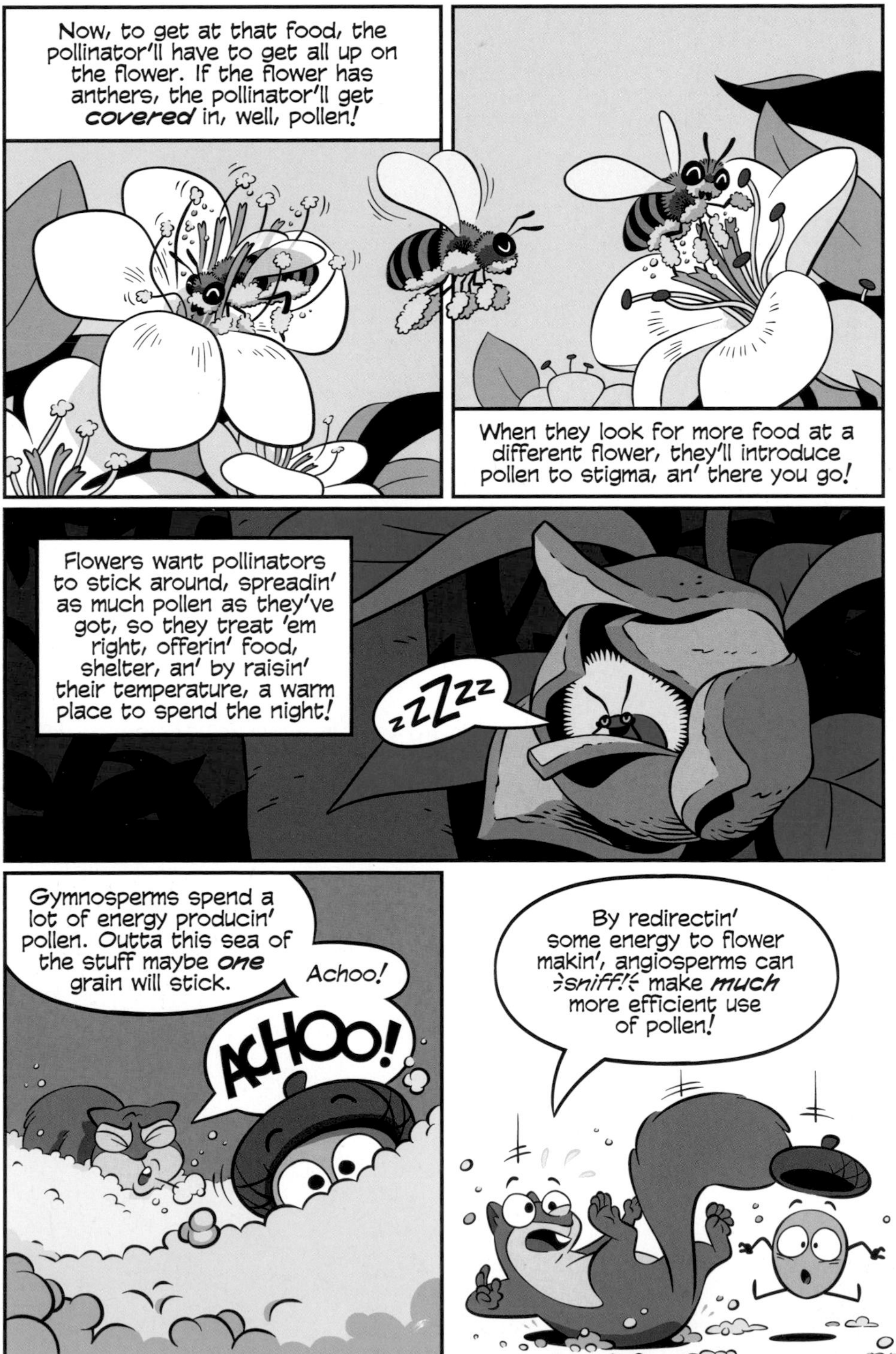

Now, to get at that food, the pollinator'll have to get all up on the flower. If the flower has anthers, the pollinator'll get *covered* in, well, pollen!
When they look for more food at a different flower, they'll introduce pollen to stigma, an' there you go!
Flowers want pollinators to stick around, spreadin' as much pollen as they've got, so they treat 'em right, offerin' food, shelter, an' by raisin' their temperature, a warm place to spend the night!
zZZzz
Gymnosperms spend a lot of energy producin' pollen. Outta this sea of the stuff maybe *one* grain will stick.
Achoo!
ACHOO!
By redirectin' some energy to flower makin', angiosperms can *sniff!* make *much* more efficient use of pollen!

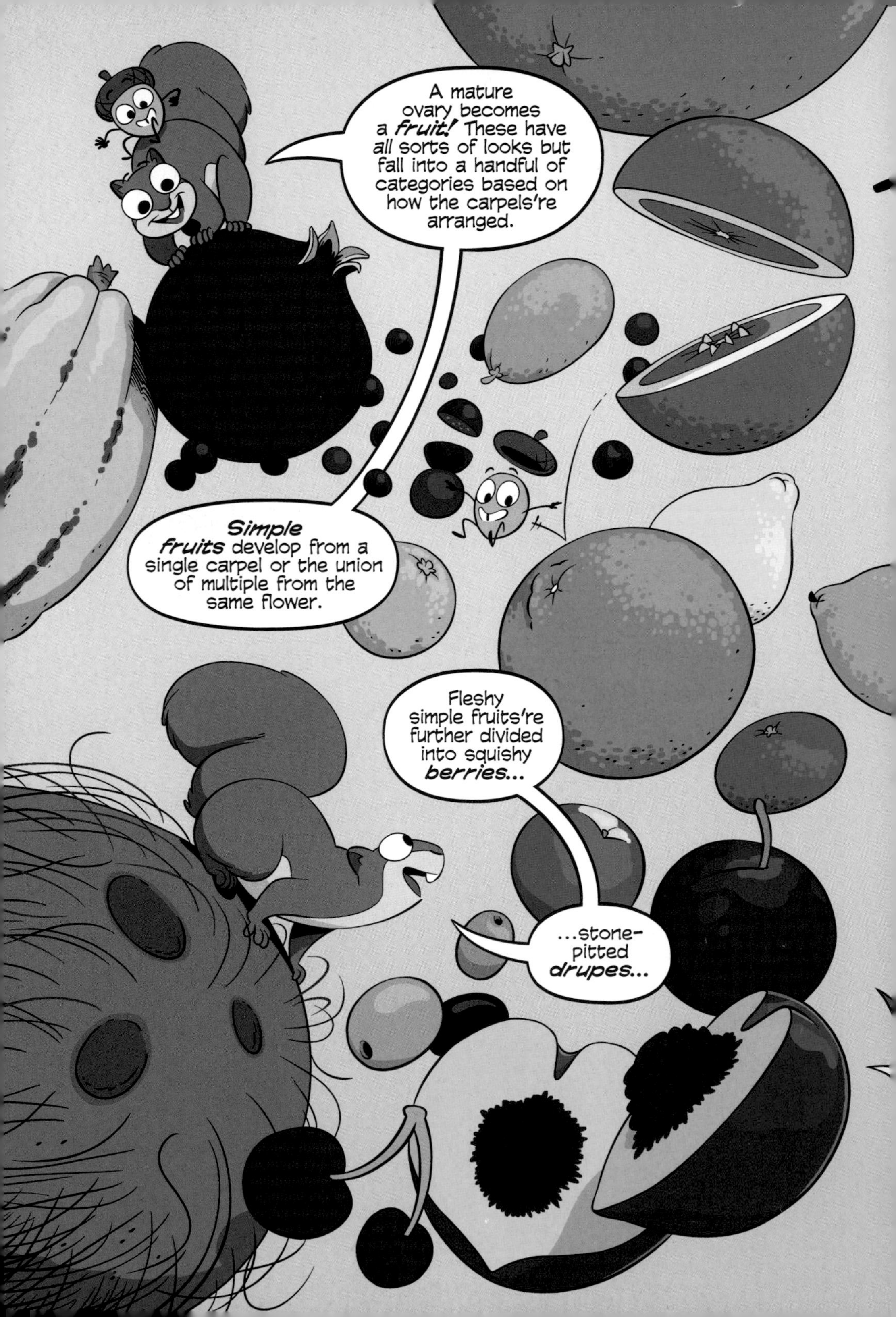
A mature ovary becomes a *fruit!* These have *all* sorts of looks but fall into a handful of categories based on how the carpels're arranged.
Simple fruits develop from a single carpel or the union of multiple from the same flower.
Fleshy simple fruits're further divided into squishy ***berries...***
...stone-pitted ***drupes...***

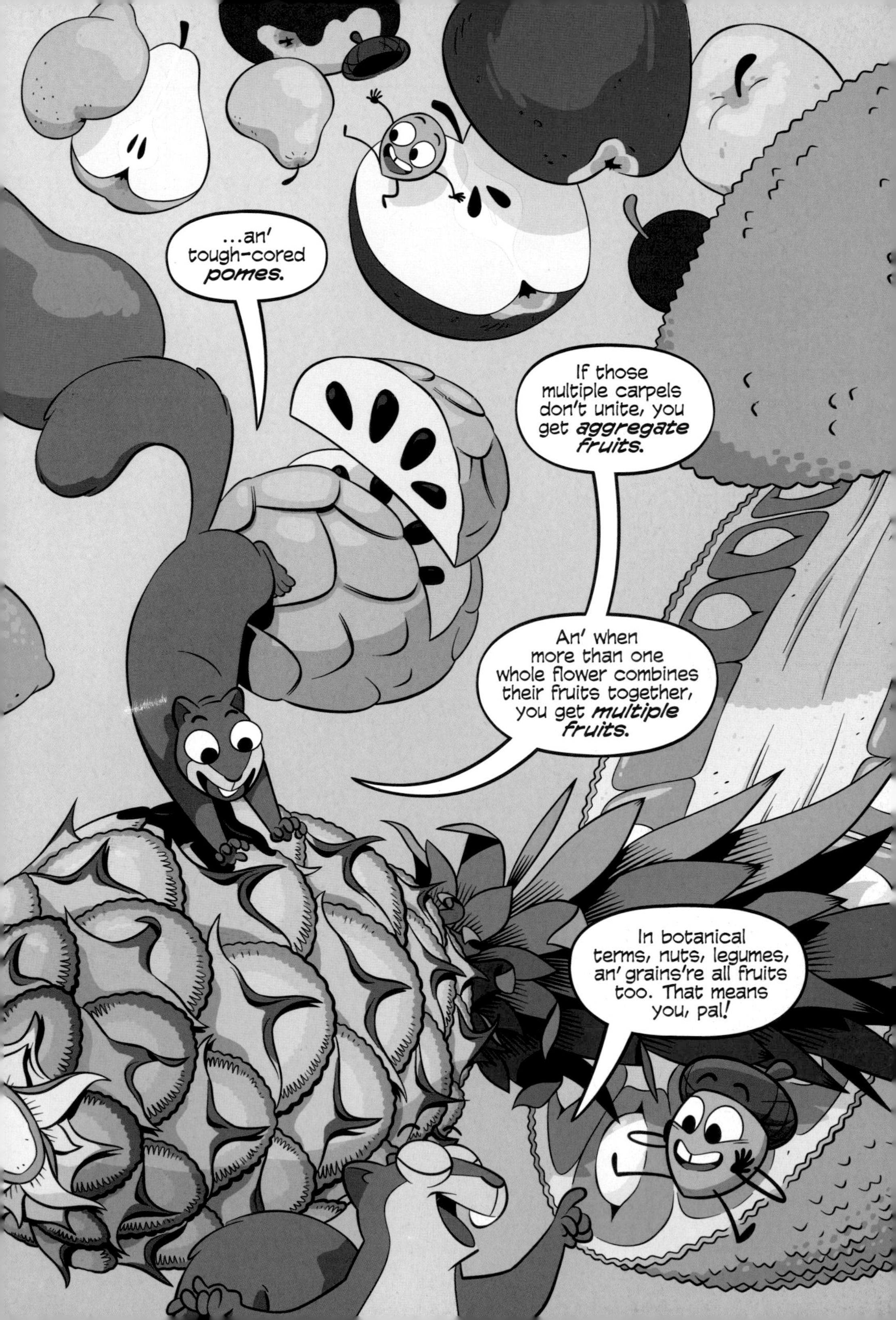
...an' tough-cored *pomes.*
If those multiple carpels don't unite, you get *aggregate fruits.*
An' when more than one whole flower combines their fruits together, you get *multiple fruits.*
In botanical terms, nuts, legumes, an' grains're all fruits too. That means you, pal!

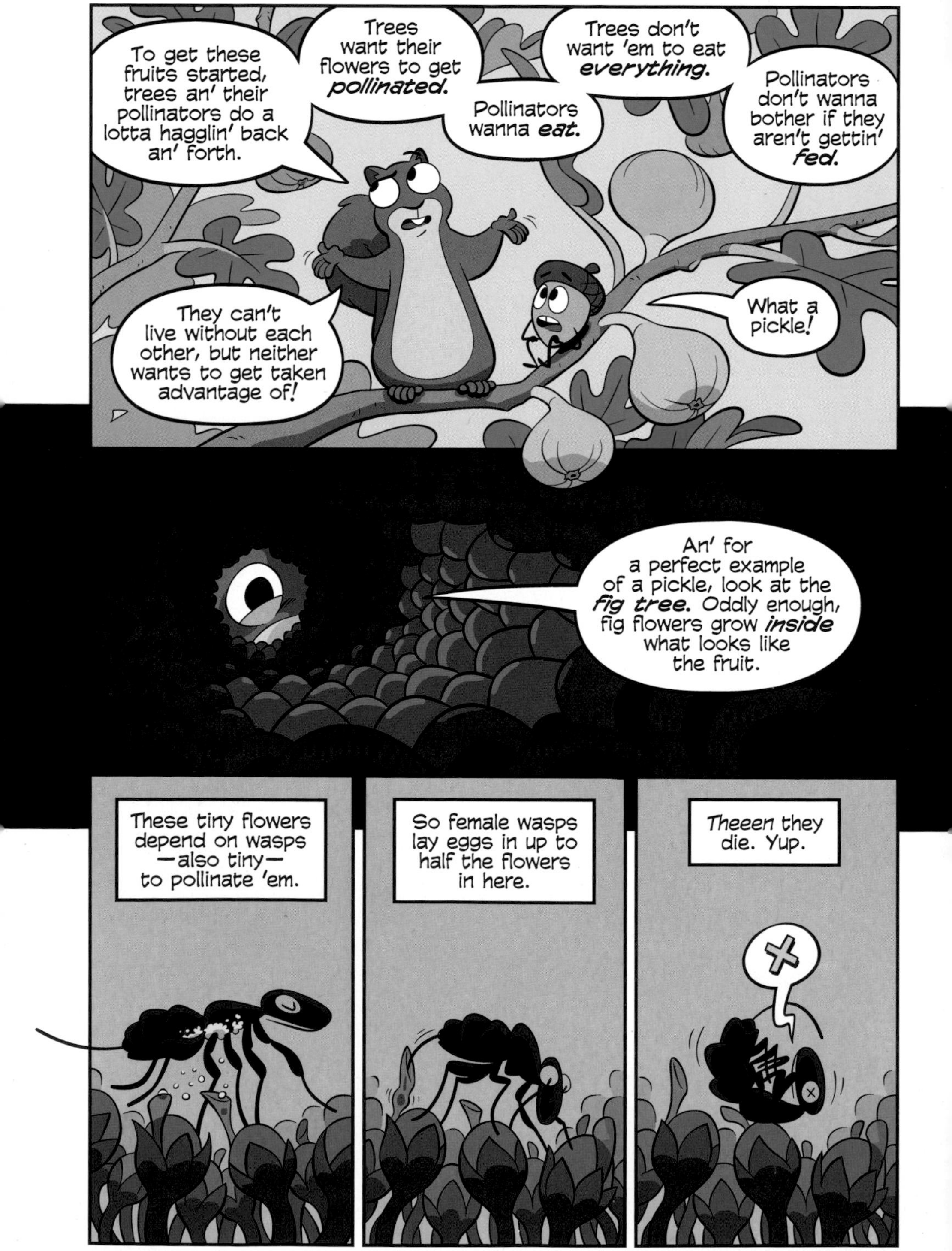
To get these fruits started, trees an' their pollinators do a lotta hagglin' back an' forth.
Trees want their flowers to get *pollinated.*
Pollinators wanna *eat.*
Trees don't want 'em to eat *everything.*
Pollinators don't wanna bother if they aren't gettin' *fed.*
They can't live without each other, but neither wants to get taken advantage of!
What a pickle!
An' for a perfect example of a pickle, look at the *fig tree.* Oddly enough, fig flowers grow *inside* what looks like the fruit.
These tiny flowers depend on wasps —also tiny— to pollinate 'em.
So female wasps lay eggs in up to half the flowers in here.
Theeen they die. Yup.

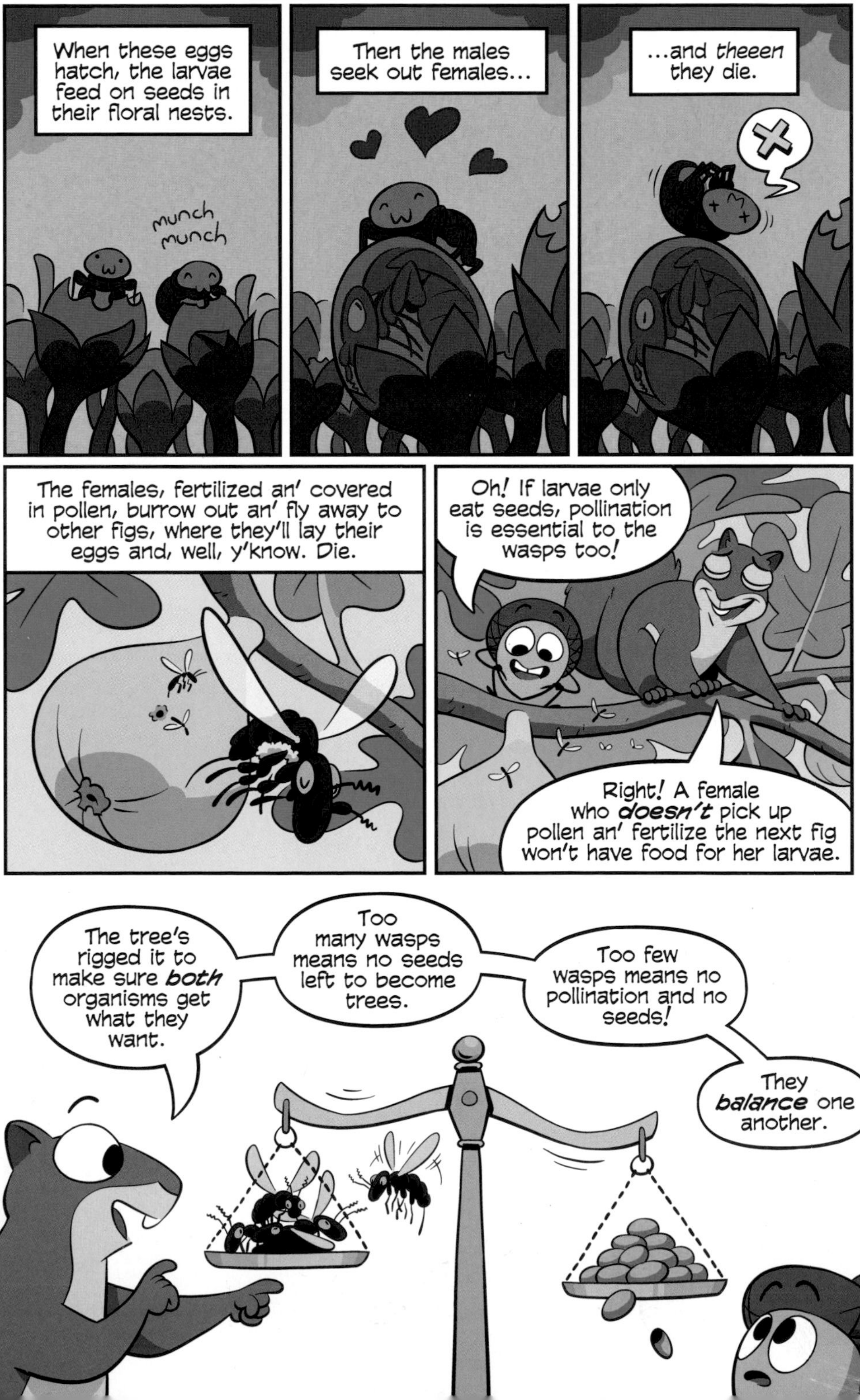
When these eggs hatch, the larvae feed on seeds in their floral nests.
munch munch
Then the males seek out females...
...and *theeen* they die.
The females, fertilized an' covered in pollen, burrow out an' fly away to other figs, where they'll lay their eggs and, well, y'know. Die.
Oh! If larvae only eat seeds, pollination is essential to the wasps too!
Right! A female who ***doesn't*** pick up pollen an' fertilize the next fig won't have food for her larvae.
The tree's rigged it to make sure ***both*** organisms get what they want.
Too many wasps means no seeds left to become trees.
Too few wasps means no pollination and no seeds!
They ***balance*** one another.

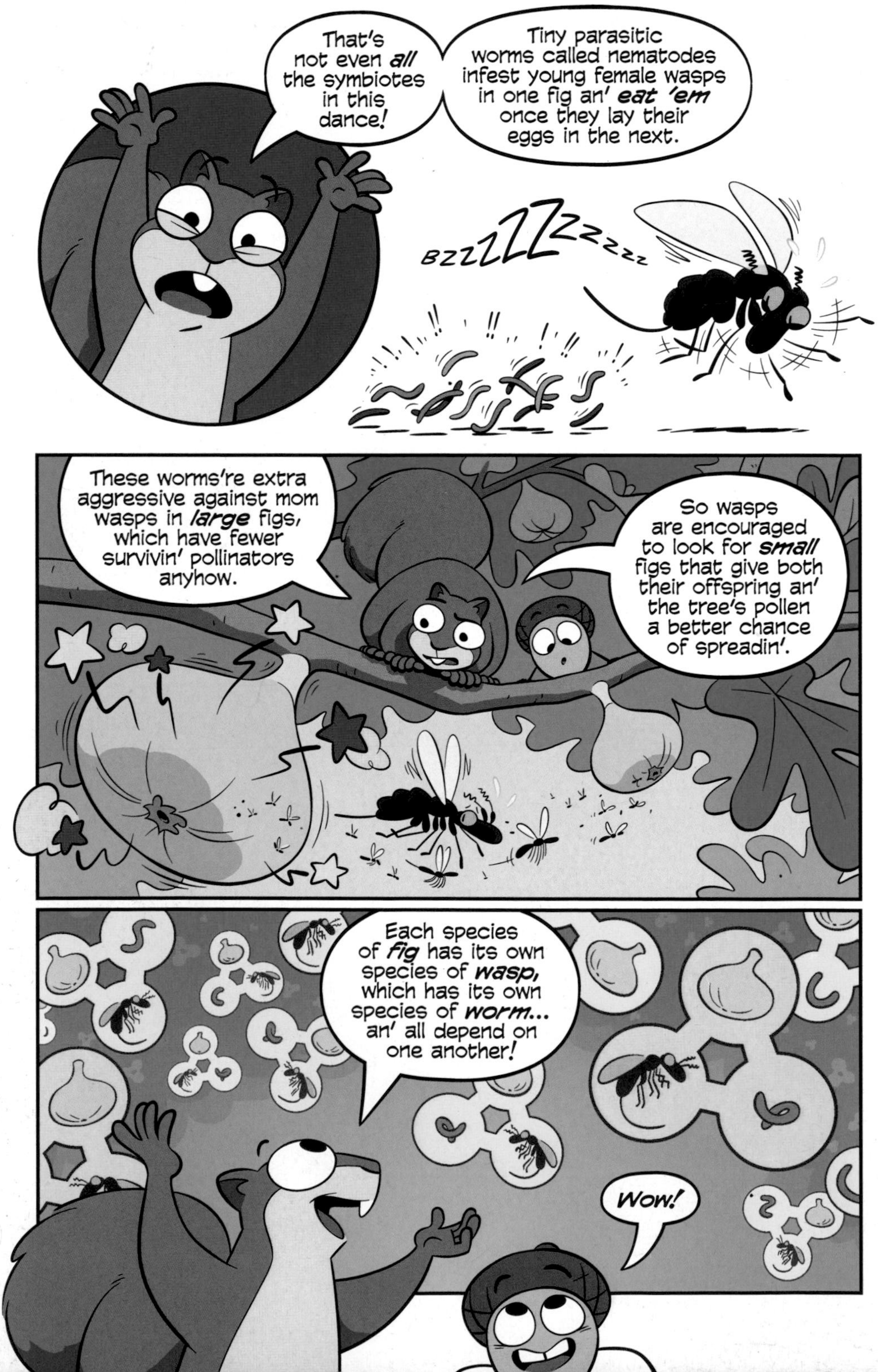
That's not even all the symbiotes in this dance!
Tiny parasitic worms called nematodes infest young female wasps in one fig an' eat 'em once they lay their eggs in the next.
BZZZZZZzzzzz
These worms're extra aggressive against mom wasps in large figs, which have fewer survivin' pollinators anyhow.
So wasps are encouraged to look for small figs that give both their offspring an' the tree's pollen a better chance of spreadin'.
Each species of fig has its own species of wasp, which has its own species of worm... an' all depend on one another!
Wow!

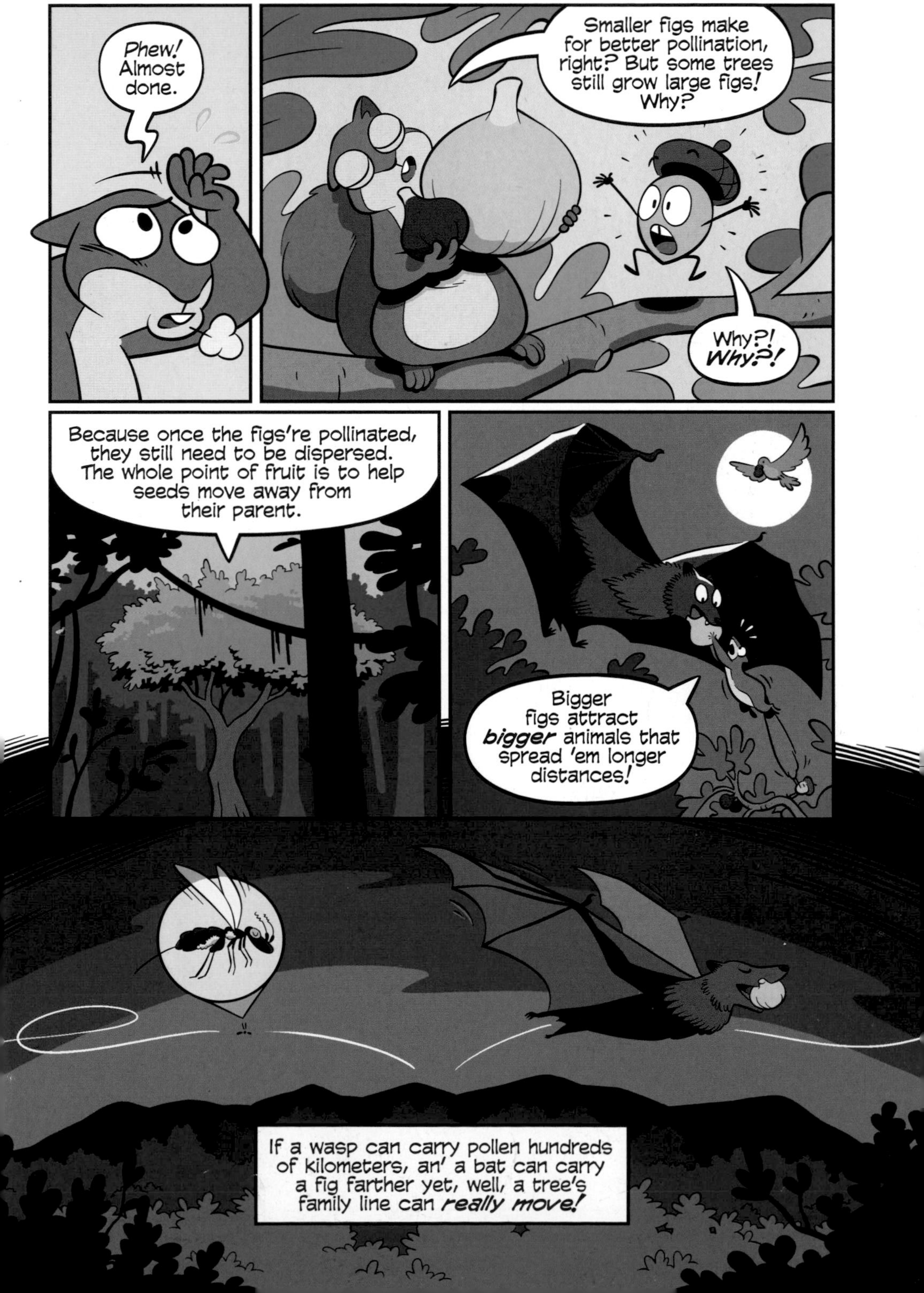
Phew! Almost done.
Smaller figs make for better pollination, right? But some trees still grow large figs! Why?
Why?! *Why?!*
Because once the figs're pollinated, they still need to be dispersed. The whole point of fruit is to help seeds move away from their parent.
Bigger figs attract ***bigger*** animals that spread 'em longer distances!
If a wasp can carry pollen hundreds of kilometers, an' a bat can carry a fig farther yet, well, a tree's family line can ***really move!***

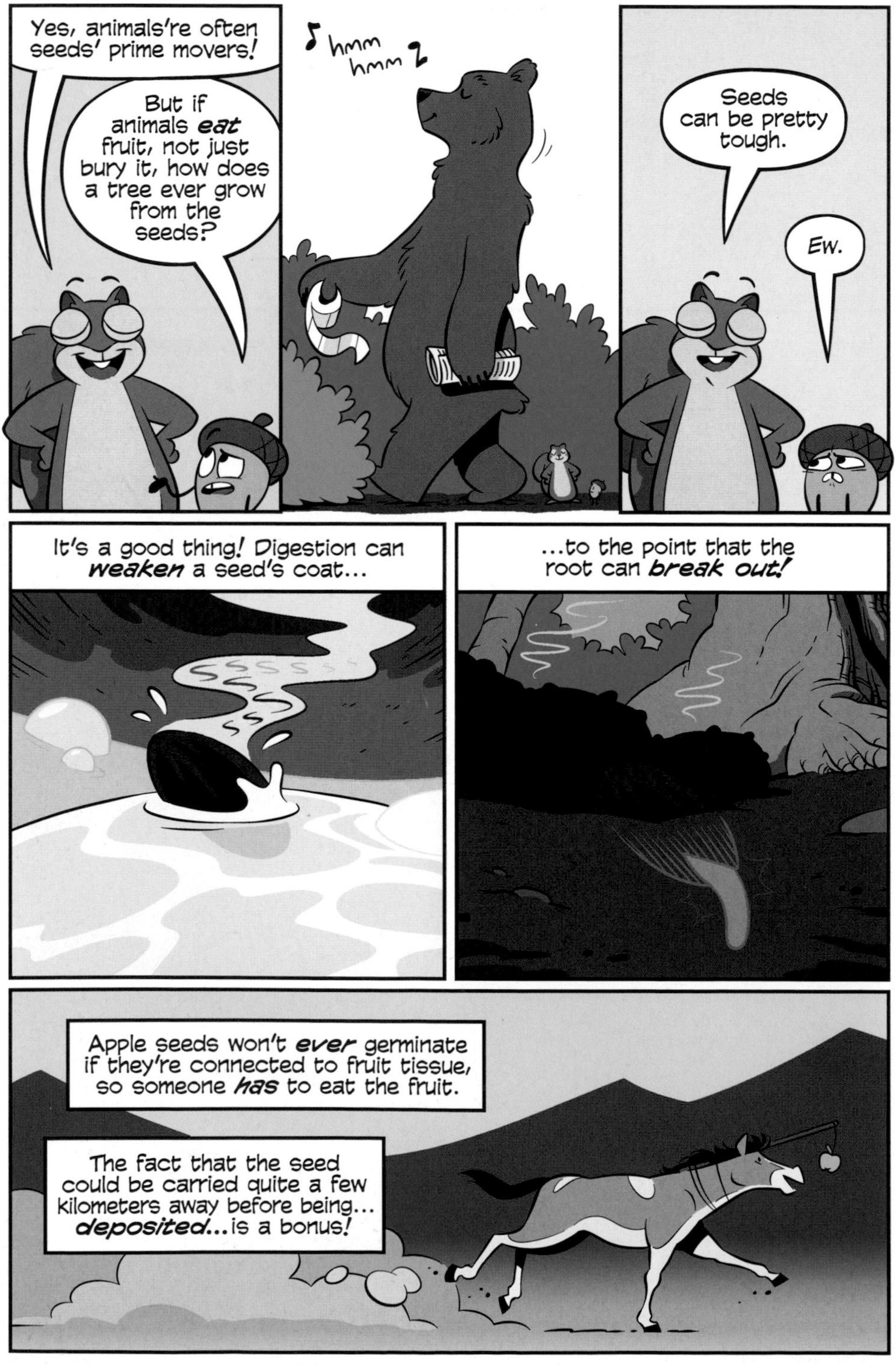

Yes, animals're often seeds' prime movers!
But if animals *eat* fruit, not just bury it, how does a tree ever grow from the seeds?
hmm hmm
Seeds can be pretty tough.
Ew.
It's a good thing! Digestion can *weaken* a seed's coat...
...to the point that the root can *break out!*
Apple seeds won't *ever* germinate if they're connected to fruit tissue, so someone *has* to eat the fruit.
The fact that the seed could be carried quite a few kilometers away before being... *deposited...* is a bonus!

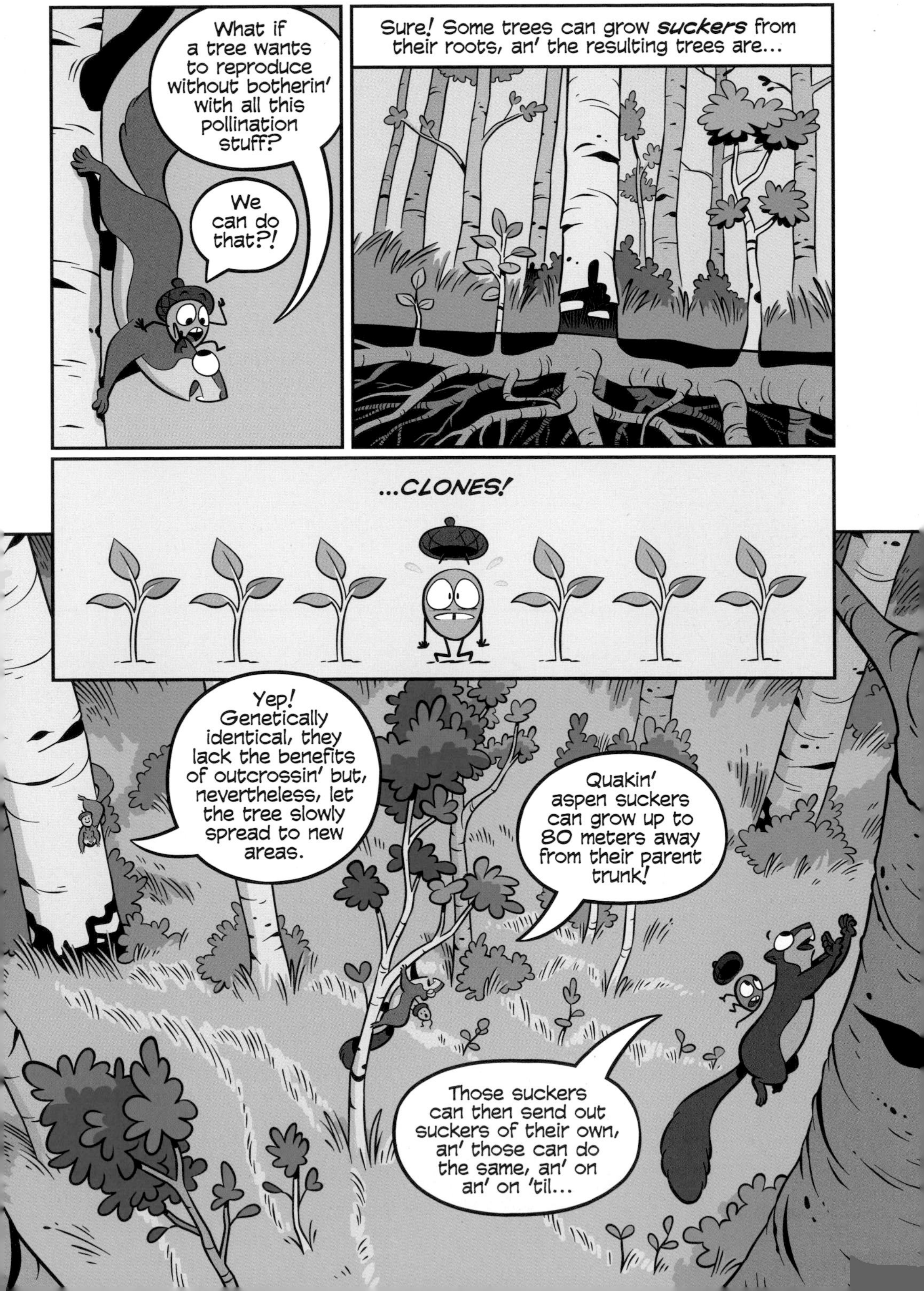
What if a tree wants to reproduce without botherin' with all this pollination stuff?
We can do that?!
Sure! Some trees can grow *suckers* from their roots, an' the resulting trees are...
...CLONES!
Yep! Genetically identical, they lack the benefits of outcrossin' but, nevertheless, let the tree slowly spread to new areas.
Quakin' aspen suckers can grow up to 80 meters away from their parent trunk!
Those suckers can then send out suckers of their own, an' those can do the same, an' on an' on 'til...

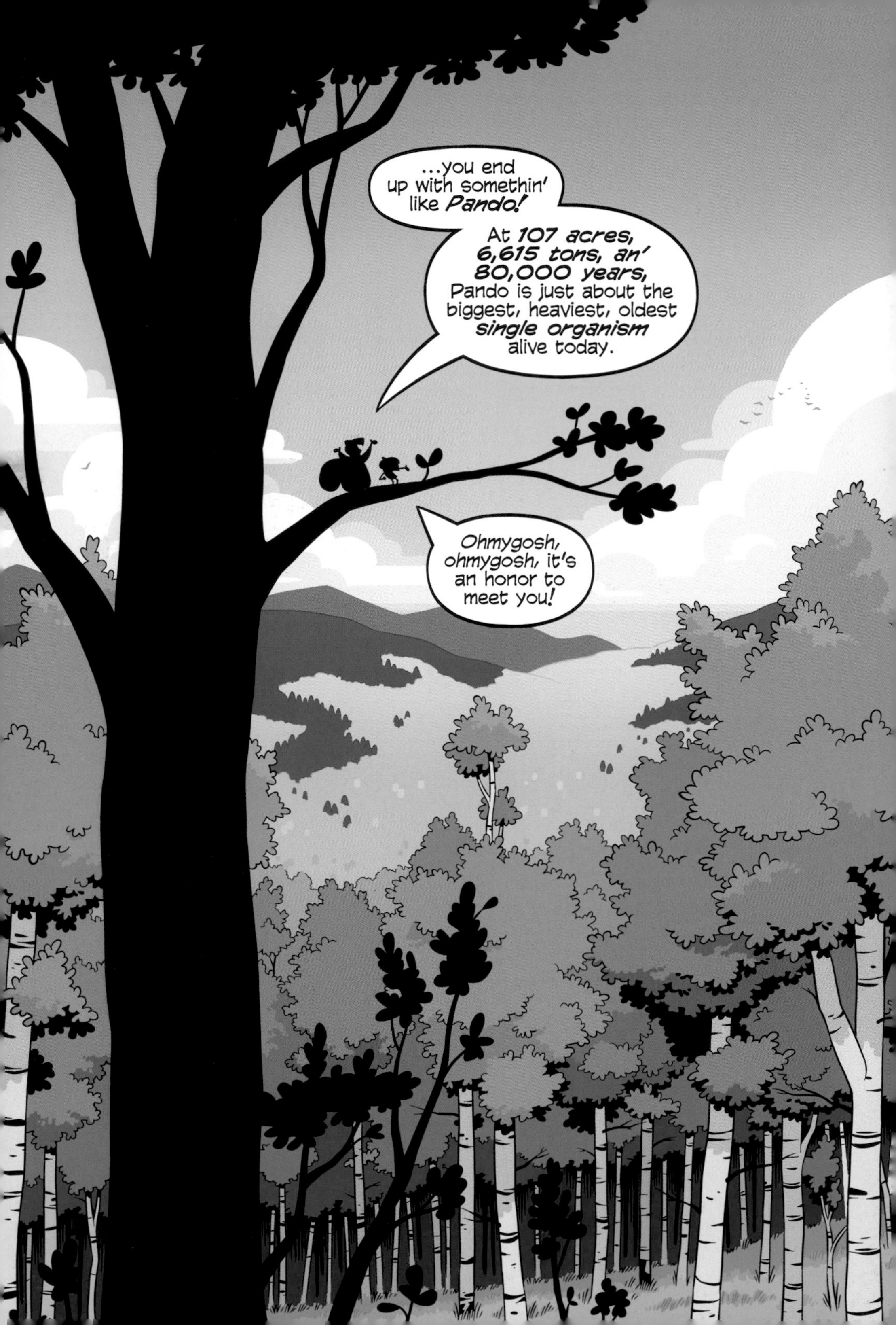
...you end up with somethin' like *Pando!*
At ***107 acres, 6,615 tons, an' 80,000 years,*** Pando is just about the biggest, heaviest, oldest ***single organism*** alive today.
Ohmygosh, ohmygosh, it's an honor to meet you!

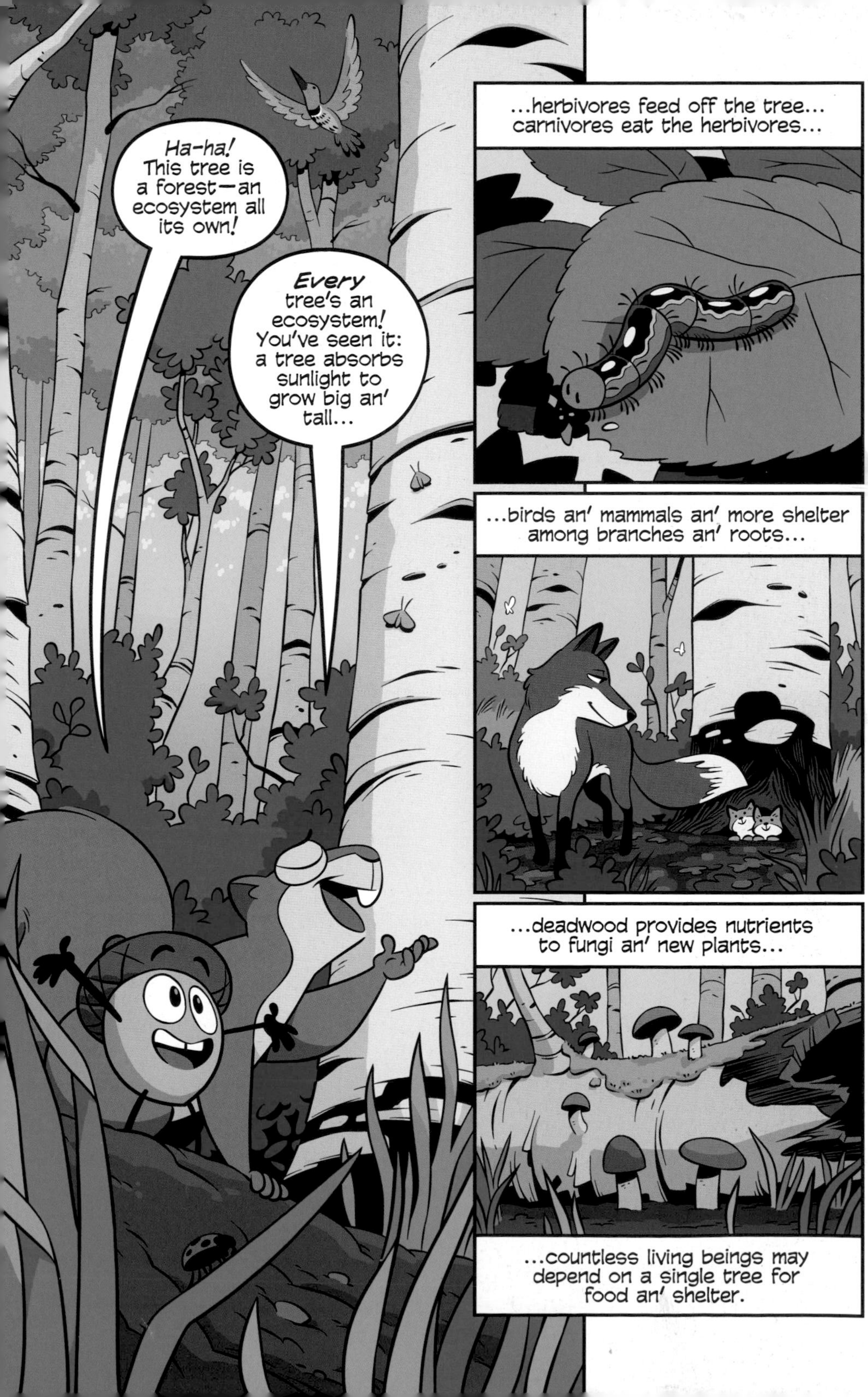

Ha-ha! This tree is a forest—an ecosystem all its own!
Every tree's an ecosystem! You've seen it: a tree absorbs sunlight to grow big an' tall...
...herbivores feed off the tree... carnivores eat the herbivores...
...birds an' mammals an' more shelter among branches an' roots...
...deadwood provides nutrients to fungi an' new plants...
...countless living beings may depend on a single tree for food an' shelter.

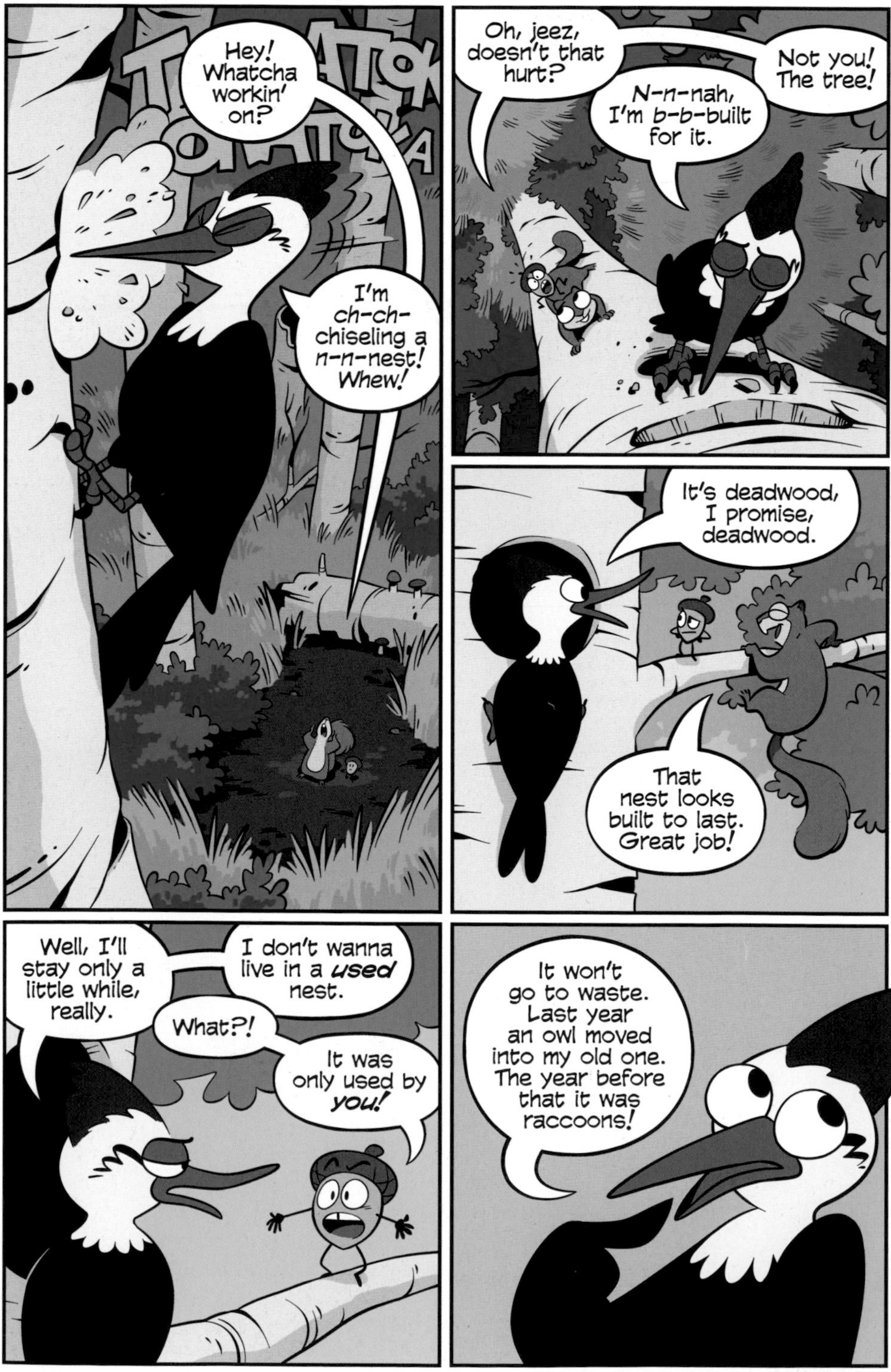
TOK TOK
Hey! Whatcha workin' on?
I'm ch-ch-chiseling a n-n-nest! Whew!
Oh, jeez, doesn't that hurt?
N-n-nah, I'm b-b-built for it.
Not you! The tree!
It's deadwood, I promise, deadwood.
That nest looks built to last. Great job!
Well, I'll stay only a little while, really.
I don't wanna live in a *used* nest.
What?!
It was only used by *you!*
It won't go to waste. Last year an owl moved into my old one. The year before that it was raccoons!

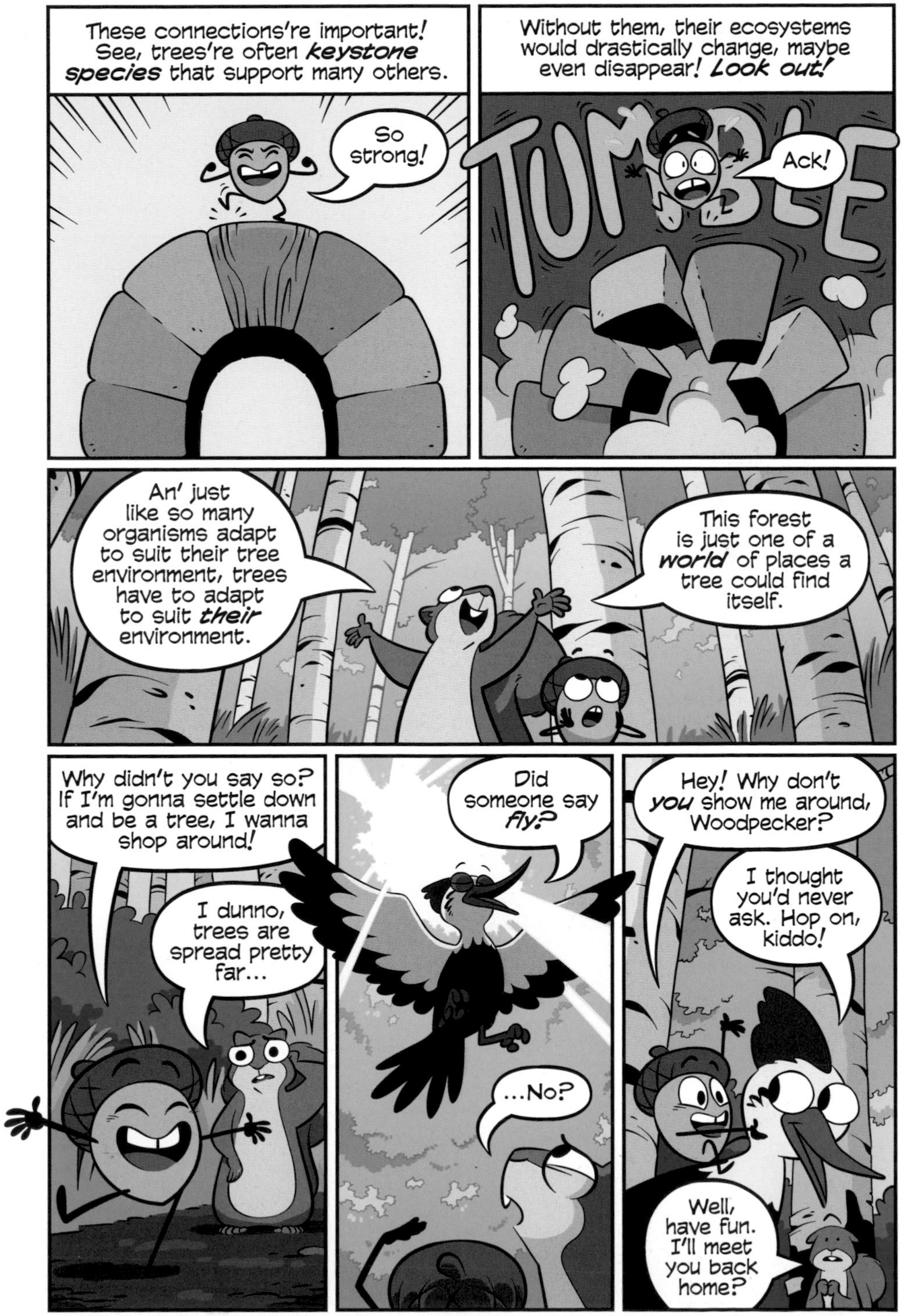
These connections're important! See, trees're often *keystone species* that support many others.
So strong!
Without them, their ecosystems would drastically change, maybe even disappear! *Look out!*
TUMBLE
Ack!
An' just like so many organisms adapt to suit their tree environment, trees have to adapt to suit *their* environment.
This forest is just one of a *world* of places a tree could find itself.
Why didn't you say so? If I'm gonna settle down and be a tree, I wanna shop around!
I dunno, trees are spread pretty far...
Did someone say *fly?*
...No?
Hey! Why don't *you* show me around, Woodpecker?
I thought you'd never ask. Hop on, kiddo!
Well, have fun. I'll meet you back home?

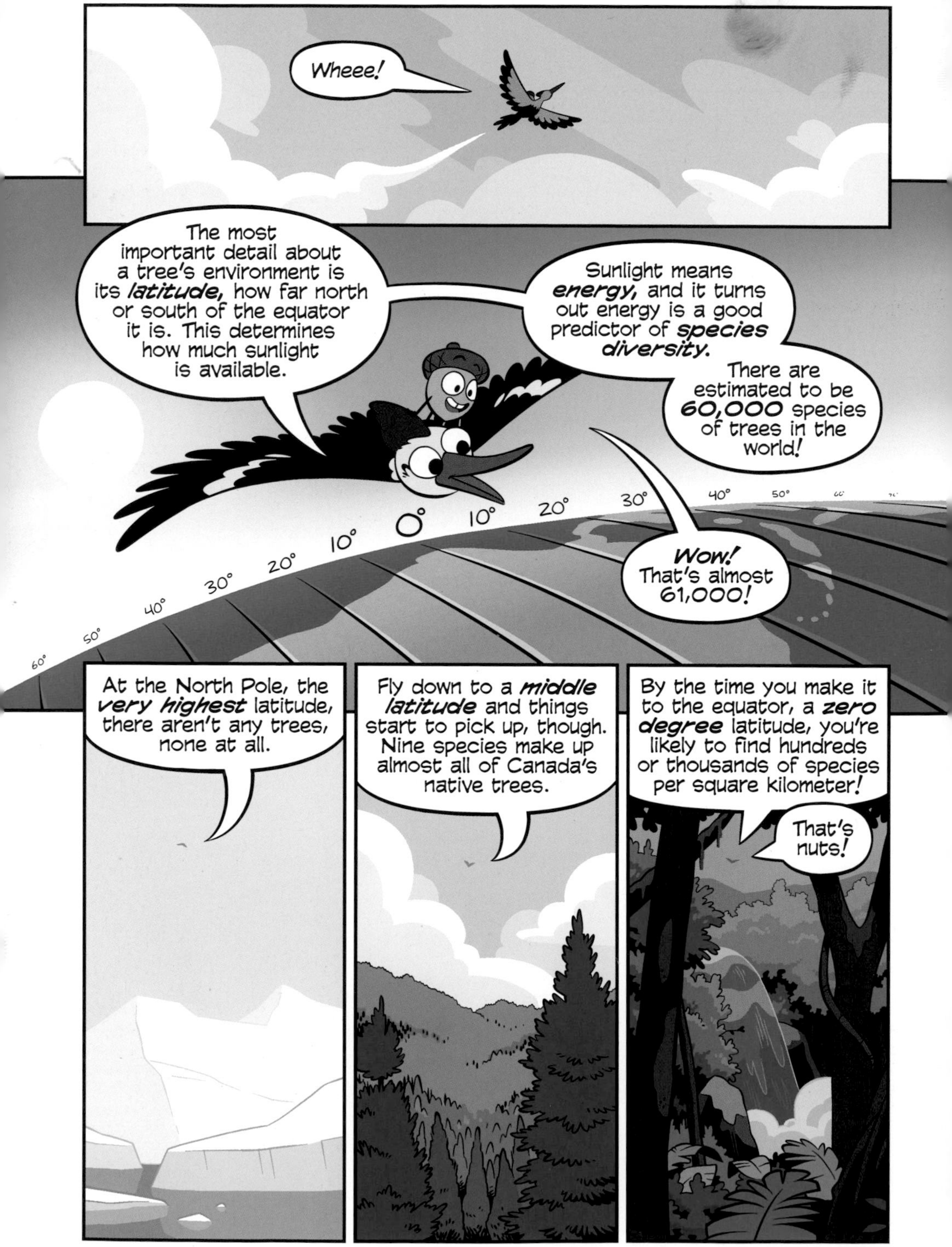
Wheee!
The most important detail about a tree's environment is its *latitude,* how far north or south of the equator it is. This determines how much sunlight is available.
Sunlight means *energy,* and it turns out energy is a good predictor of *species diversity.*
There are estimated to be **60,000** species of trees in the world!
Wow! That's almost 61,000!
60° 50° 40° 30° 20° 10° 0° 10° 20° 30° 40° 50°
At the North Pole, the *very highest* latitude, there aren't any trees, none at all.
Fly down to a *middle latitude* and things start to pick up, though. Nine species make up almost all of Canada's native trees.
By the time you make it to the equator, a *zero degree* latitude, you're likely to find hundreds or thousands of species per square kilometer!
That's nuts!

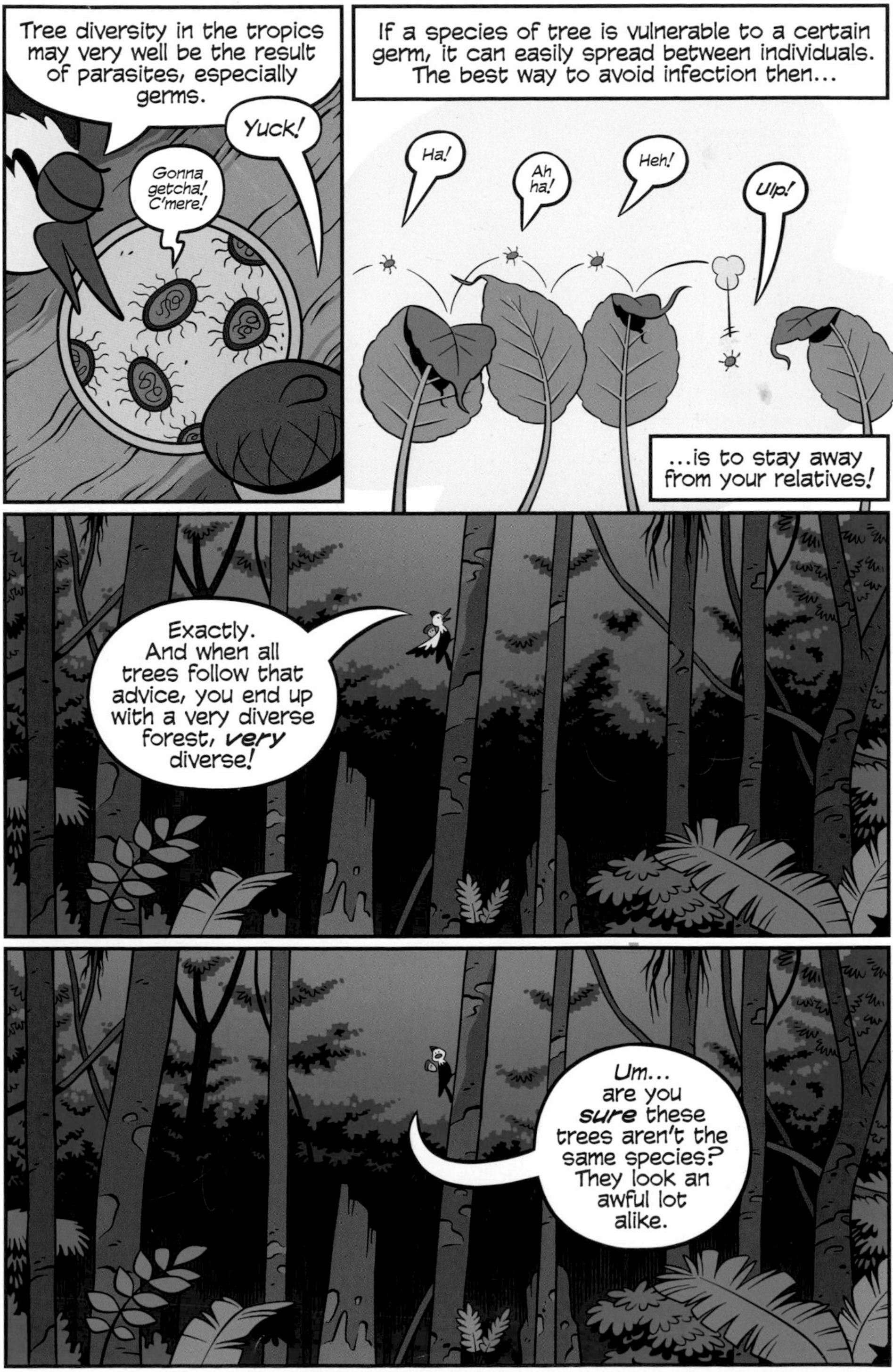
Tree diversity in the tropics may very well be the result of parasites, especially germs.
Yuck!
Gonna getcha! C'mere!
If a species of tree is vulnerable to a certain germ, it can easily spread between individuals. The best way to avoid infection then...
Ha!
Ah ha!
Heh!
Ulp!
...is to stay away from your relatives!
Exactly. And when all trees follow that advice, you end up with a very diverse forest, *very* diverse!
Um... are you *sure* these trees aren't the same species? They look an awful lot alike.

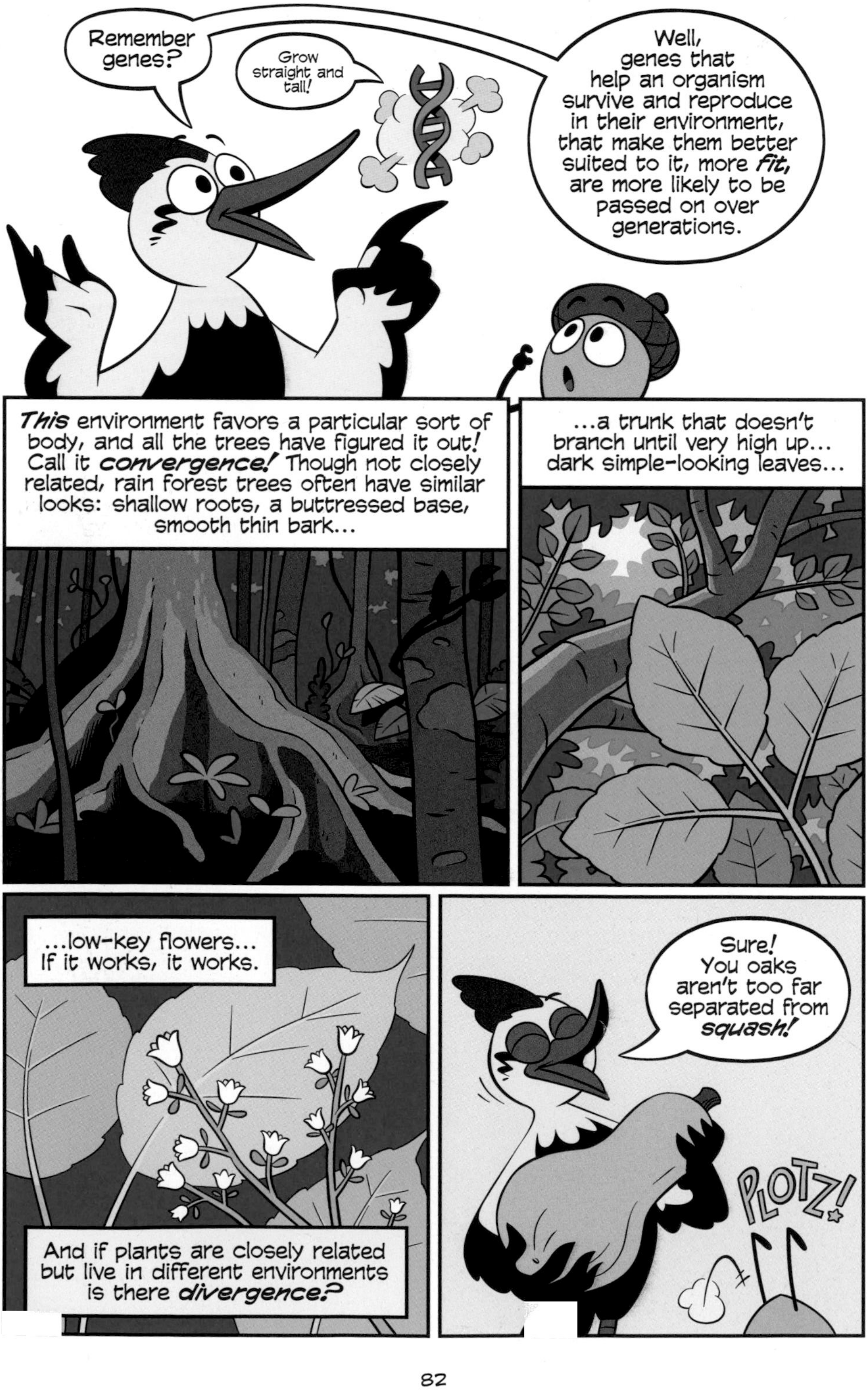
Remember genes?
Grow straight and tall!
Well, genes that help an organism survive and reproduce in their environment, that make them better suited to it, more *fit,* are more likely to be passed on over generations.
This environment favors a particular sort of body, and all the trees have figured it out! Call it *convergence!* Though not closely related, rain forest trees often have similar looks: shallow roots, a buttressed base, smooth thin bark...
...a trunk that doesn't branch until very high up... dark simple-looking leaves...
...low-key flowers... If it works, it works.
And if plants are closely related but live in different environments is there *divergence?*
Sure! You oaks aren't too far separated from *squash!*
PLOTZ!

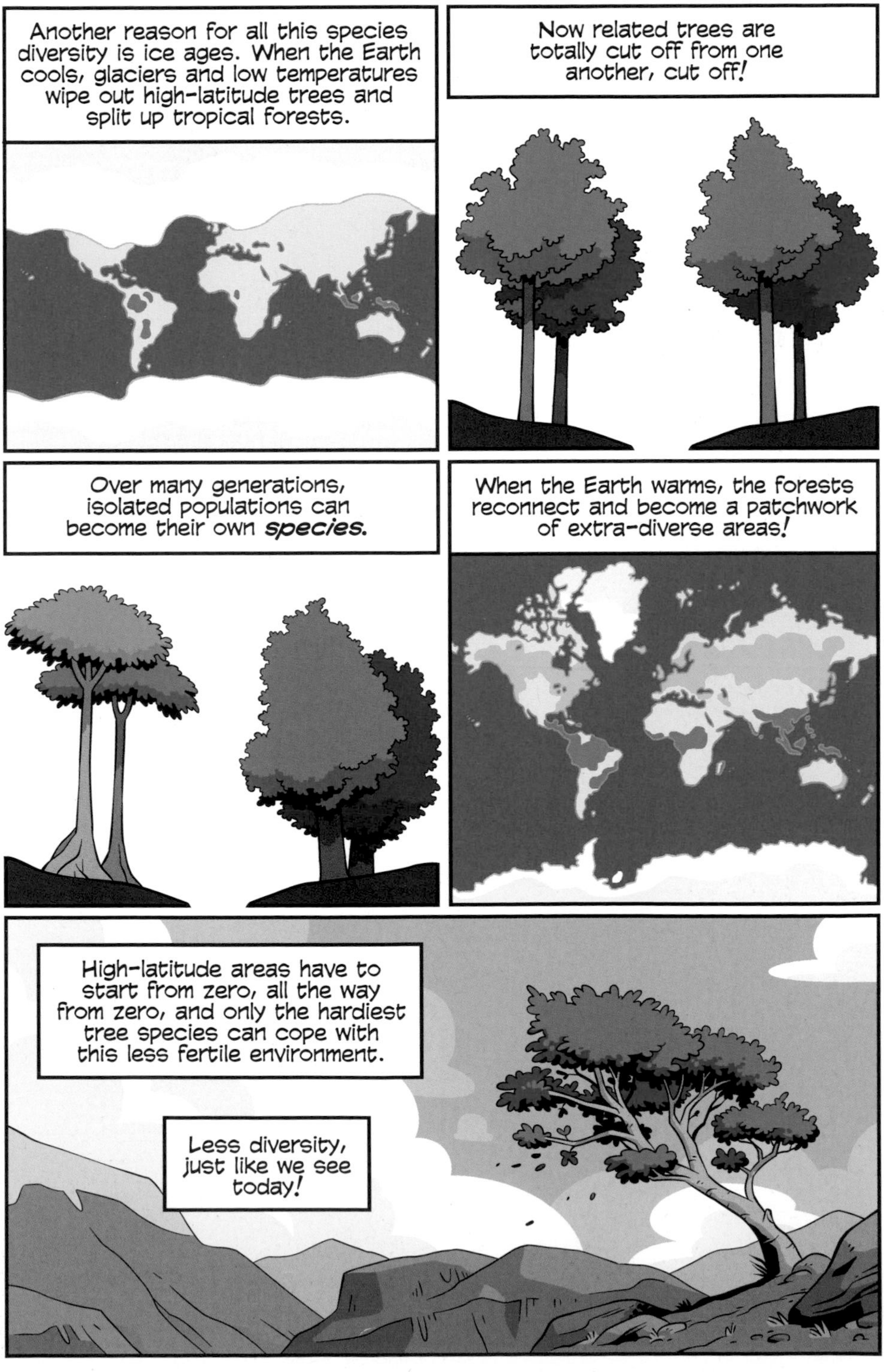
Another reason for all this species diversity is ice ages. When the Earth cools, glaciers and low temperatures wipe out high-latitude trees and split up tropical forests.
Now related trees are totally cut off from one another, cut off!
Over many generations, isolated populations can become their own ***species.***
When the Earth warms, the forests reconnect and become a patchwork of extra-diverse areas!
High-latitude areas have to start from zero, all the way from zero, and only the hardiest tree species can cope with this less fertile environment.
Less diversity, just like we see today!

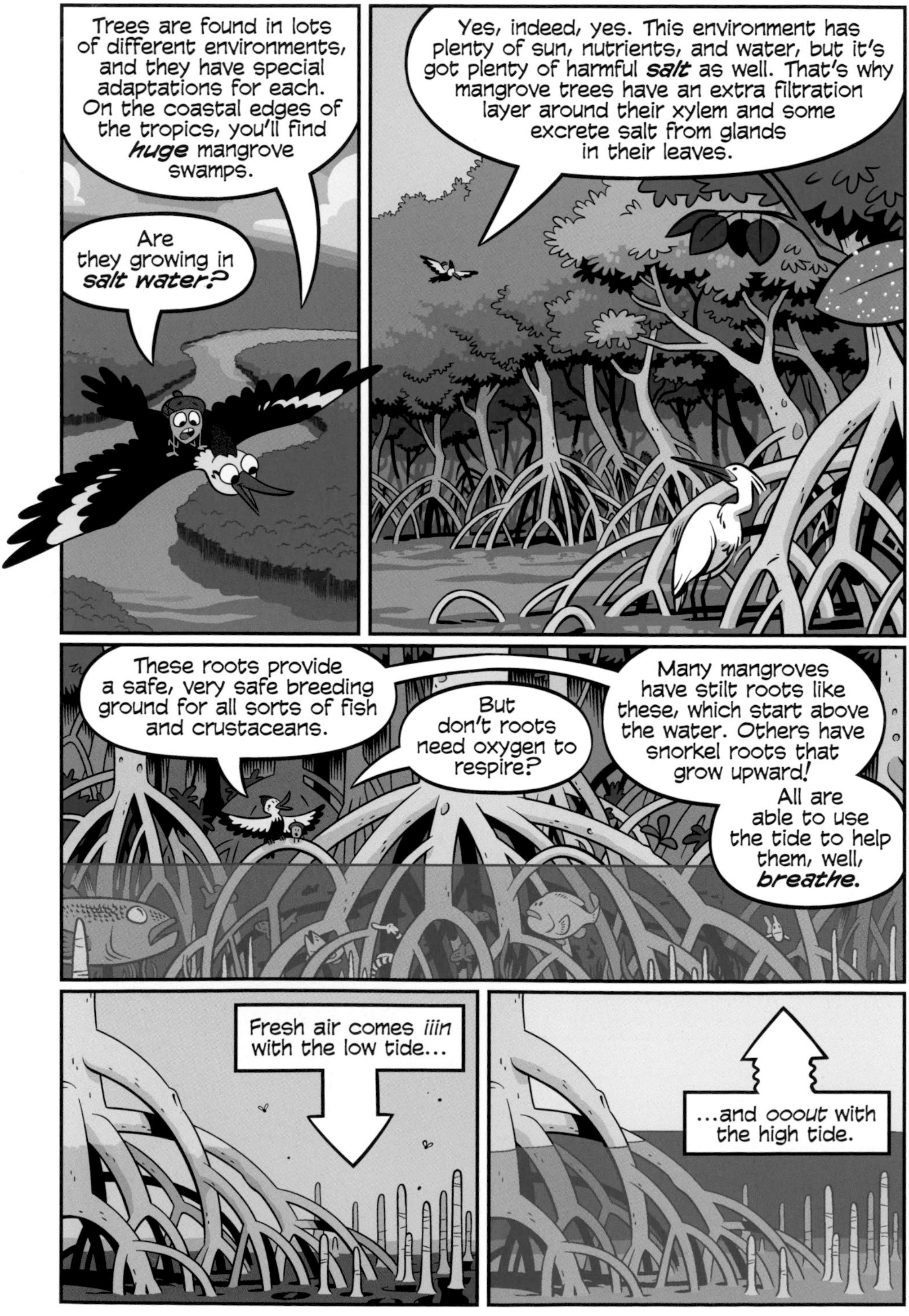

Trees are found in lots of different environments, and they have special adaptations for each. On the coastal edges of the tropics, you'll find ***huge*** mangrove swamps.
Are they growing in ***salt water?***
Yes, indeed, yes. This environment has plenty of sun, nutrients, and water, but it's got plenty of harmful ***salt*** as well. That's why mangrove trees have an extra filtration layer around their xylem and some excrete salt from glands in their leaves.
These roots provide a safe, very safe breeding ground for all sorts of fish and crustaceans.
But don't roots need oxygen to respire?
Many mangroves have stilt roots like these, which start above the water. Others have snorkel roots that grow upward!
All are able to use the tide to help them, well, ***breathe.***
Fresh air comes *iiin* with the low tide...
...and *ooout* with the high tide.

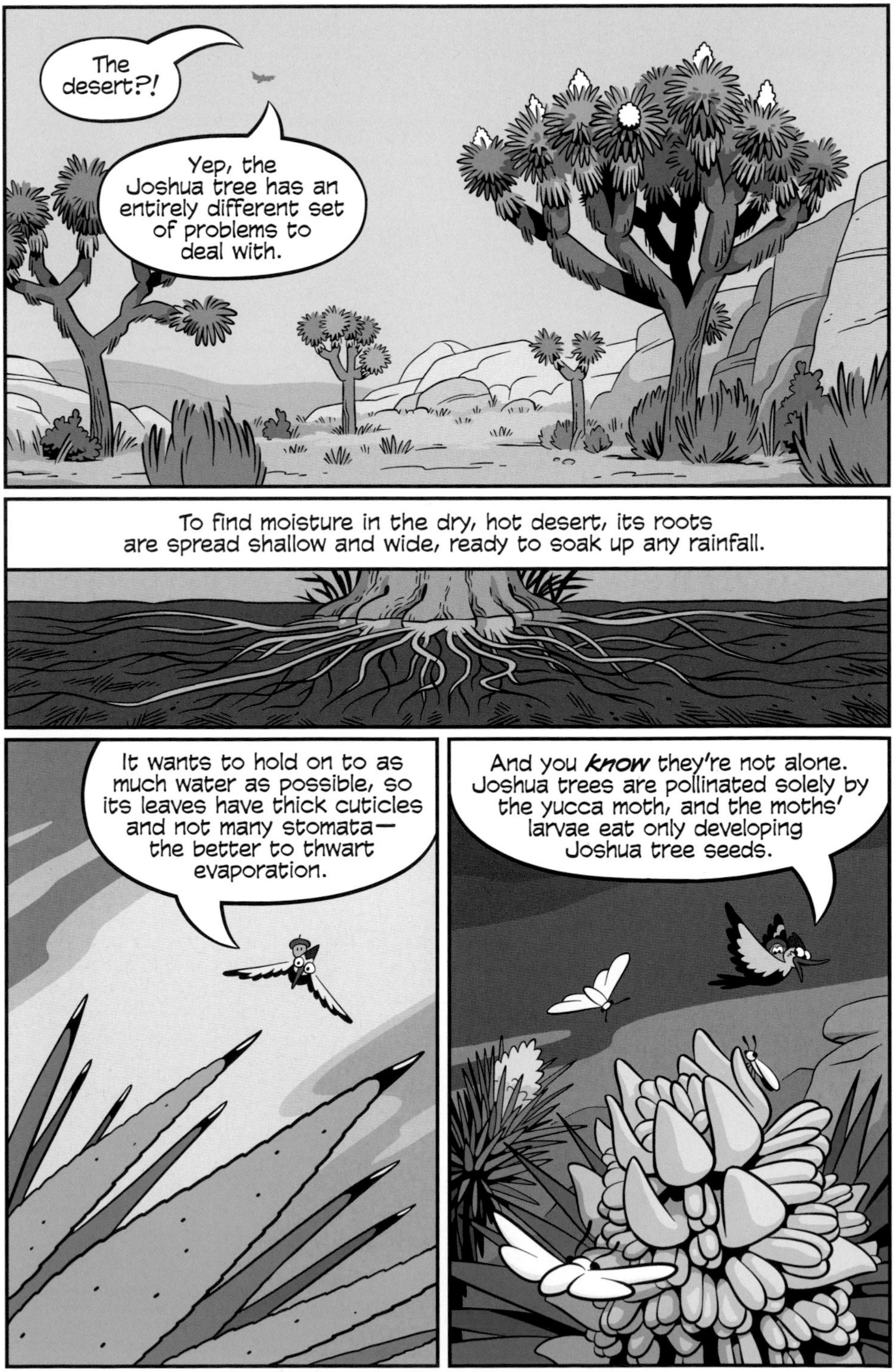
The desert?!
Yep, the Joshua tree has an entirely different set of problems to deal with.
To find moisture in the dry, hot desert, its roots are spread shallow and wide, ready to soak up any rainfall.
It wants to hold on to as much water as possible, so its leaves have thick cuticles and not many stomata— the better to thwart evaporation.
And you *know* they're not alone. Joshua trees are pollinated solely by the yucca moth, and the moths' larvae eat only developing Joshua tree seeds.

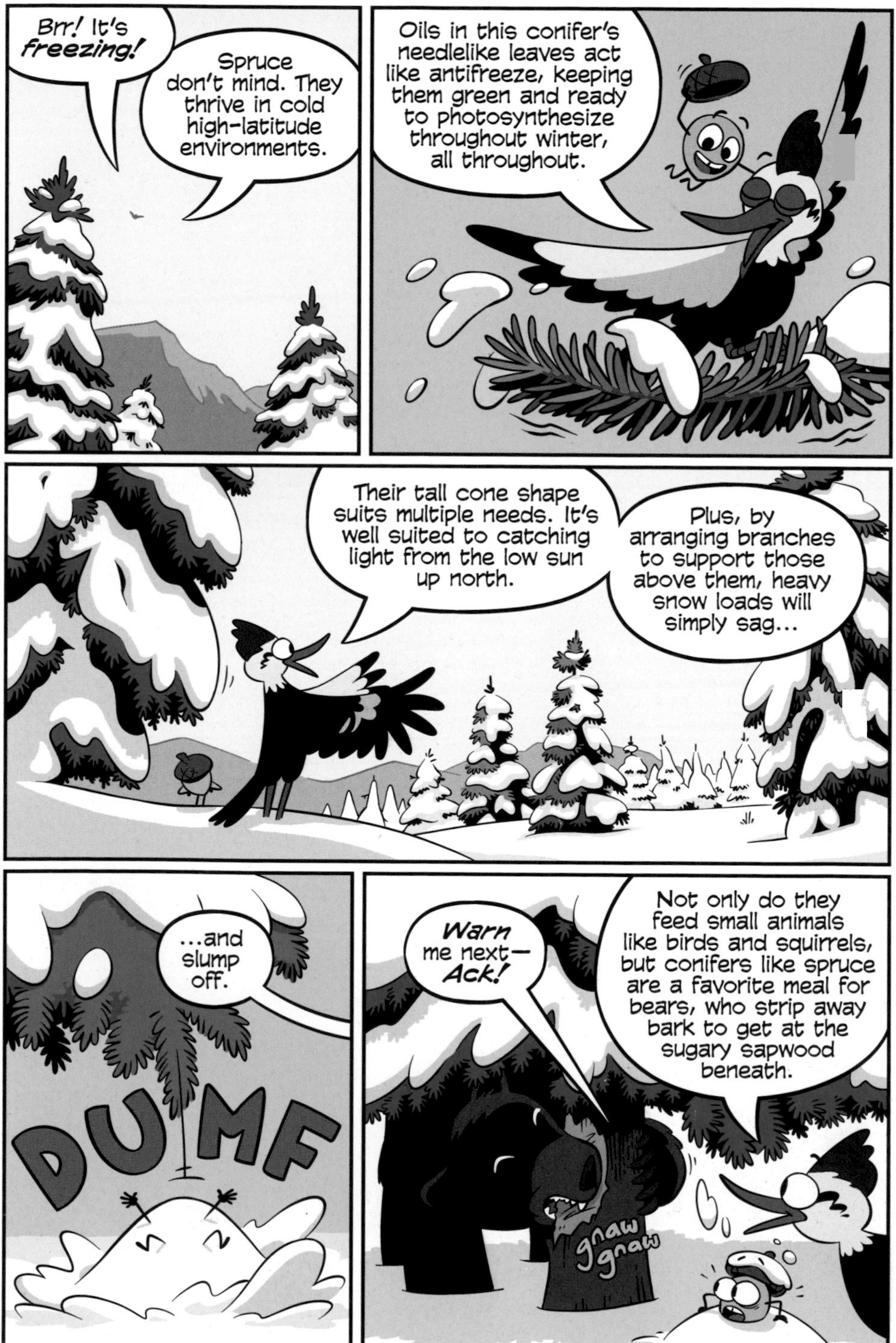
Brr! It's *freezing!*
Spruce don't mind. They thrive in cold high-latitude environments.
Oils in this conifer's needlelike leaves act like antifreeze, keeping them green and ready to photosynthesize throughout winter, all throughout.
Their tall cone shape suits multiple needs. It's well suited to catching light from the low sun up north.
Plus, by arranging branches to support those above them, heavy snow loads will simply sag...
...and slump off.
DUMF
Warn me next— *Ack!*
Not only do they feed small animals like birds and squirrels, but conifers like spruce are a favorite meal for bears, who strip away bark to get at the sugary sapwood beneath.
gnaw gnaw

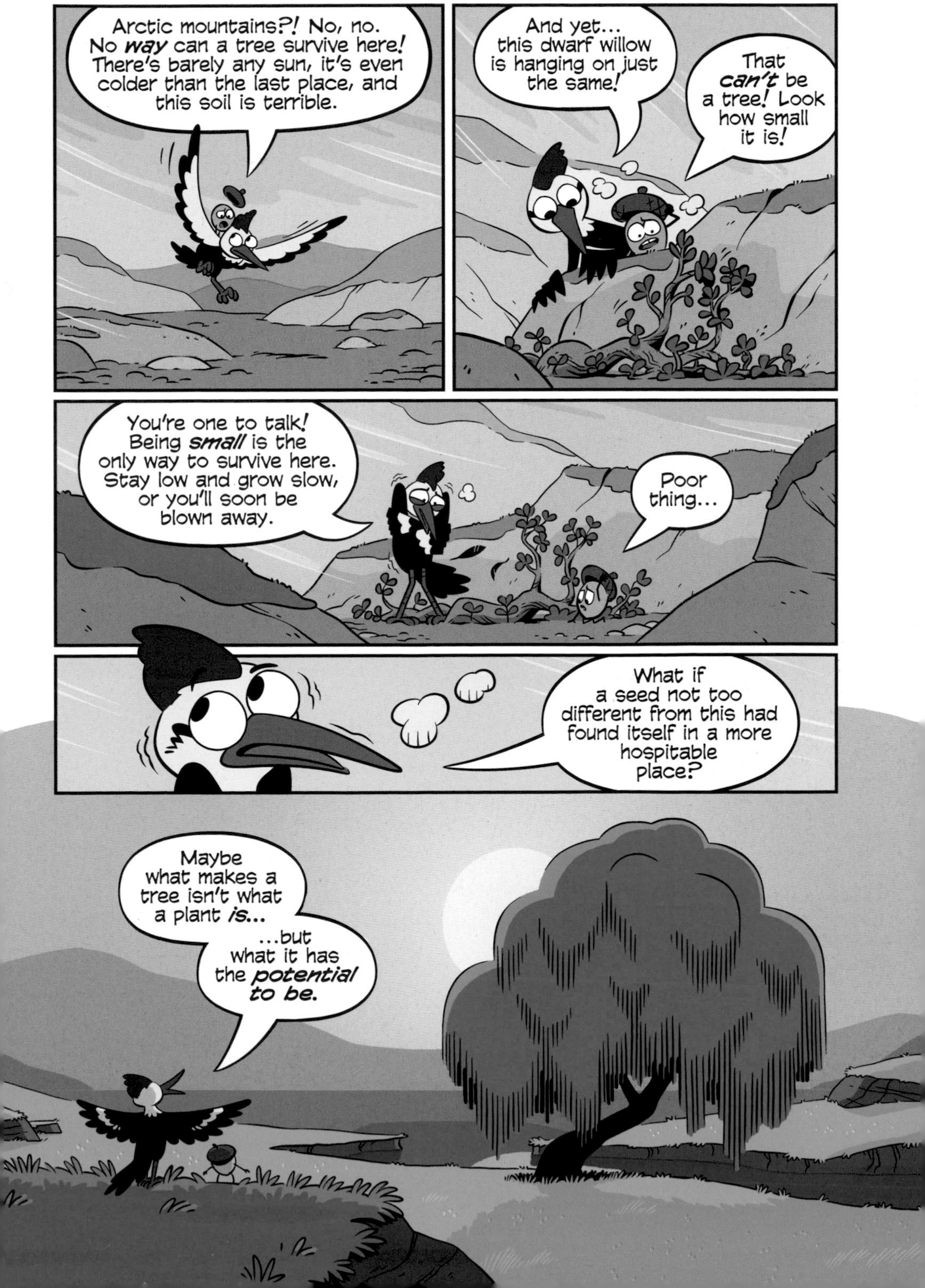
Arctic mountains?! No, no. No *way* can a tree survive here! There's barely any sun, it's even colder than the last place, and this soil is terrible.
And yet... this dwarf willow is hanging on just the same!
That *can't* be a tree! Look how small it is!
You're one to talk! Being *small* is the only way to survive here. Stay low and grow slow, or you'll soon be blown away.
Poor thing...
What if a seed not too different from this had found itself in a more hospitable place?
Maybe what makes a tree isn't what a plant *is*...
...but what it has the *potential to be.*

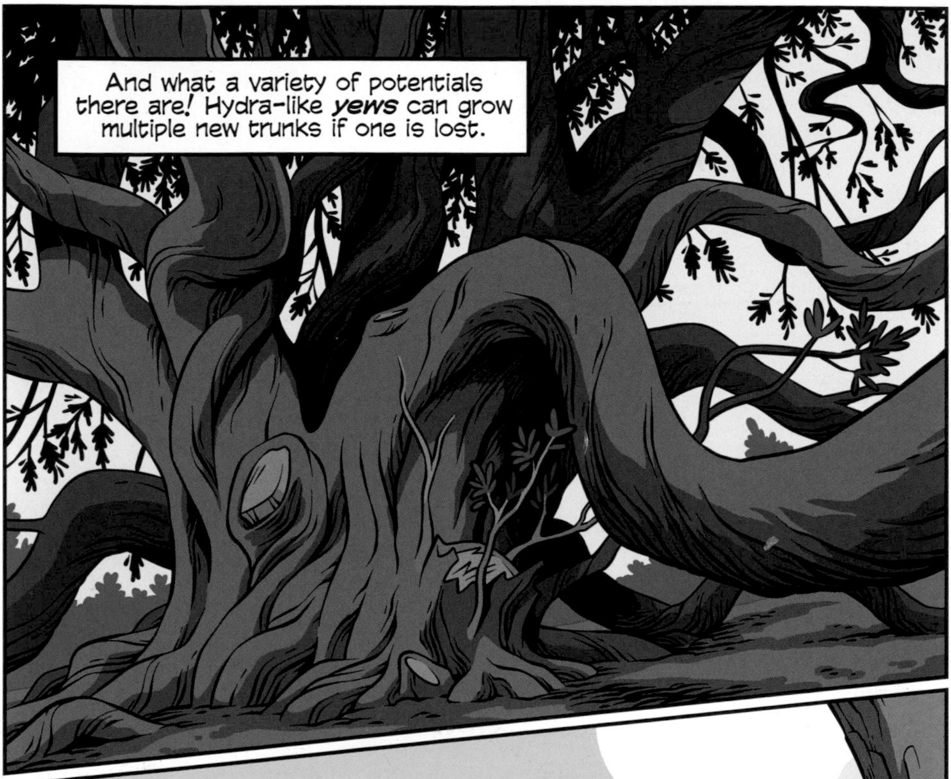
And what a variety of potentials there are! Hydra-like *yews* can grow multiple new trunks if one is lost.

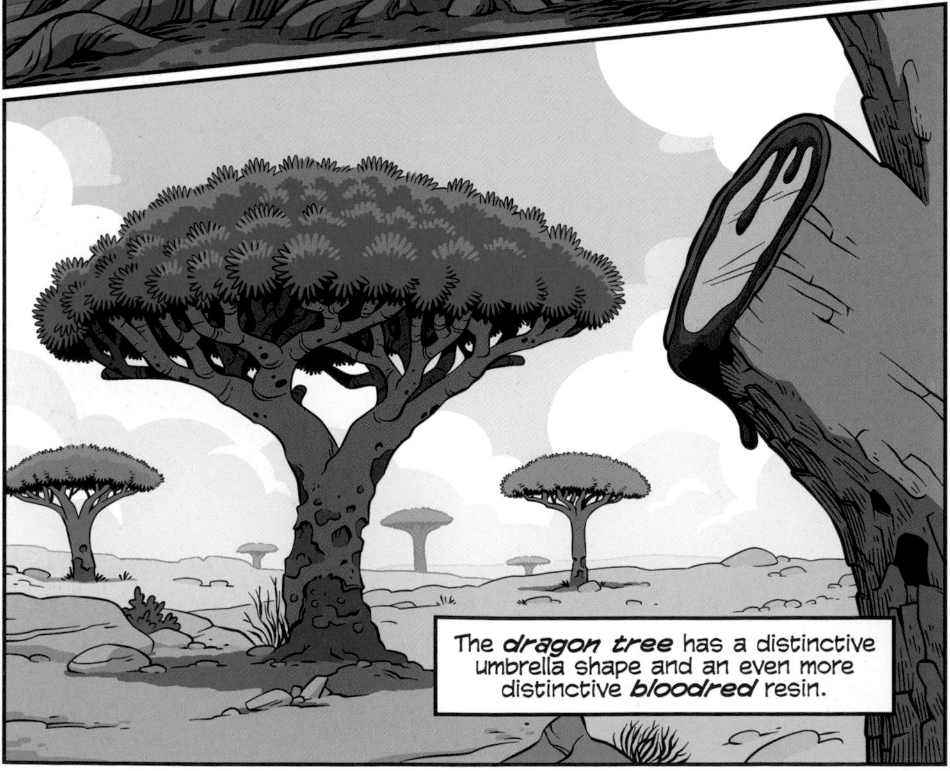
The *dragon tree* has a distinctive umbrella shape and an even more distinctive *bloodred* resin.

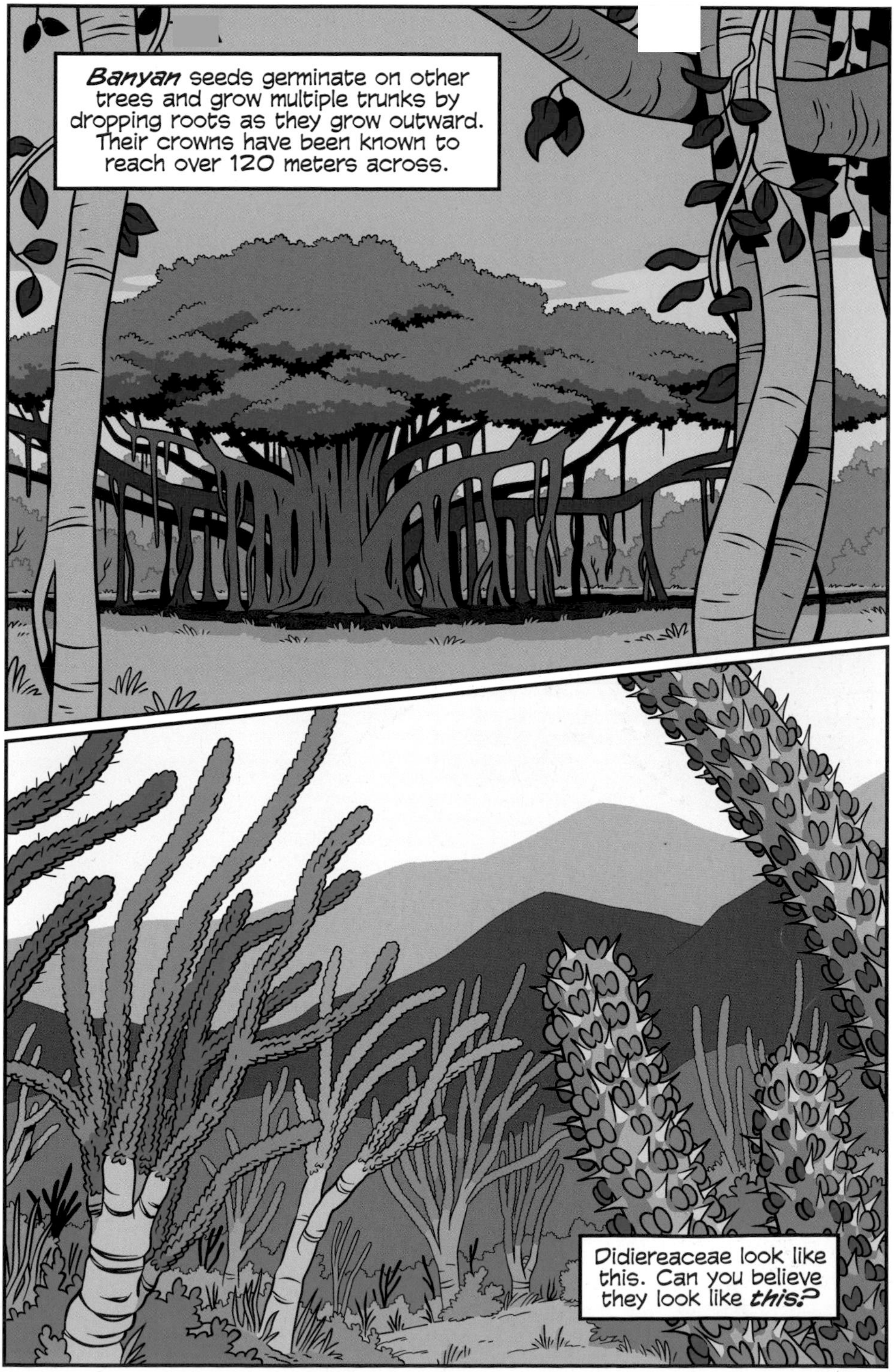
Banyan seeds germinate on other trees and grow multiple trunks by dropping roots as they grow outward. Their crowns have been known to reach over 120 meters across.
Didiereaceae look like this. Can you believe they look like ***this?***

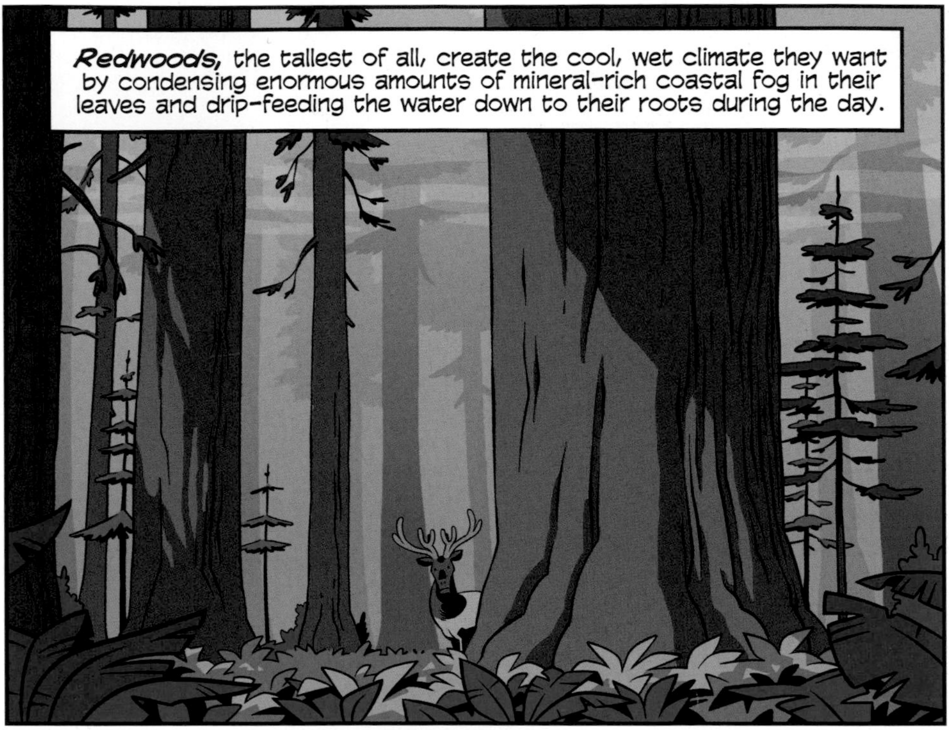
Redwoods, the tallest of all, create the cool, wet climate they want by condensing enormous amounts of mineral-rich coastal fog in their leaves and drip-feeding the water down to their roots during the day.

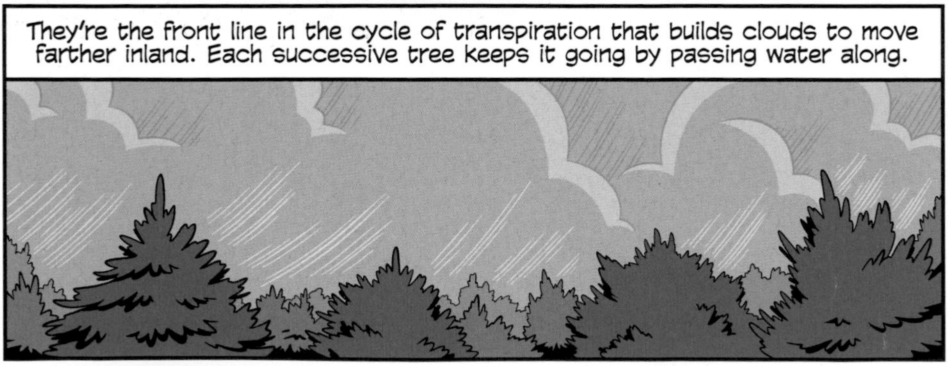
They're the front line in the cycle of transpiration that builds clouds to move farther inland. Each successive tree keeps it going by passing water along.

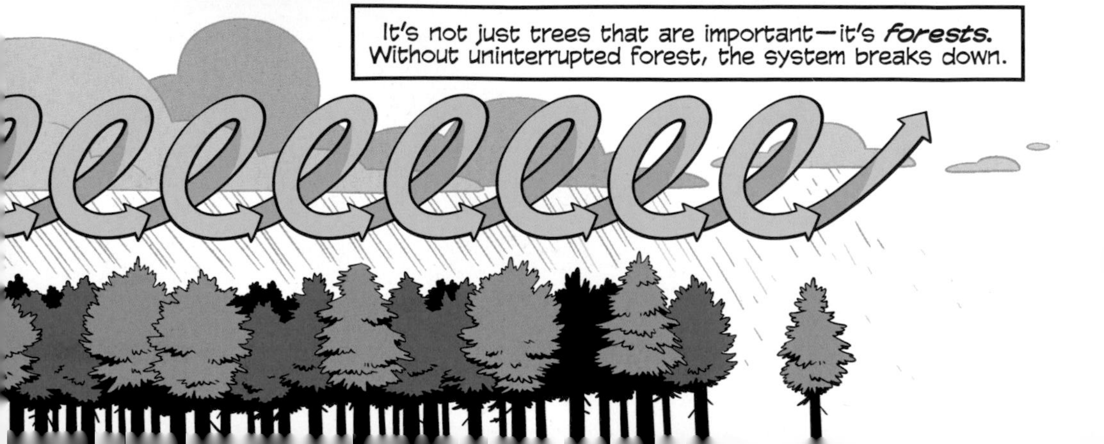
It's not just trees that are important—it's *forests.* Without uninterrupted forest, the system breaks down.

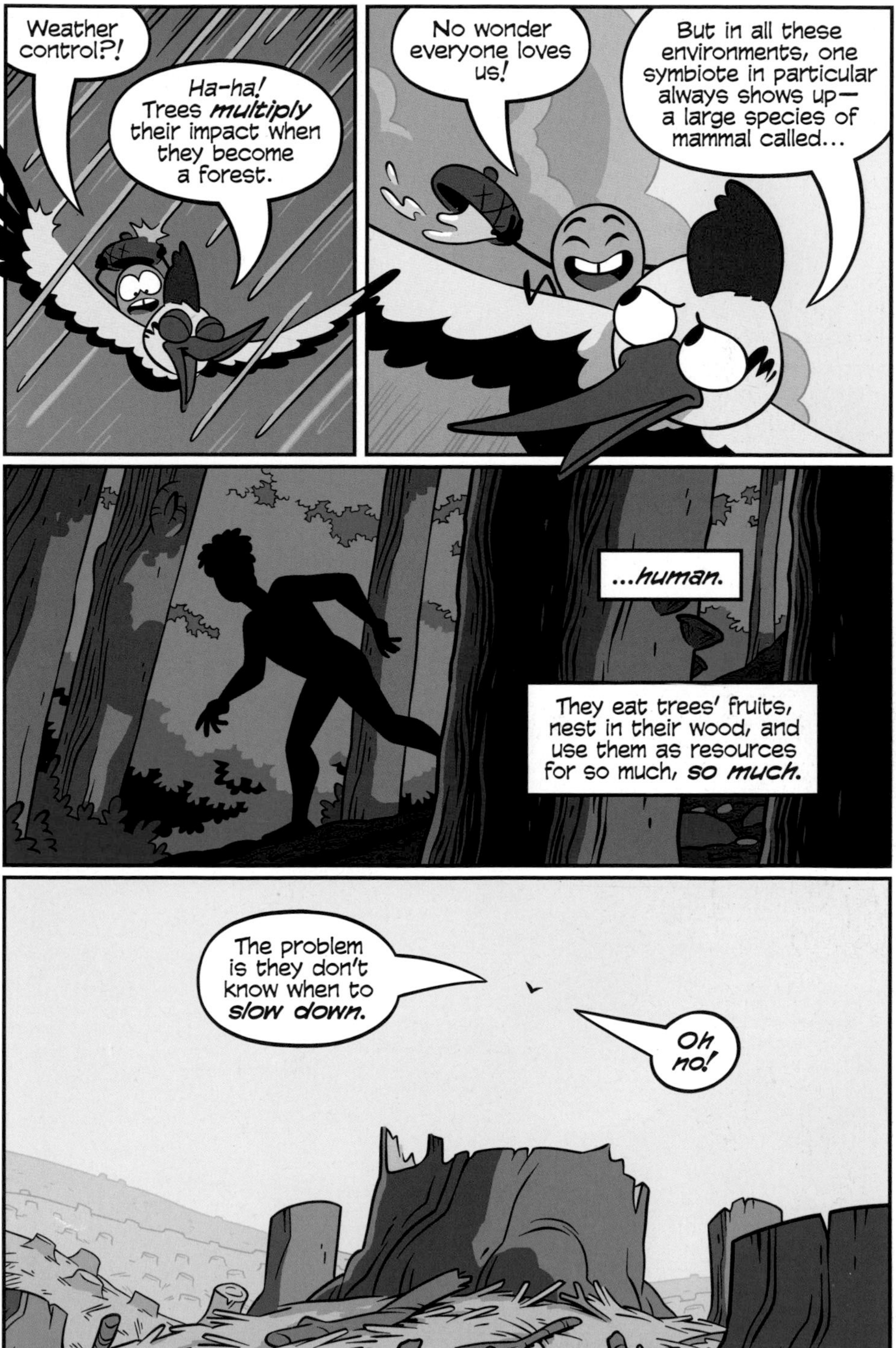
Weather control?!
Ha-ha! Trees *multiply* their impact when they become a forest.
No wonder everyone loves us!
But in all these environments, one symbiote in particular always shows up— a large species of mammal called...
...*human.*
They eat trees' fruits, nest in their wood, and use them as resources for so much, *so much.*
The problem is they don't know when to *slow down.*
Oh no!

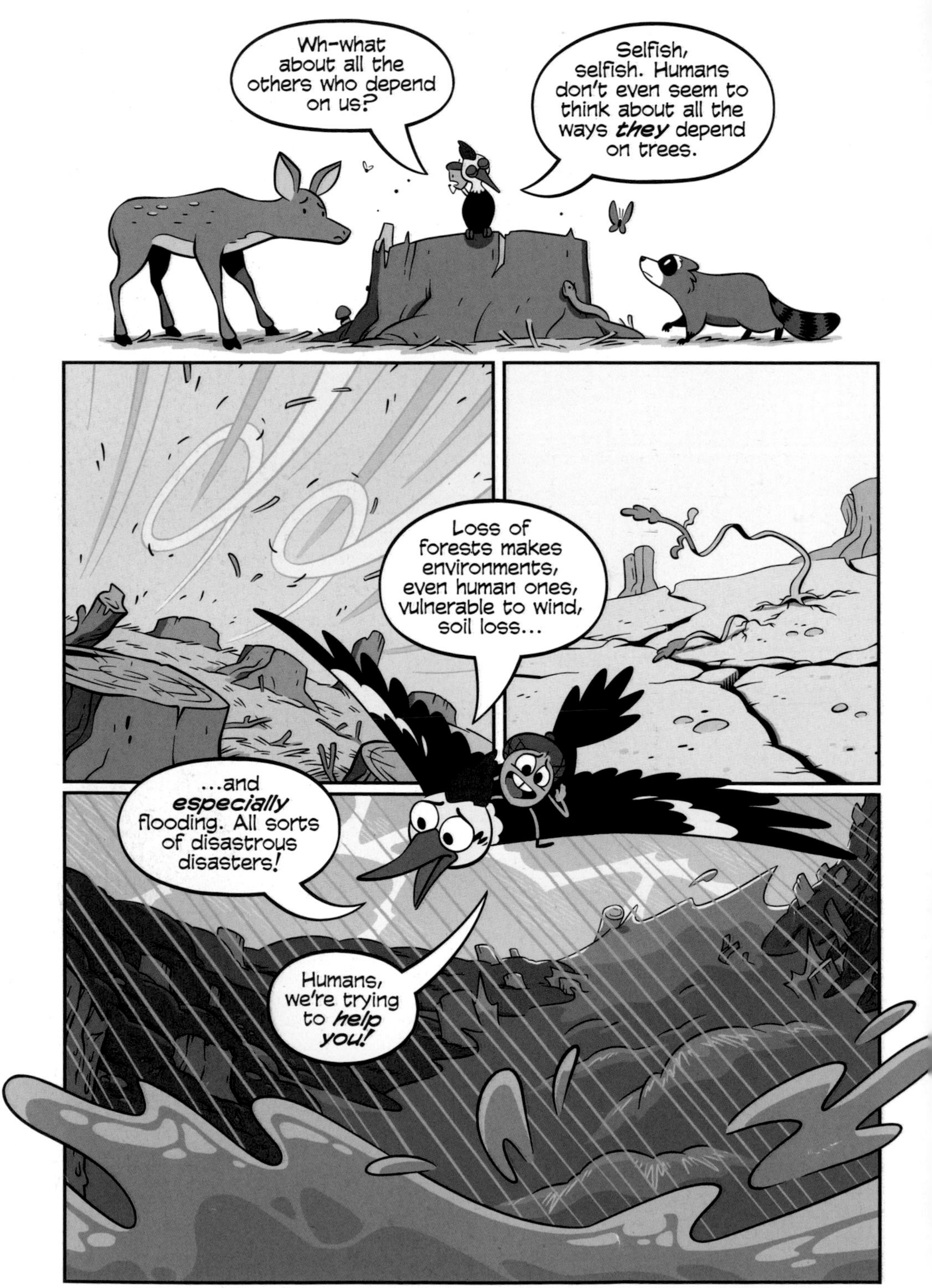
Wh-what about all the others who depend on us?
Selfish, selfish. Humans don't even seem to think about all the ways *they* depend on trees.
Loss of forests makes environments, even human ones, vulnerable to wind, soil loss...
...and *especially* flooding. All sorts of disastrous disasters!
Humans, we're trying to *help you!*

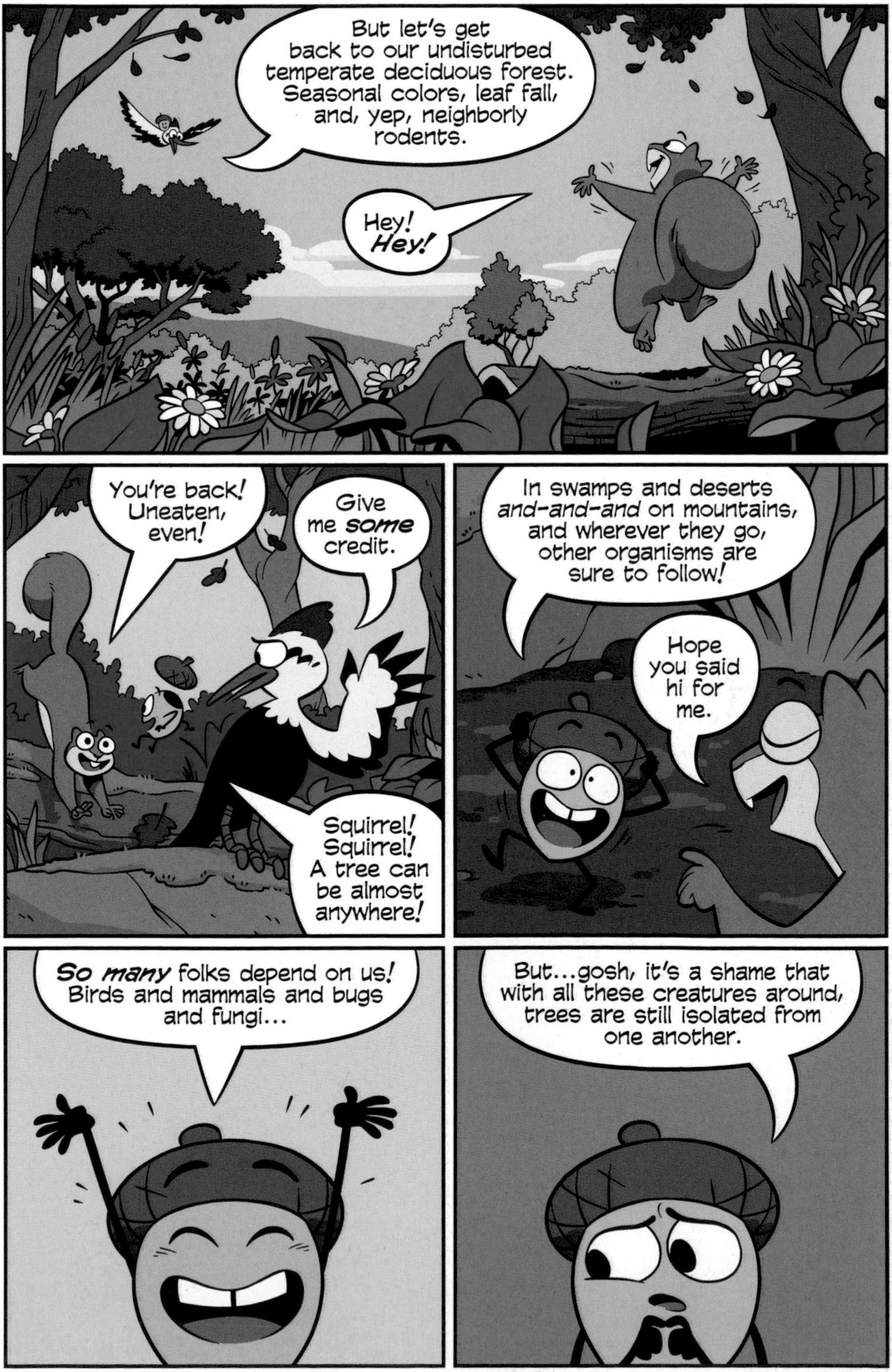
But let's get back to our undisturbed temperate deciduous forest. Seasonal colors, leaf fall, and, yep, neighborly rodents.
Hey! ***Hey!***
You're back! Uneaten, even!
Give me ***some*** credit.
Squirrel! Squirrel! A tree can be almost anywhere!
In swamps and deserts *and-and-and* on mountains, and wherever they go, other organisms are sure to follow!
Hope you said hi for me.
So many folks depend on us! Birds and mammals and bugs and fungi...
But...gosh, it's a shame that with all these creatures around, trees are still isolated from one another.

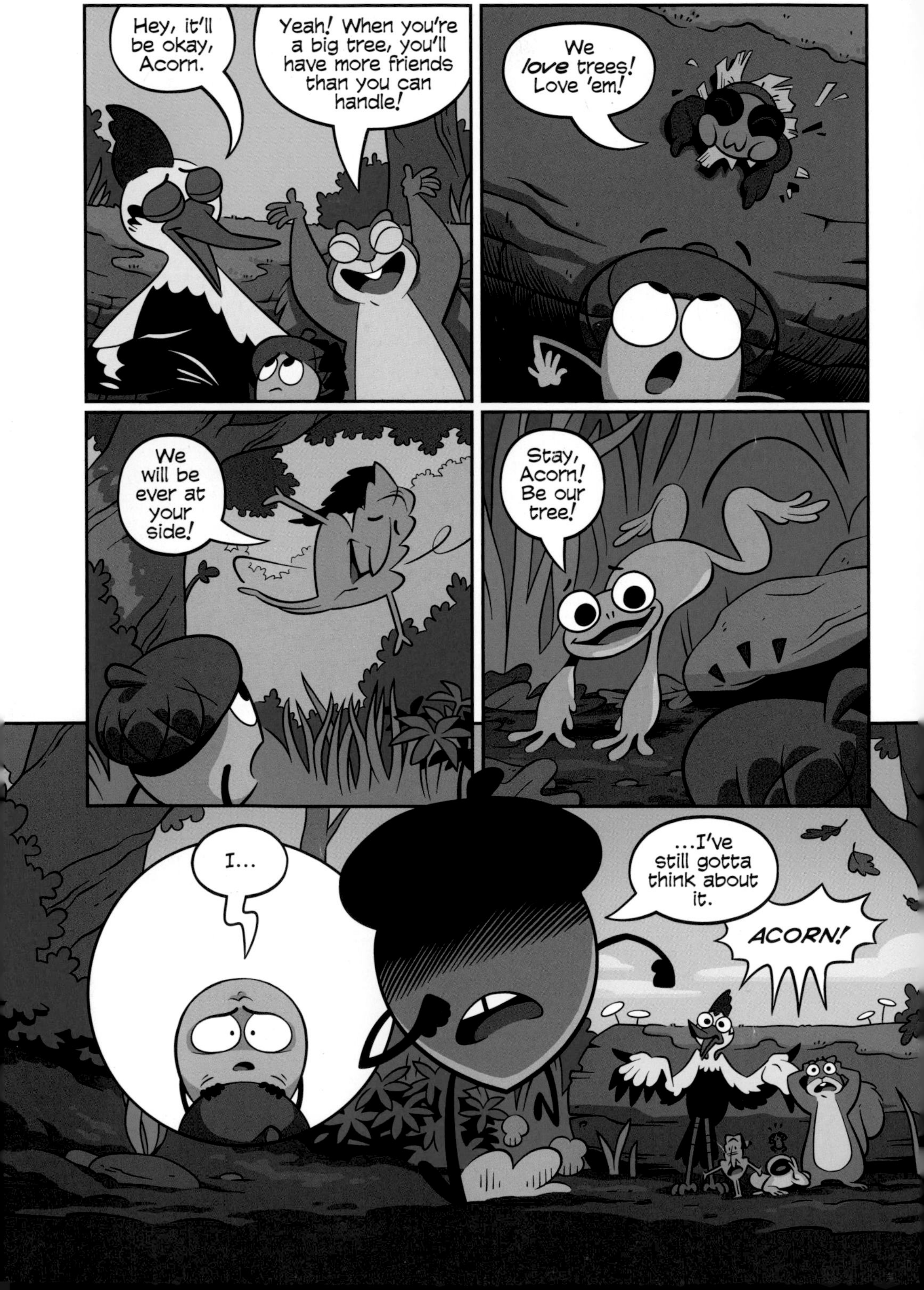
Hey, it'll be okay, Acorn.
Yeah! When you're a big tree, you'll have more friends than you can handle!
We *love* trees! Love 'em!
We will be ever at your side!
Stay, Acorn! Be our tree!
I...
...I've still gotta think about it.
ACORN!

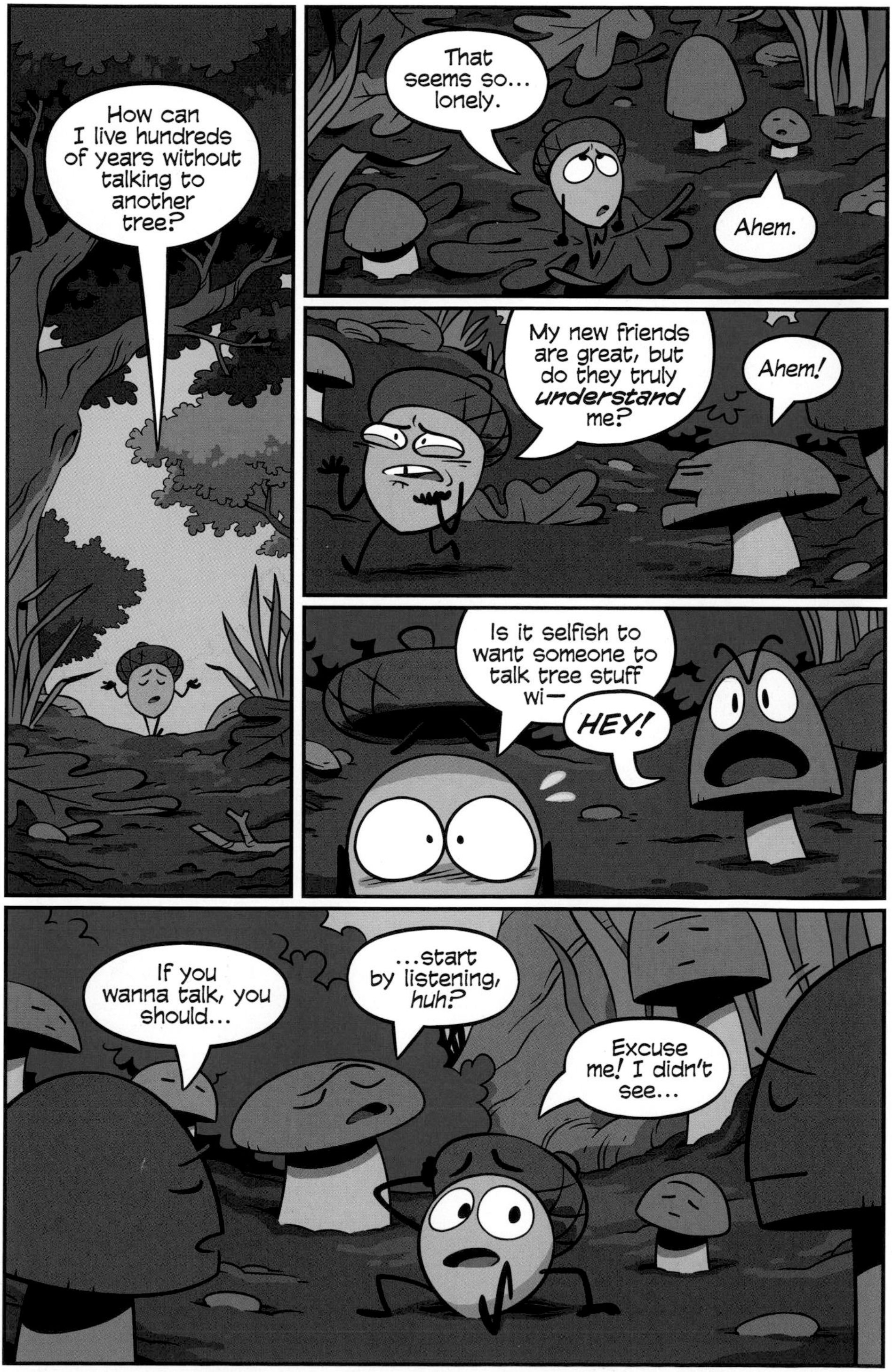
How can I live hundreds of years without talking to another tree?
That seems so... lonely.
Ahem.
My new friends are great, but do they truly *understand* me?
Ahem!
Is it selfish to want someone to talk tree stuff wi—
HEY!
If you wanna talk, you should...
...start by listening, *huh?*
Excuse me! I didn't see...

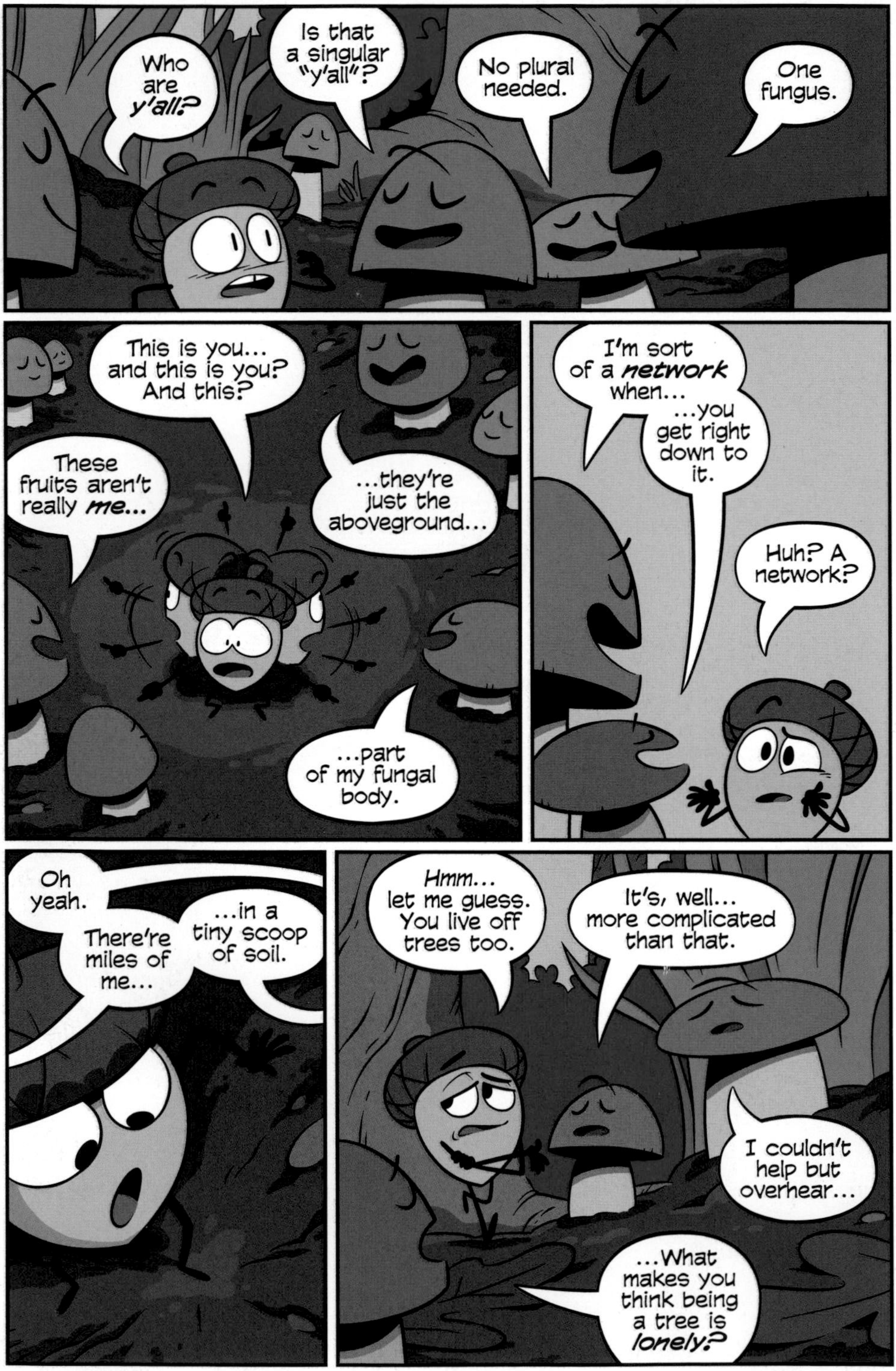

Who are *y'all?*
Is that a singular "y'all"?
No plural needed.
One fungus.
This is you... and this is you? And this?
These fruits aren't really *me*...
...they're just the aboveground...
...part of my fungal body.
I'm sort of a ***network*** when...
...you get right down to it.
Huh? A network?
Oh yeah.
There're miles of me...
...in a tiny scoop of soil.
Hmm... let me guess. You live off trees too.
It's, well... more complicated than that.
I couldn't help but overhear...
...What makes you think being a tree is ***lonely?***

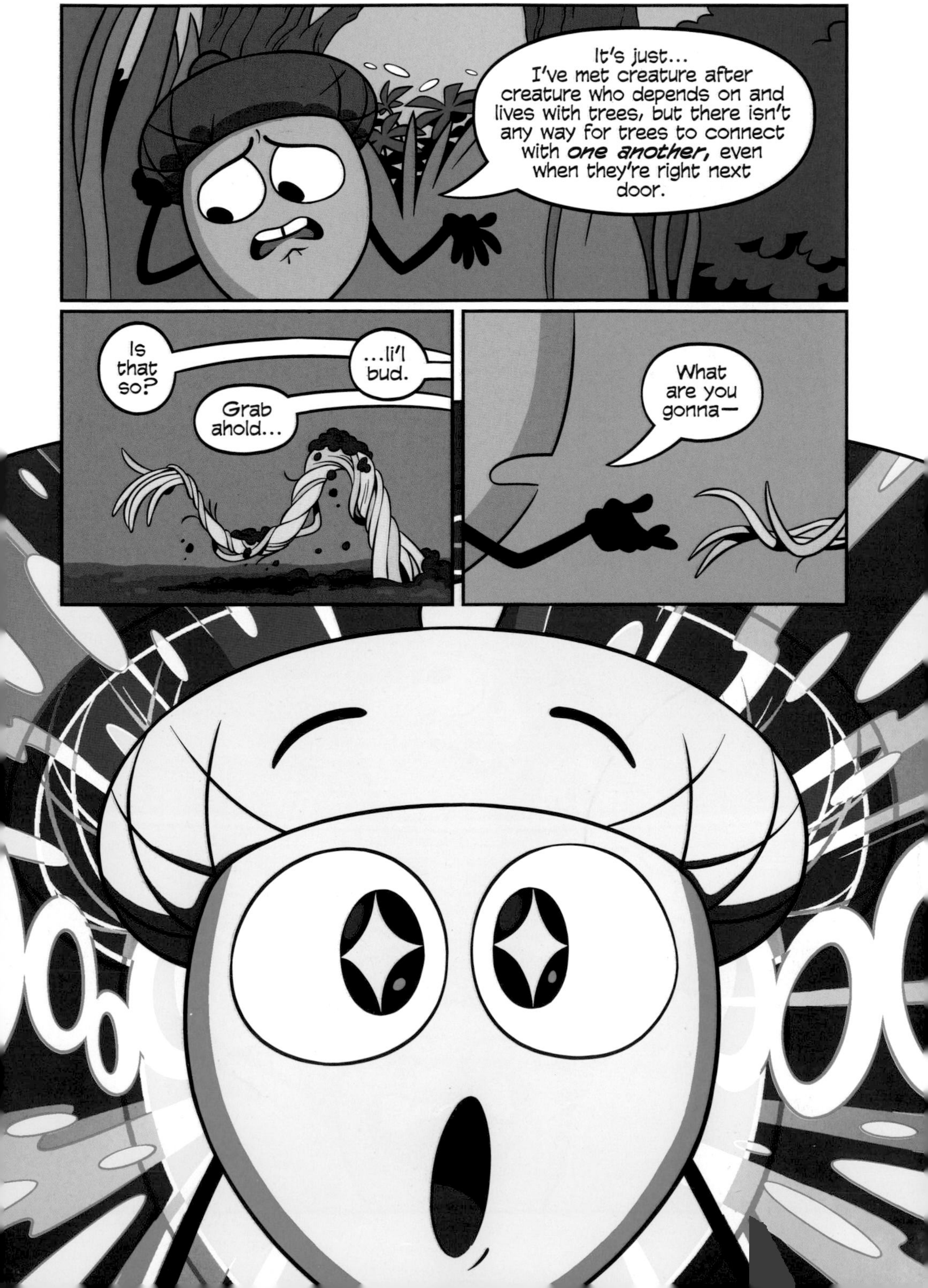
It's just... I've met creature after creature who depends on and lives with trees, but there isn't any way for trees to connect with *one another,* even when they're right next door.
Is that so?
Grab ahold...
...li'l bud.
What are you gonna—

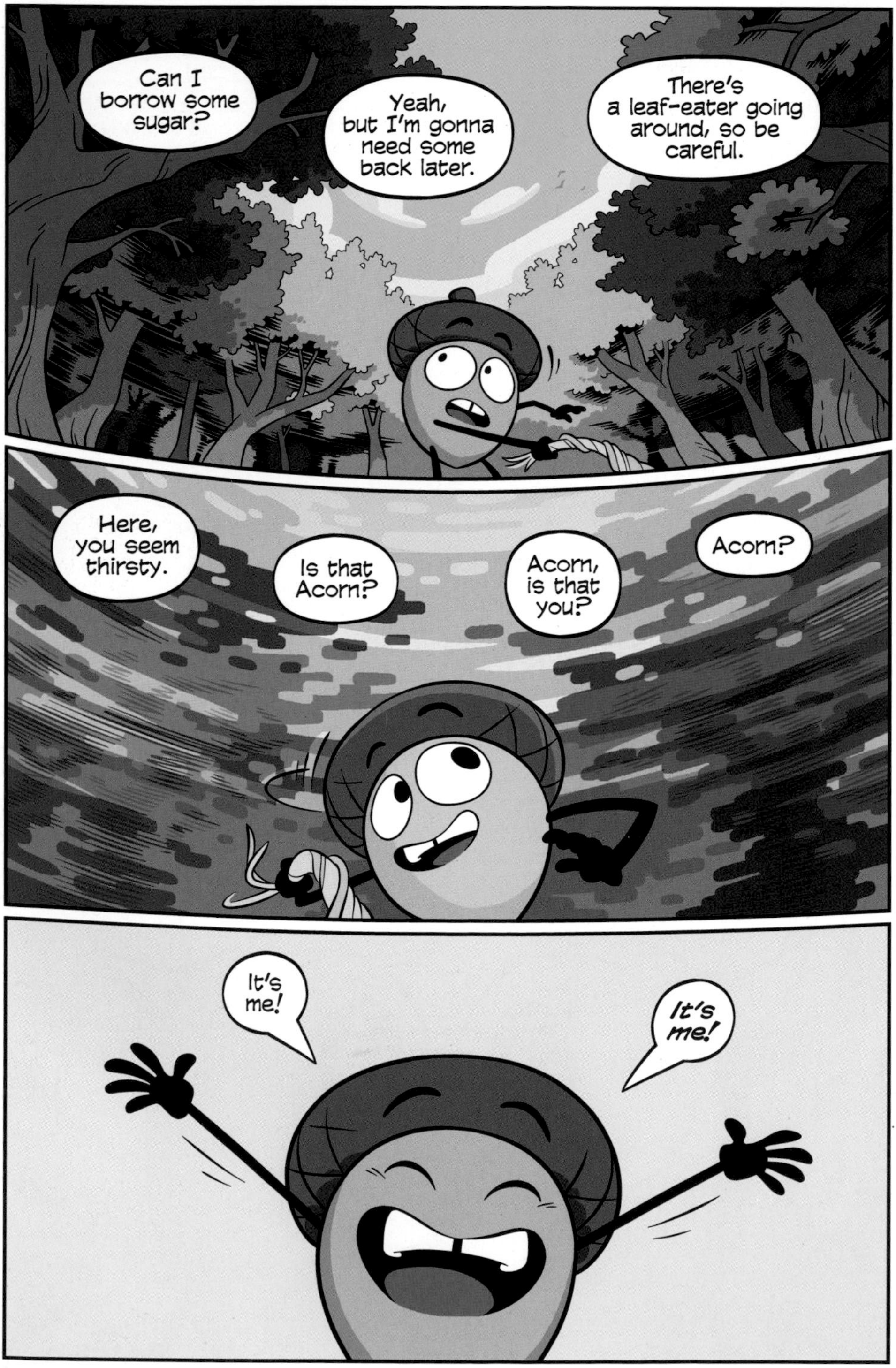
Can I borrow some sugar?
Yeah, but I'm gonna need some back later.
There's a leaf-eater going around, so be careful.
Here, you seem thirsty.
Is that Acorn?
Acorn, is that you?
Acorn?
It's me!
It's me!

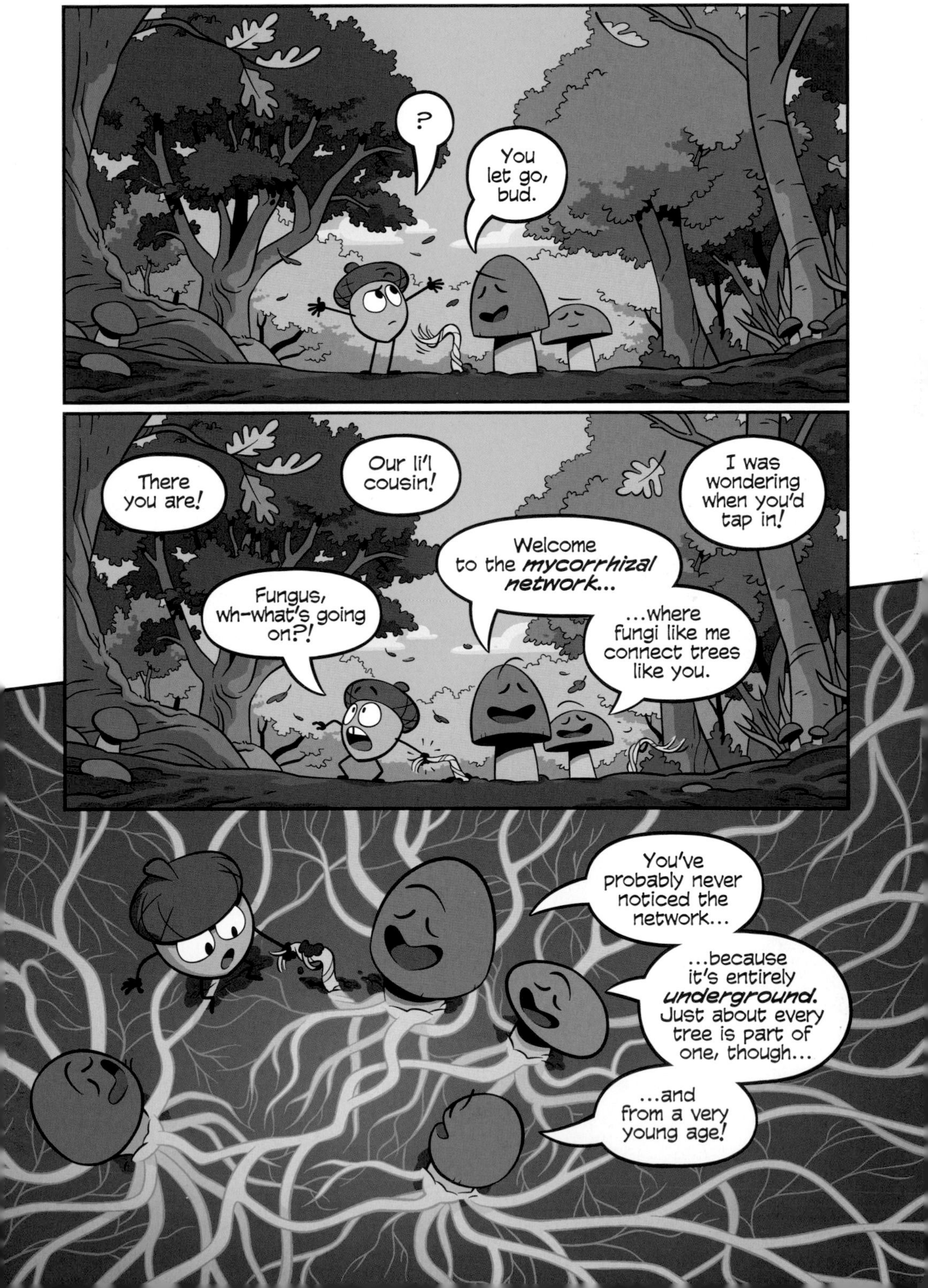
?
You let go, bud.
There you are!
Our li'l cousin!
I was wondering when you'd tap in!
Fungus, wh-what's going on?!
Welcome to the *mycorrhizal network*...
...where fungi like me connect trees like you.
You've probably never noticed the network...
...because it's entirely *underground.* Just about every tree is part of one, though...
...and from a very young age!

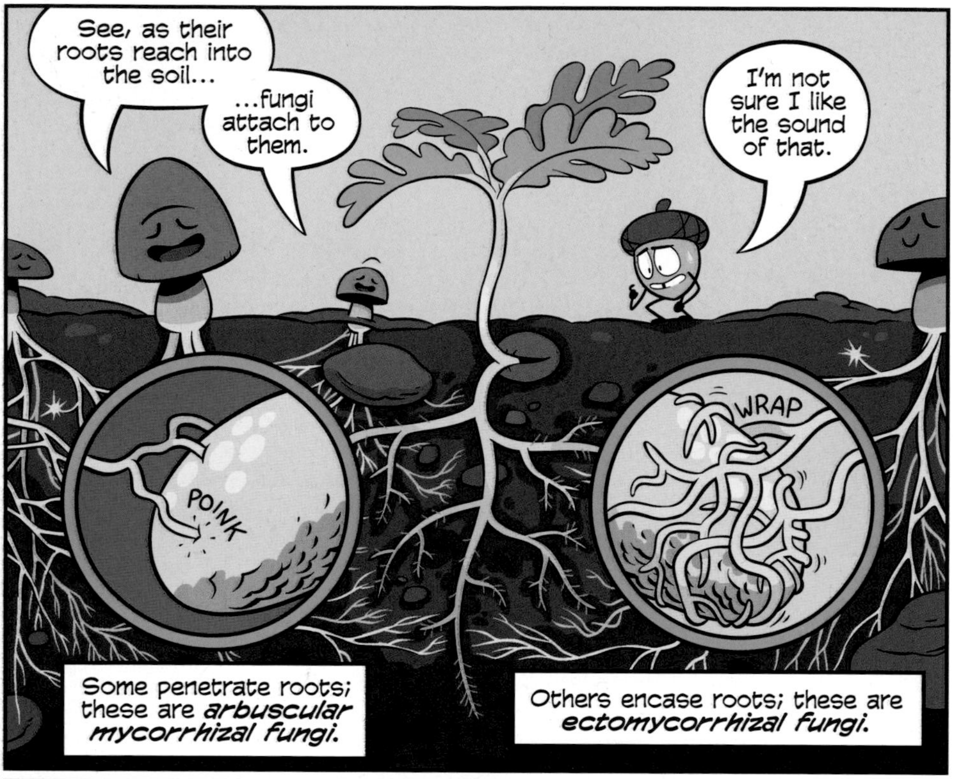
See, as their roots reach into the soil...
...fungi attach to them.
I'm not sure I like the sound of that.
POINK
WRAP
Some penetrate roots; these are *arbuscular mycorrhizal fungi.*
Others encase roots; these are *ectomycorrhizal fungi.*

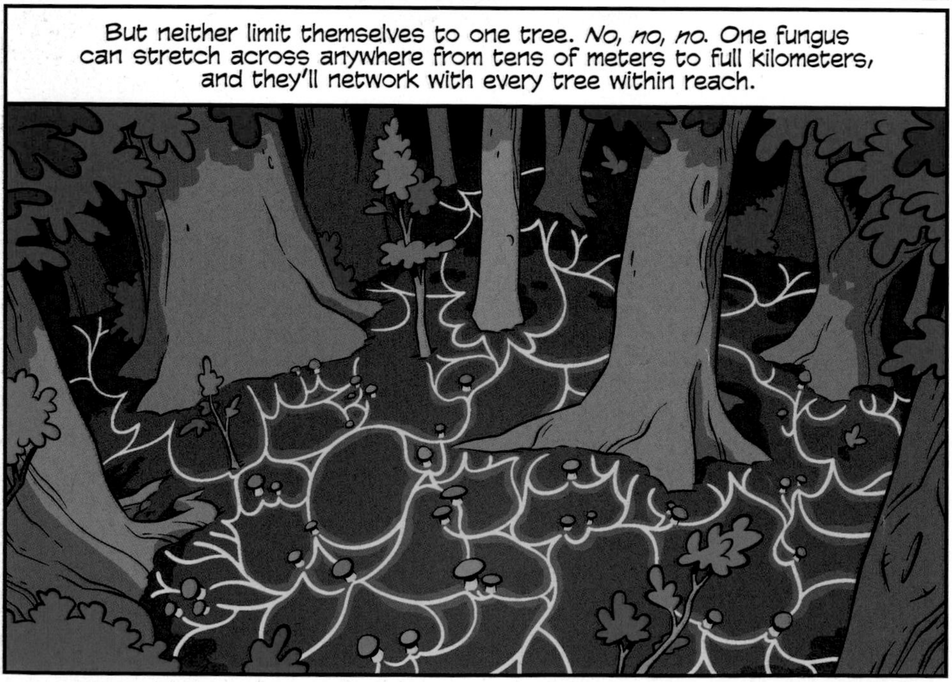
But neither limit themselves to one tree. *No, no, no.* One fungus can stretch across anywhere from tens of meters to full kilometers, and they'll network with every tree within reach.

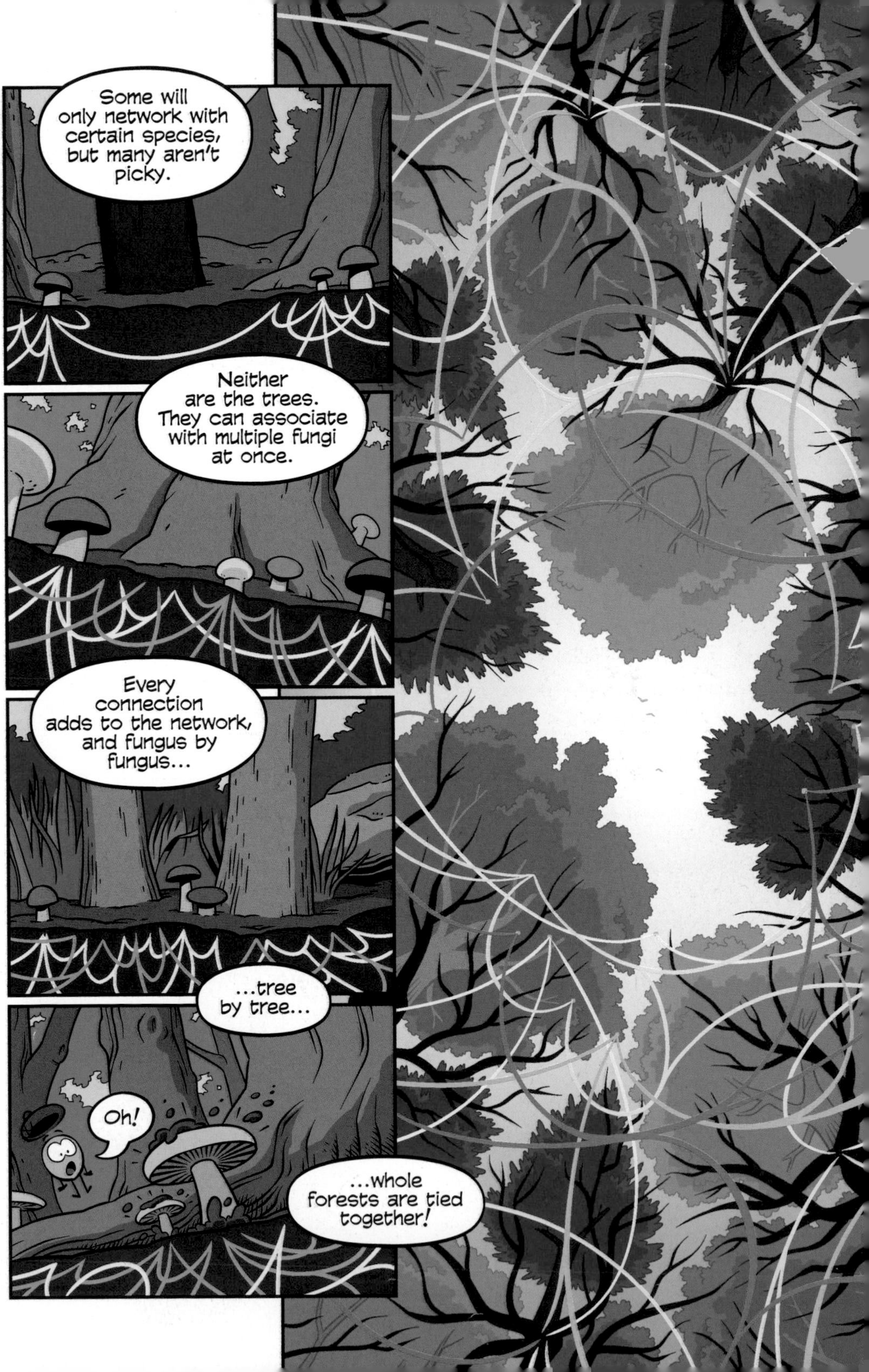
Some will only network with certain species, but many aren't picky.
Neither are the trees. They can associate with multiple fungi at once.
Every connection adds to the network, and fungus by fungus...
...tree by tree...
Oh!
...whole forests are tied together!

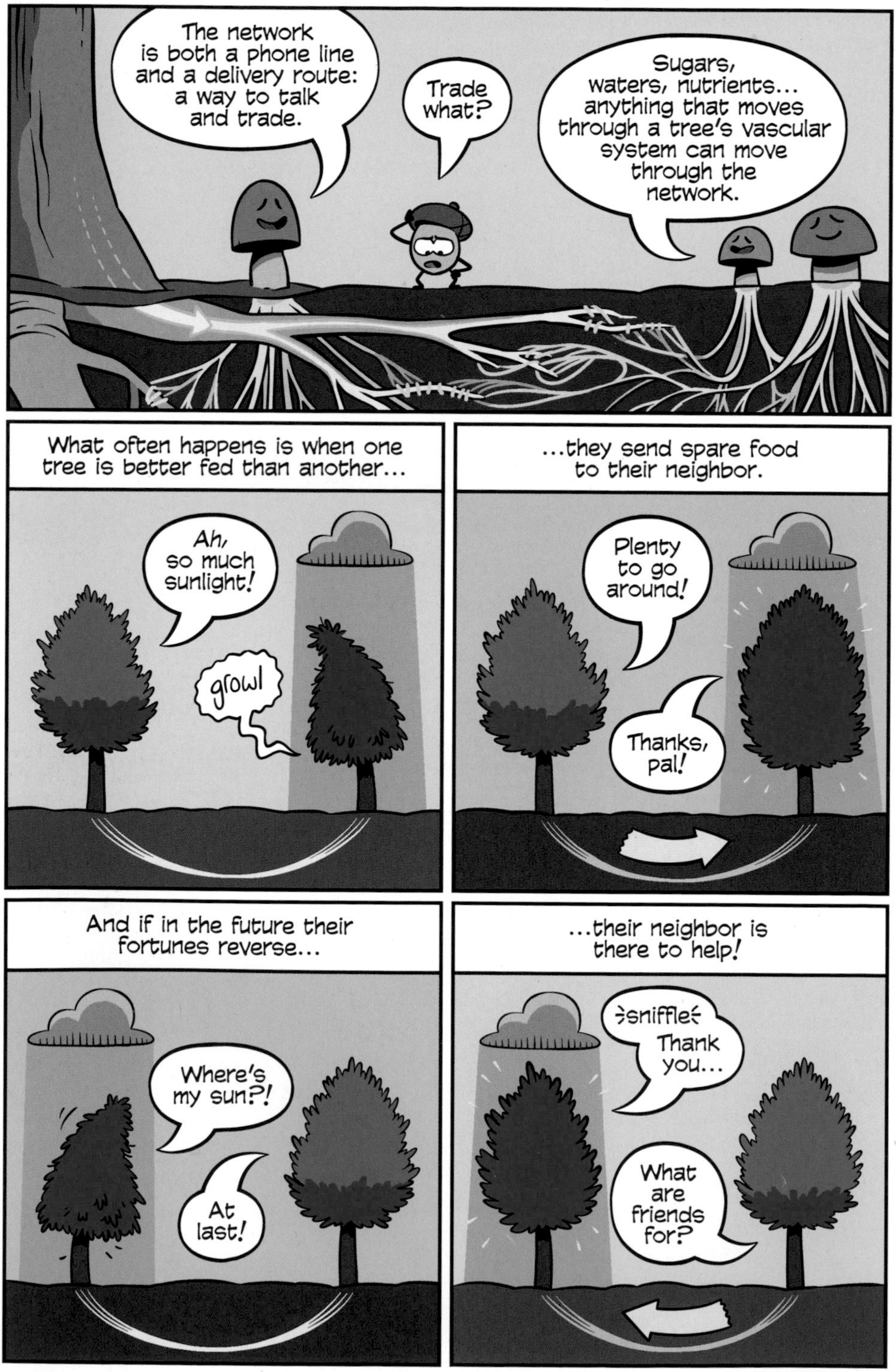
The network is both a phone line and a delivery route: a way to talk and trade.
Trade what?
Sugars, waters, nutrients... anything that moves through a tree's vascular system can move through the network.
What often happens is when one tree is better fed than another...
Ah, so much sunlight!
growl
...they send spare food to their neighbor.
Plenty to go around!
Thanks, pal!
And if in the future their fortunes reverse...
Where's my sun?!
At last!
...their neighbor is there to help!
sniffle
Thank you...
What are friends for?

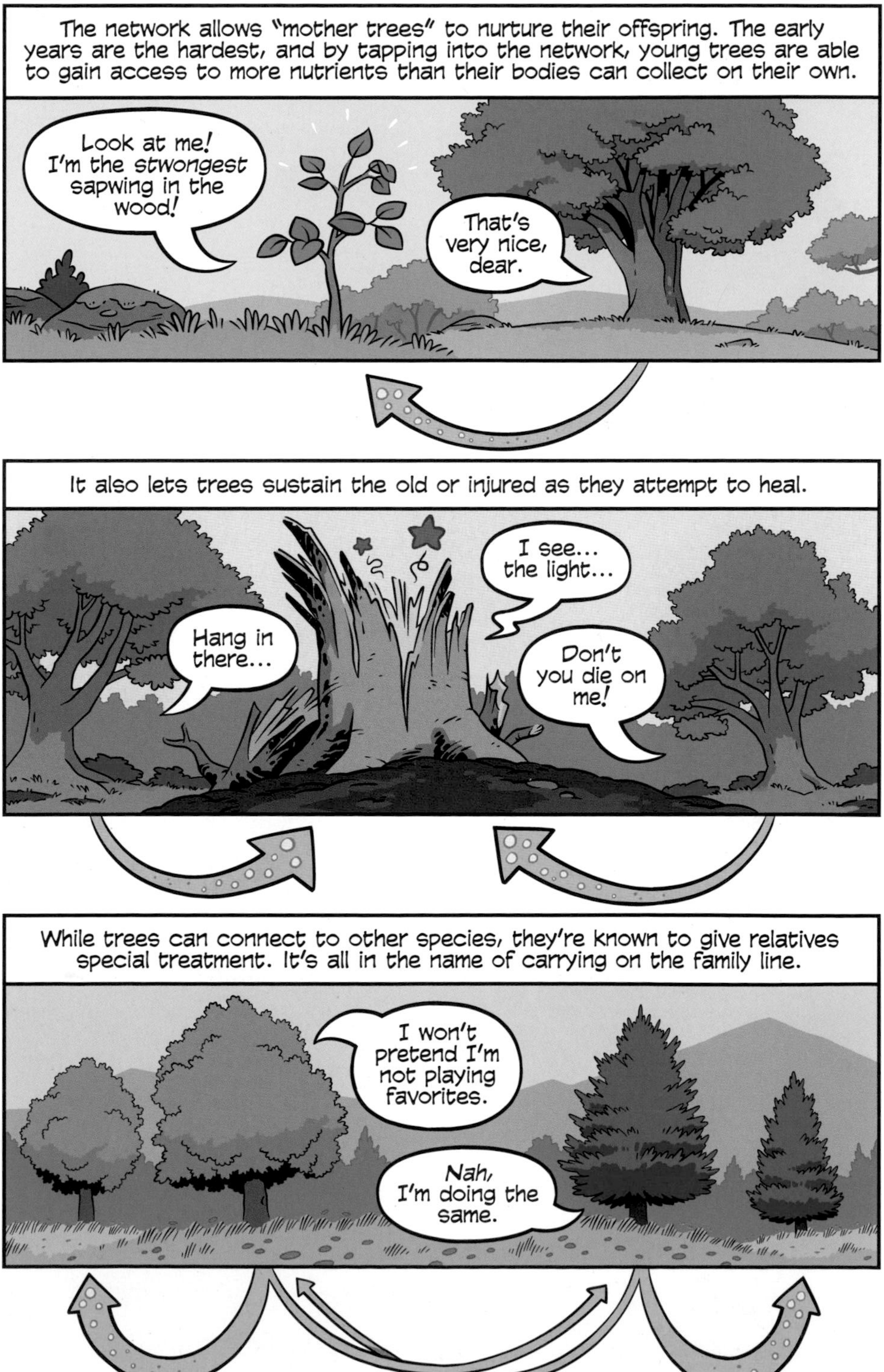
The network allows "mother trees" to nurture their offspring. The early years are the hardest, and by tapping into the network, young trees are able to gain access to more nutrients than their bodies can collect on their own.
Look at me! I'm the *stwongest* sapwing in the wood!
That's very nice, dear.
It also lets trees sustain the old or injured as they attempt to heal.
Hang in there...
I see... the light...
Don't you die on me!
While trees can connect to other species, they're known to give relatives special treatment. It's all in the name of carrying on the family line.
I won't pretend I'm not playing favorites.
Nah, I'm doing the same.

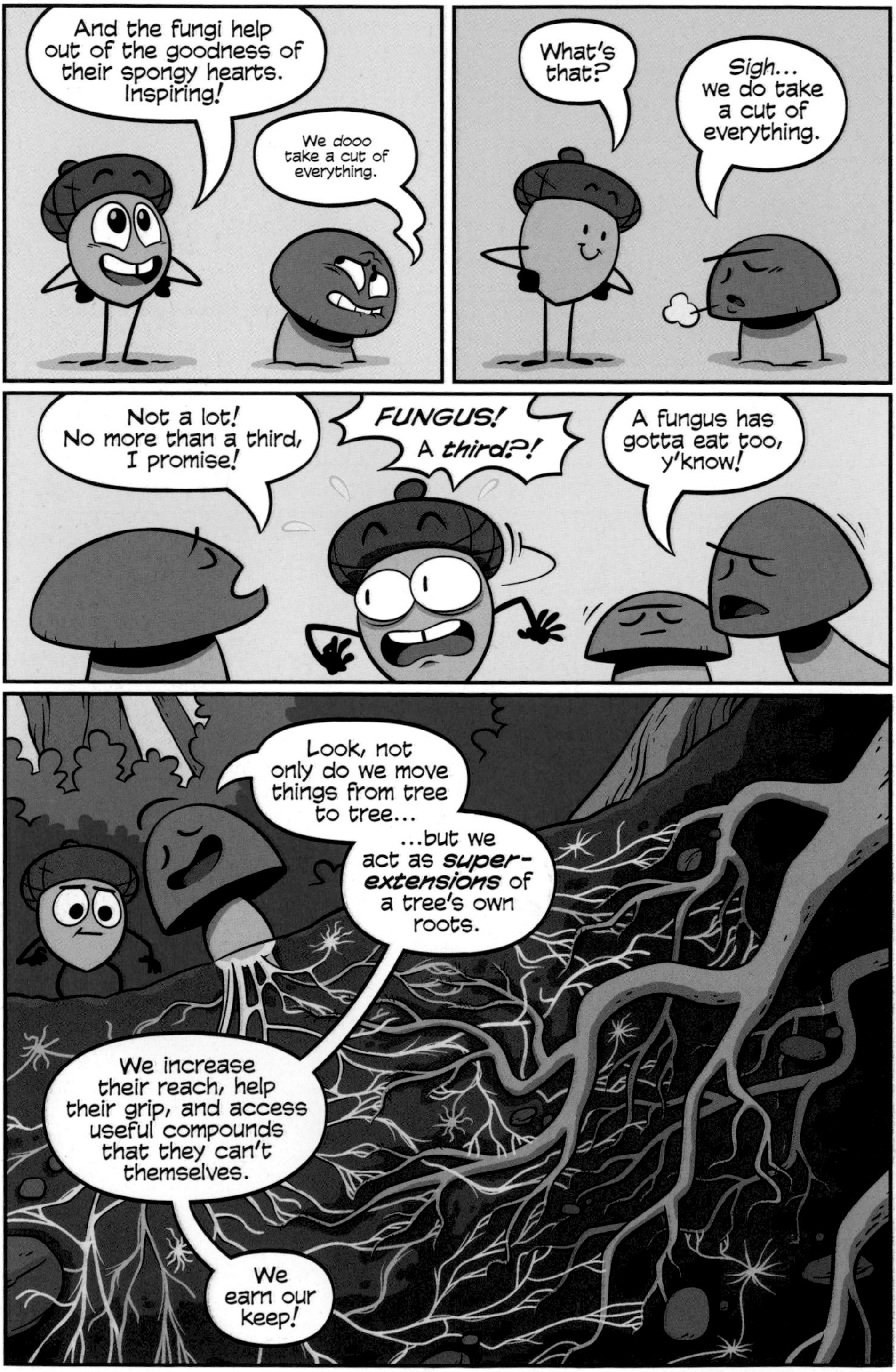
And the fungi help out of the goodness of their spongy hearts. Inspiring!
We *dooo* take a cut of everything.
What's that?
Sigh... we do take a cut of everything.
Not a lot! No more than a third, I promise!
FUNGUS! A ***third?!***
A fungus has gotta eat too, y'know!
Look, not only do we move things from tree to tree...
...but we act as ***super-extensions*** of a tree's own roots.
We increase their reach, help their grip, and access useful compounds that they can't themselves.
We earn our keep!

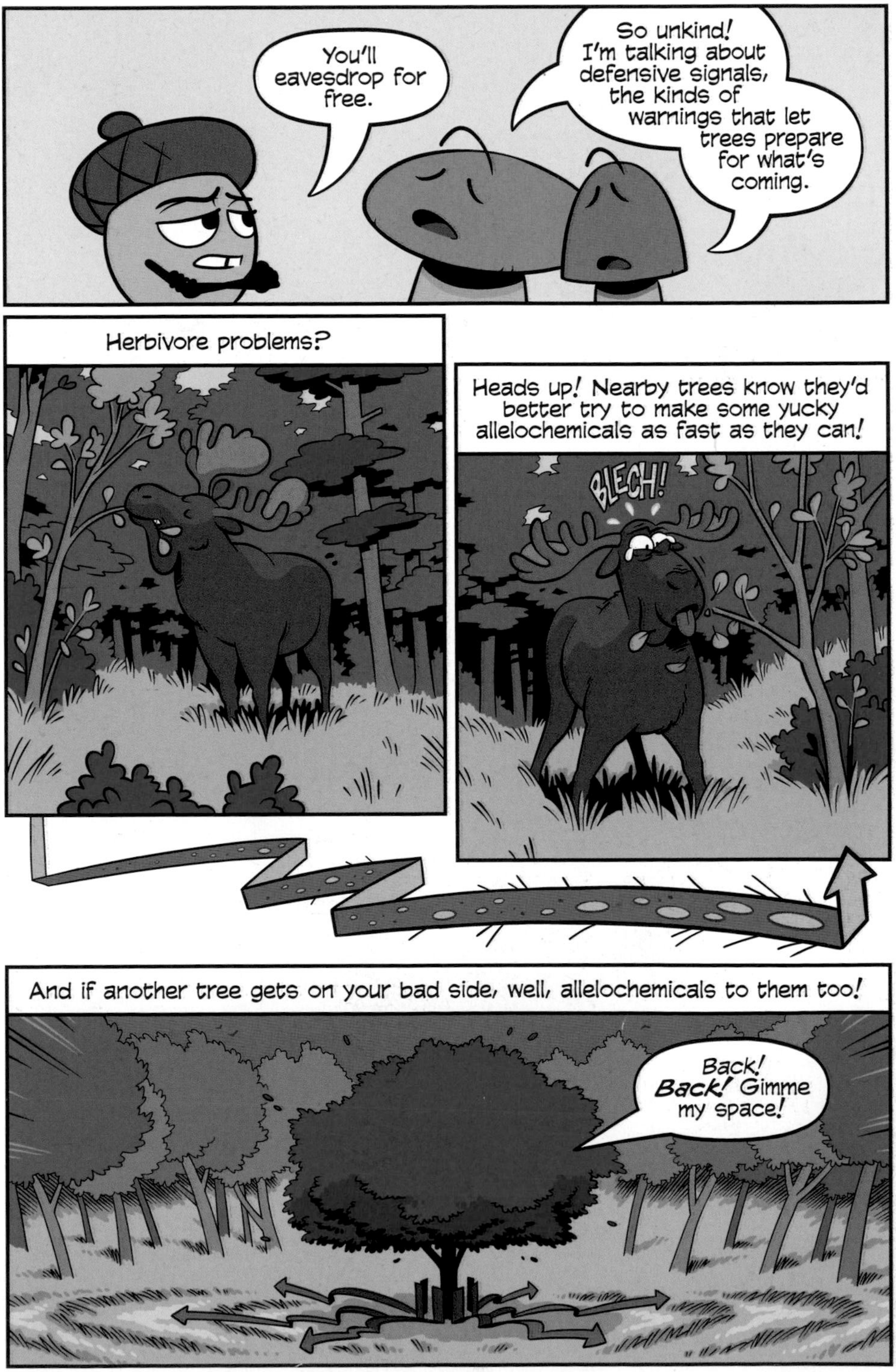
You'll eavesdrop for free.
So unkind! I'm talking about defensive signals, the kinds of warnings that let trees prepare for what's coming.
Herbivore problems?
Heads up! Nearby trees know they'd better try to make some yucky allelochemicals as fast as they can!
BLECH!
And if another tree gets on your bad side, well, allelochemicals to them too!
Back! Back! Gimme my space!

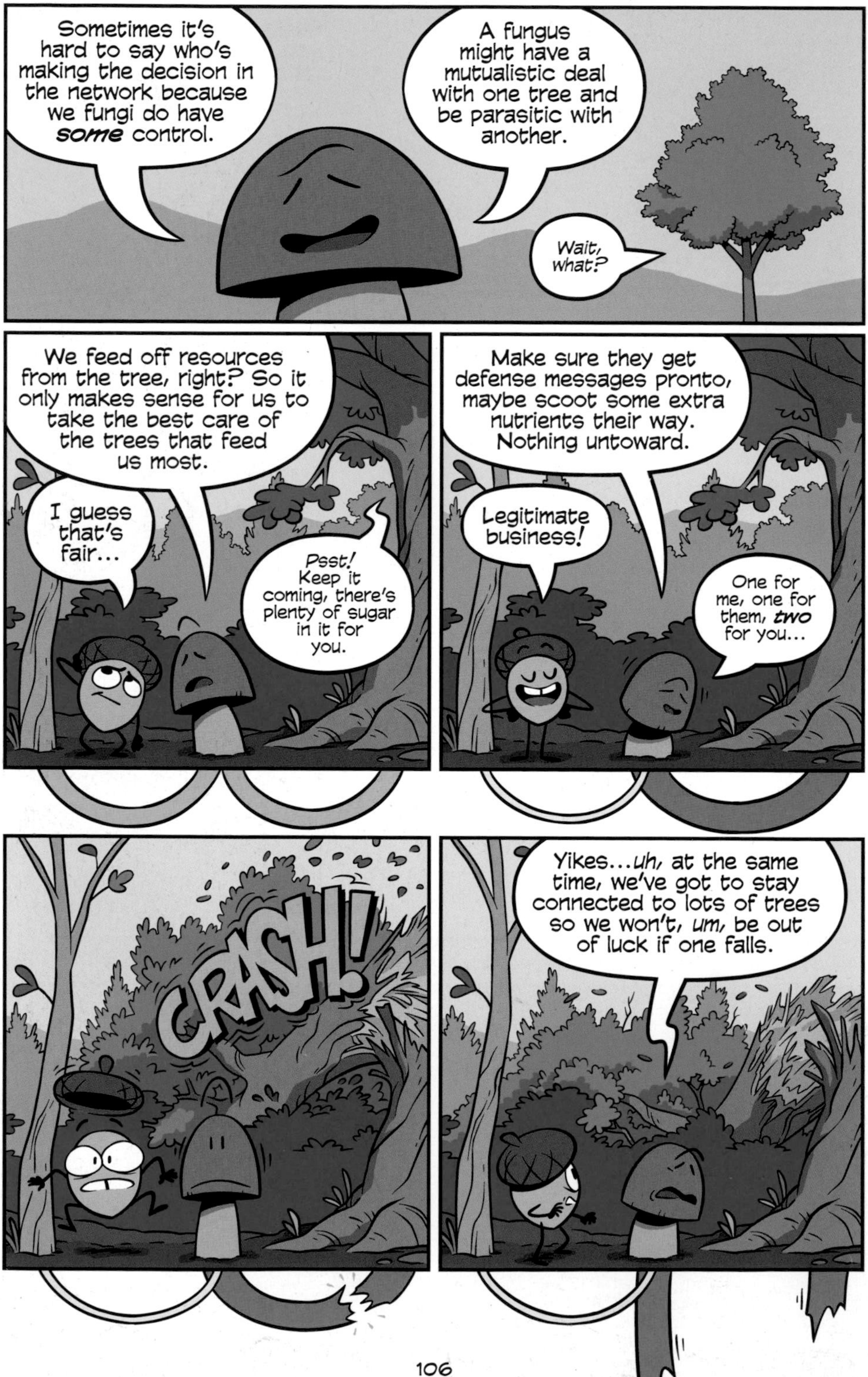
Sometimes it's hard to say who's making the decision in the network because we fungi do have *some* control.
A fungus might have a mutualistic deal with one tree and be parasitic with another.
Wait, what?
We feed off resources from the tree, right? So it only makes sense for us to take the best care of the trees that feed us most.
I guess that's fair...
Psst! Keep it coming, there's plenty of sugar in it for you.
Make sure they get defense messages pronto, maybe scoot some extra nutrients their way. Nothing untoward.
Legitimate business!
One for me, one for them, *two* for you...
CRASH!
Yikes...*uh,* at the same time, we've got to stay connected to lots of trees so we won't, *um,* be out of luck if one falls.

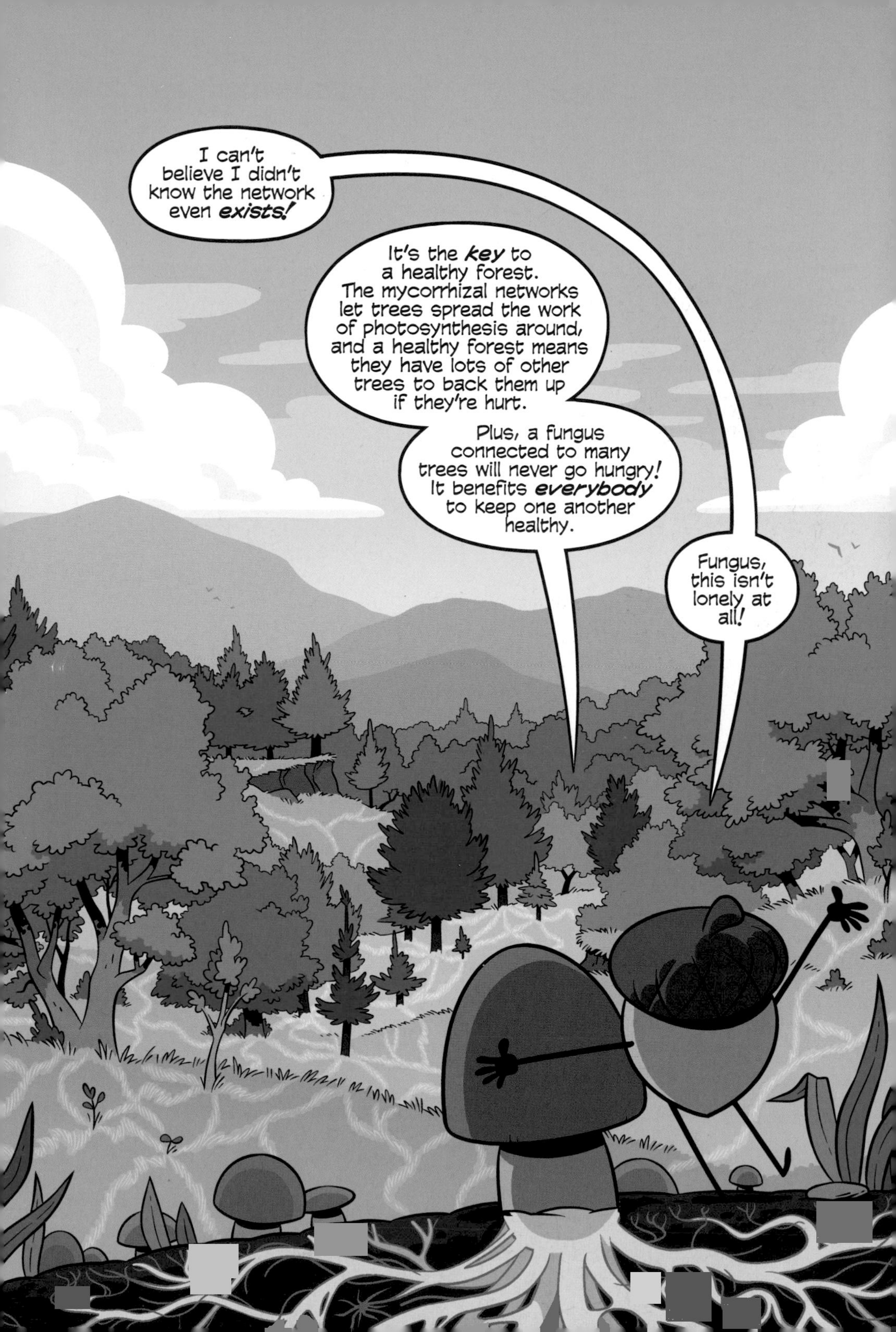
I can't believe I didn't know the network even *exists!*
It's the *key* to a healthy forest. The mycorrhizal networks let trees spread the work of photosynthesis around, and a healthy forest means they have lots of other trees to back them up if they're hurt.
Plus, a fungus connected to many trees will never go hungry! It benefits *everybody* to keep one another healthy.
Fungus, this isn't lonely at all!

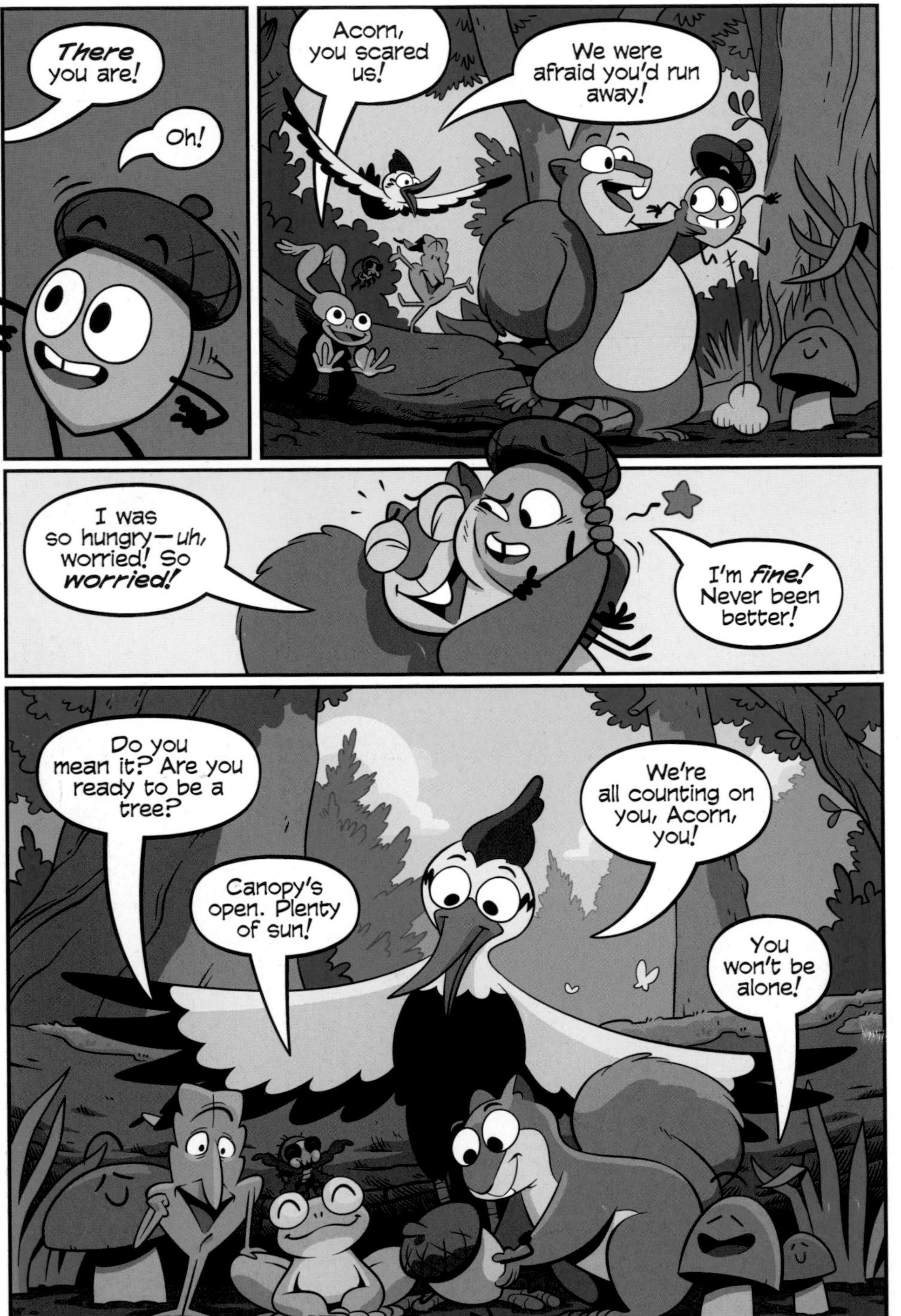

There you are!
Oh!
Acorn, you scared us!
We were afraid you'd run away!
I was so hungry—*uh,* worried! So ***worried!***
I'm ***fine!*** Never been better!
Do you mean it? Are you ready to be a tree?
Canopy's open. Plenty of sun!
We're all counting on you, Acorn, you!
You won't be alone!

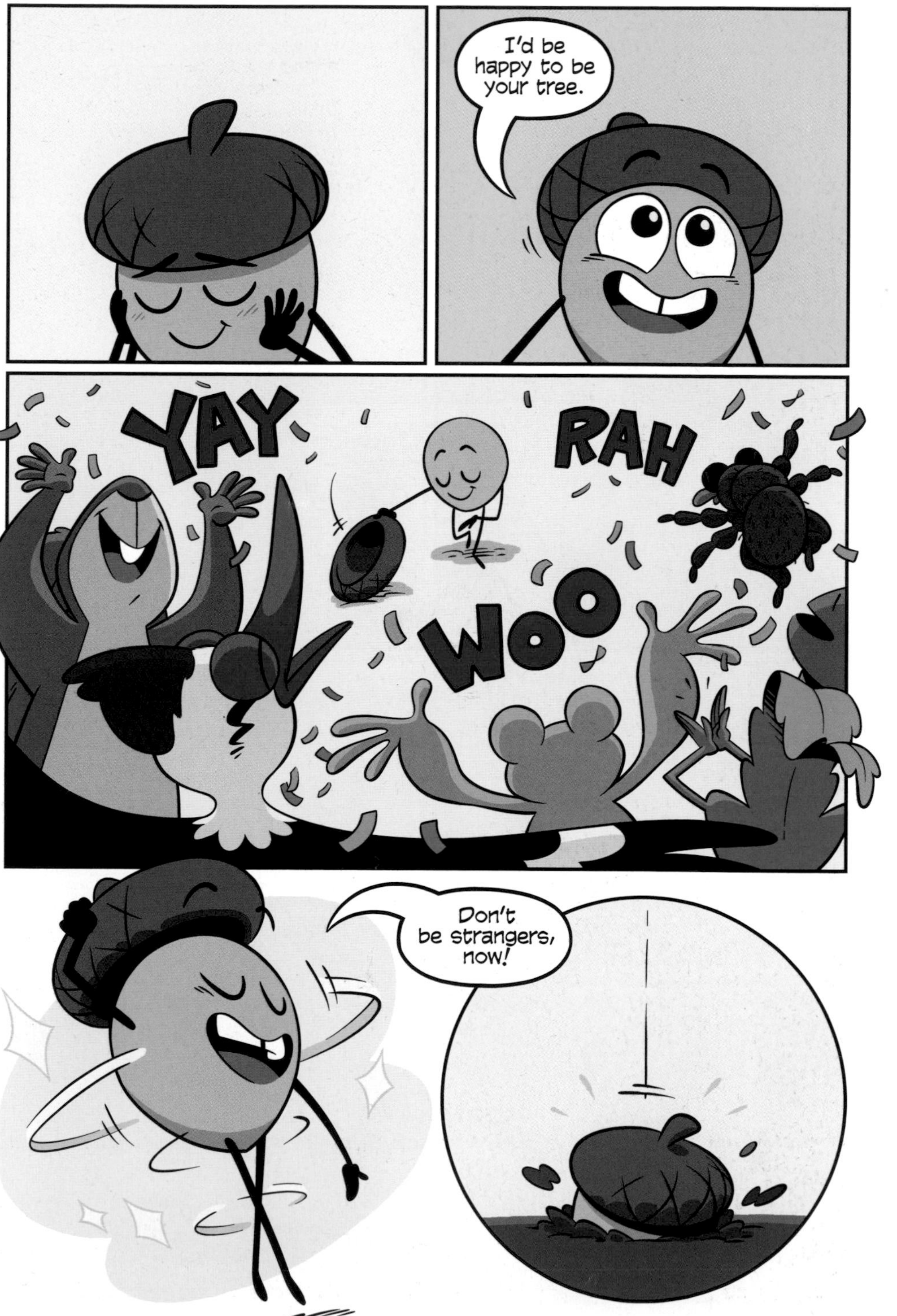
I'd be happy to be your tree.
YAY
RAH
WOO
Don't be strangers, now!

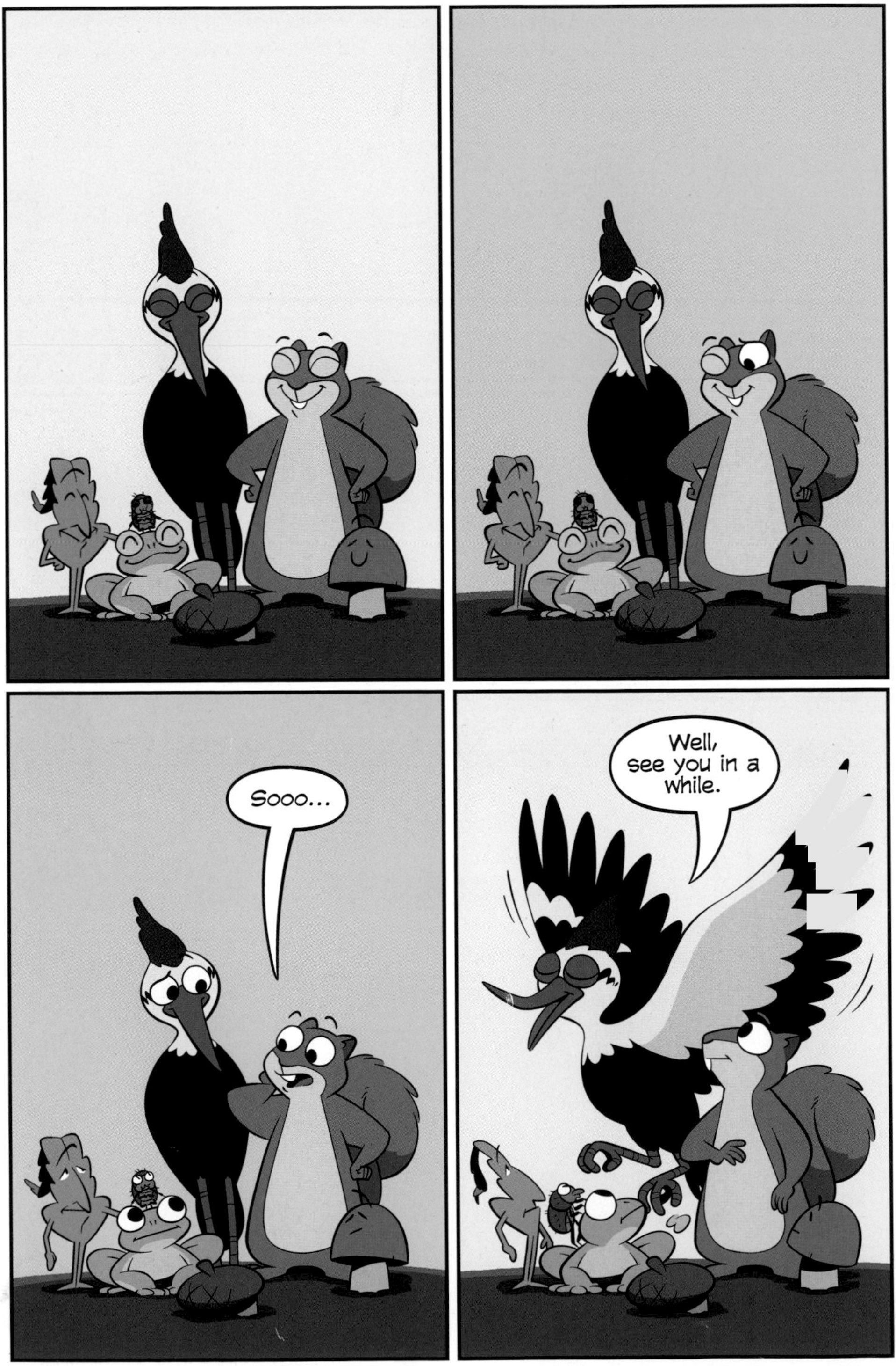
Sooo...
Well, see you in a while.

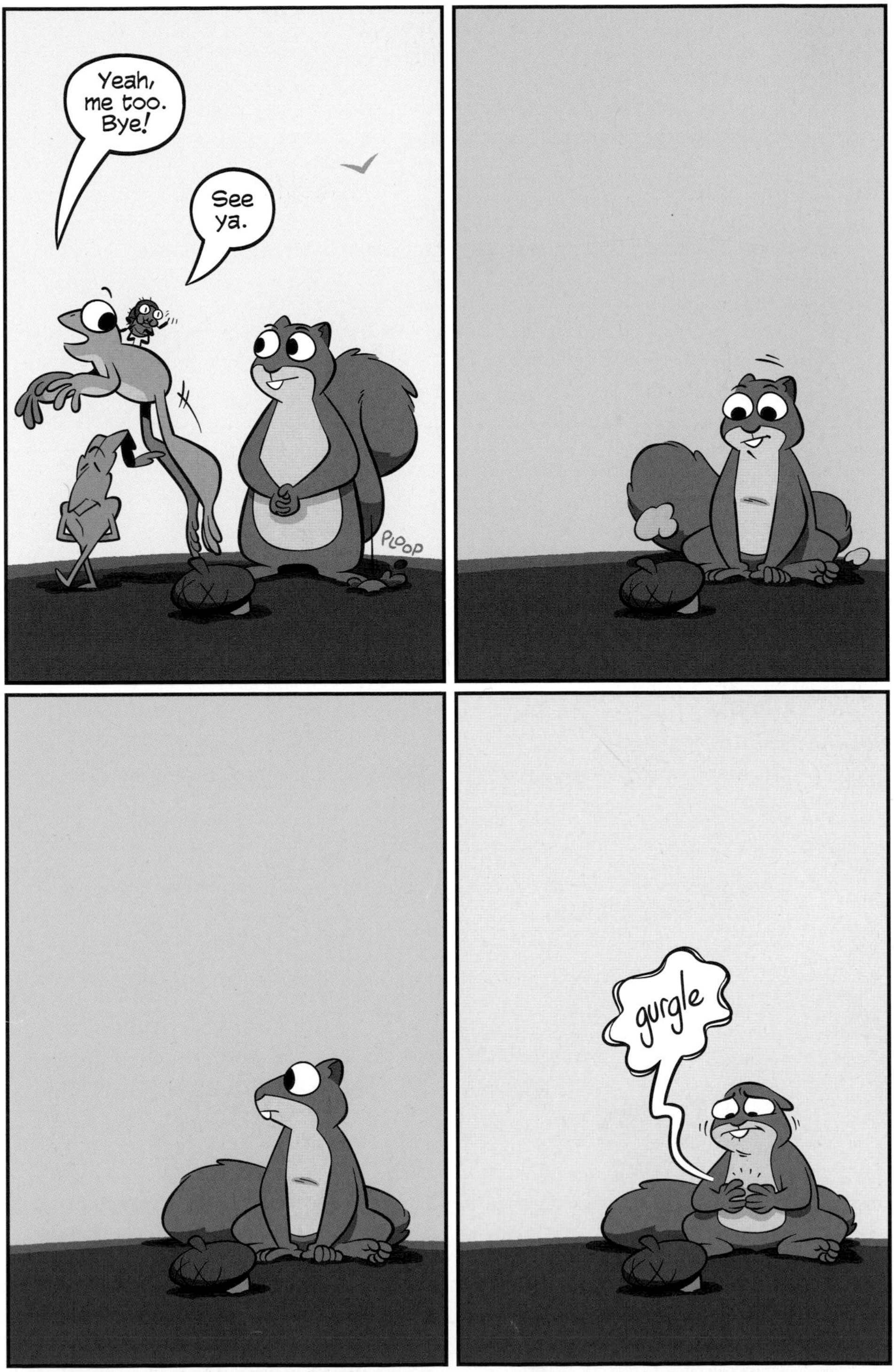
Yeah, me too. Bye!
See ya.
PLOOP
gurgle

—GLOSSARY—

Allelochemicals

Chemicals produced by plants for defensive purposes. These can be antibiotic, insecticidal, or otherwise unpleasant to eat.

Apical Dominance

The chemical inhibition of secondary growth by the lead shoot. Along with environmental factors, this determines what shape the tree's body takes.

Angiosperm

A category of tree also known as broadleaves or hardwoods. They reproduce through flowers, the ovaries of which enclose their seeds, and are often pollinated by animals.

Auxin

A growth-regulating chemical essential to plant growth. In different concentrations, it can encourage or impede growth in order to direct it.

Bark

The portion of secondary wood formed outward from the vascular cambium. It is divided by the cork cambium into phloem and cork.

Bud

An undeveloped leaf, flower, or shoot. These form at shoots' apical meristems and may remain dormant for long periods of time.

Compartmentalization

The process by which a tree seals off damaged areas of itself to prevent rot and infection.

Cone

The reproductive organ of a gymnosperm. Female cones are larger than males and will seal up after being pollinated.

Convergence
The evolutionary principle whereby unrelated species develop similar forms as a result of similar responses to their environment. The opposite principle applied to closely related species is divergence.

Cotyledon
A plant's first leaves enclosed within the seed. They hold the plant's initial food supply and do not last long after germination.

Deciduous
A type of tree that drops its leaves each year.

Flower
The reproductive organ of an angiosperm. For more details see page 65.

Fruit
The mature ovary of an angiosperm. It encourages seed dispersal and comes in many forms. For more details see pages 68 and 69.

Germination
The beginning of a plant's growth from a seed.

Gymnosperm
A category of tree also known as conifers or softwoods. They reproduce through cones, which hold their naked seeds and wind-borne pollen.

Herbivore
An animal that eats plants.

Intelligence
The capacity for an organism to choose an action based on awareness of its environment and past experience.

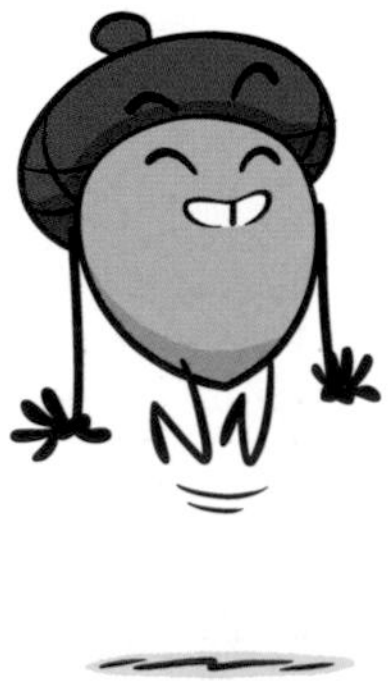

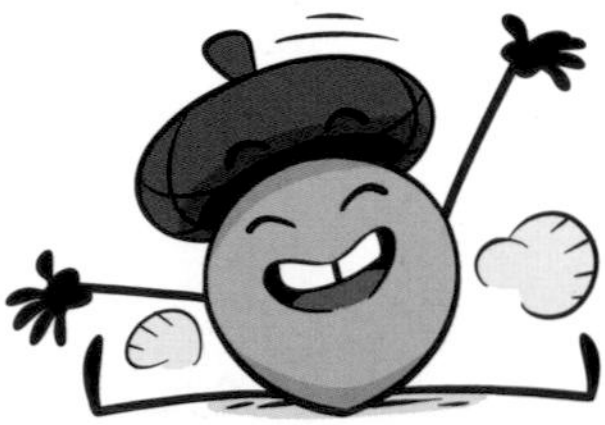

Keystone species

A species essential for the survival of many others.

Leaf

A plant organ that grows from shoots and generally acts as the site of photosynthesis. Small openings called stomata allow for the intake of carbon dioxide.

Meristem

A tissue capable of producing any kind of plant cell. Apical meristems are found only at the ends of shoots and roots, and lateral meristems, the vascular and cork cambiums, are found within the length of the tree's limbs.

Monocot

A type of tree whose seeds contain only one cotyledon. They generally do not undergo secondary growth to create wood so may not be considered "true" trees.

Mycorrhizal network

The underground web that connects trees to one another. Formed by symbiotic relationships with fungi, it allows for the transfer of nutrients and chemical messages between individuals. It is the key to a healthy forest.

Periderm

The protective layer of bark formed outward from the cork cambium. It includes cork, which insulates the tree from pests, germs, and fire.

Phloem

A tissue formed outward from the vascular cambium that facilitates the movement of sugars down the tree for use and storage.

Photoperiod

The duration of darkness. Plants measure this to determine the season and schedule events such as flowering and leaf drop.

Photosynthesis

The process by which a plant combines carbon dioxide, water, and sunlight to form oxygen and digestible sugars. Its counterpart is respiration.

Plant cell

The basic unit of the plant surrounded by a cellulose cell wall. Cells contain many organelles, tissues, and pigments. For more details see pages 28 and 29.

Pollination

The process of tree fertilization. Pollen makes its way from a male cone or floral organ to a corresponding female. Trees are capable of self-pollination, when the same tree has both male and female organs, as well as outcrossing, when the organs are found on separate individuals.

Primary growth

Growth from apical meristems. This is how a plant gets longer and taller.

Respiration

The process by which a plant combines digestible sugars with oxygen to form carbon dioxide, water, and energy. Its counterpart is photosynthesis.

Root

A plant's typically underground limbs. They gather water, oxygen, and minerals while holding the plant in place.

Secondary growth

Growth from lateral meristems. This is how a tree gets thicker.

Seed

The protective container for a newly developing plant.

Shoots

A plant's stem, trunk, and branches. They are divided into nodes, where new leaves, flowers, and shoots develop, and internodes, where the shoot is focused on primary growth.

Spore

A tiny organism created between generations of trees. They produce the single-celled gametes that combine to form a seed.

Symbiosis

A relationship in which one organism depends on another for survival. Three types of symbiosis are mutualism, when both organisms benefit; commensalism, when one organism benefits with no effect on the other; and parasitism, when one organism benefits and the other is harmed.

Transpiration

The process by which water moves upward through a tree. Water taken in at the roots is pulled upward as a result of water evaporating from the leaves.

Tropism

Directional growth. This is how plants move their bodies in reaction to gravity (gravitropism), light (phototropism), and touch (thigmotropism).

Wood

A tissue resulting from secondary growth in trees. It allows for the movement of substances within trees and provides structural support. For more details see page 43.

Xylem

A tissue formed inward from the vascular cambium that facilitates the movement of water and nutrients up the tree. Old xylem becomes mineralized heartwood and functions as structural support.

That's a **LOT** of acorns!

The tallest redwood is **3,500** acorns tall!

The deepest fig tree's roots reach nearly **3,700** acorns down!

The heaviest jackfruit weighs more than **5,000** acorns!

The largest banyan tree's crown is more than **12,000** acorns around!

The biggest giant sequoia has a trunk volume of over **130,000,000** acorns!

Look! I'm life-sized!

The oldest bristlecone pine is **5,067** years old! You can't measure *that* in acorns!

For those with a calculator, Acorn is 33mm tall, 25mm across, and weighs 8g. That's a humble start for a mighty oak!

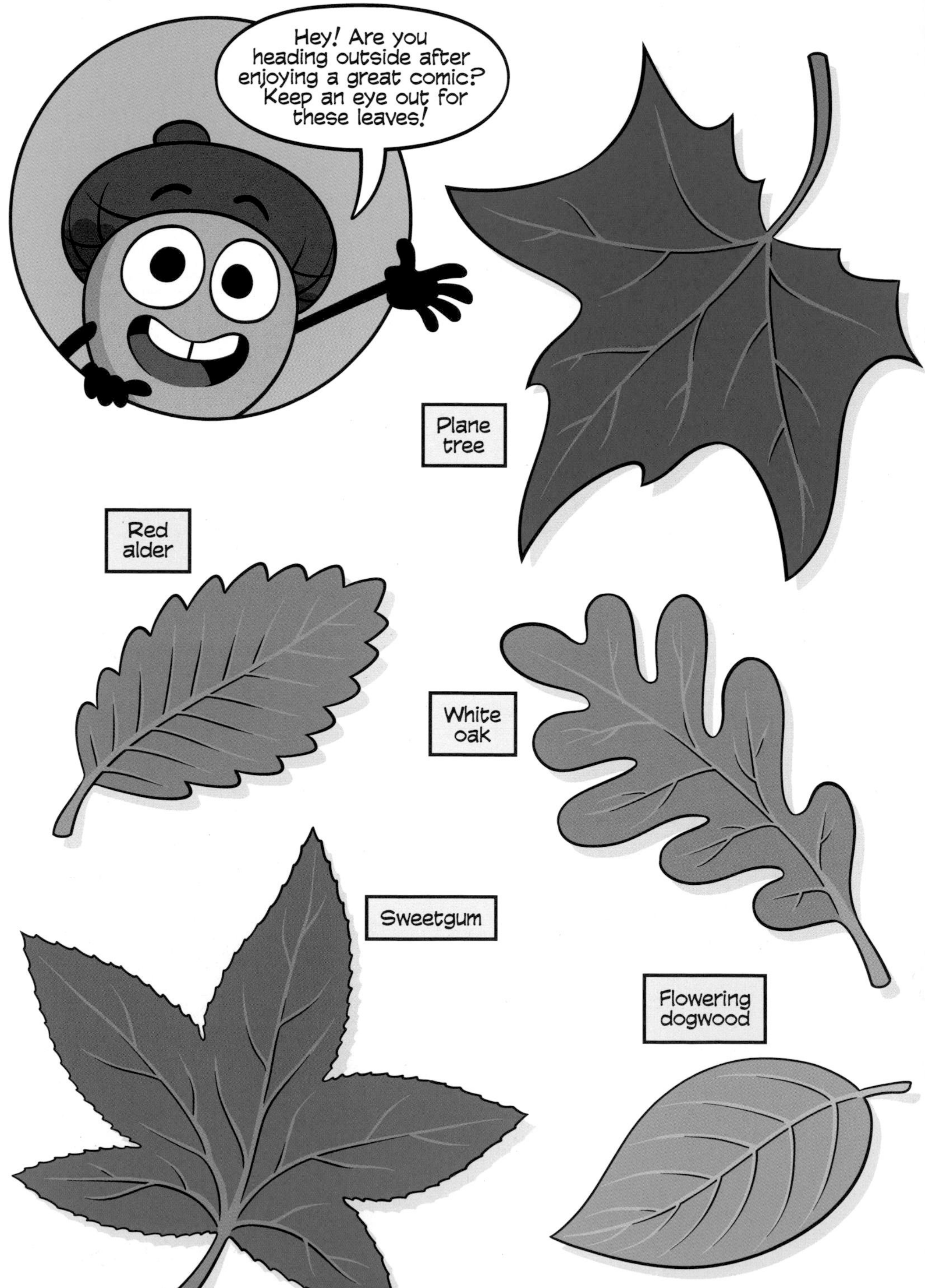

Hey! Are you heading outside after enjoying a great comic? Keep an eye out for these leaves!
Plane tree
Red alder
White oak
Sweetgum
Flowering dogwood

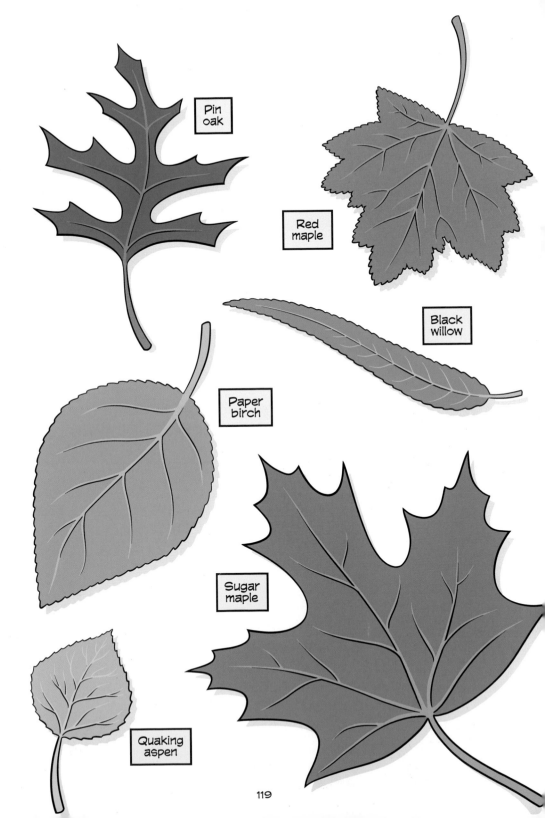

Pin
oak

Red
maple

Black
willow

Paper
birch

Sugar
maple

Quaking
aspen

—BIBLIOGRAPHY—

Books

Chamovitz, Daniel. *What a Plant Knows: A Field Guide to the Senses*. New York: Scientific American / Farrar, Straus and Giroux, 2012.

Raven, Peter H., et al. *Biology of Plants*. 8th ed. New York: W.H. Freeman and Company, 2013.

Tudge, Colin. *The Tree: A Natural History of What Trees Are, How They Live, and Why They Matter*. New York: Crown Publishers, 2005.

Wohlleben, Peter. *The Hidden Life of Trees: What They Feel, How They Communicate—Discoveries from a Secret World*. Translated by Jane Billinghurst. Vancouver: Greystone Books / David Suzuki Institute, 2016.

Other publications

Brown, Peter M. "OLDLIST." Rocky Mountain Tree-Ring Research. Web accessed August 8, 2017.

"General Sherman, the Biggest Tree in the World." Monumental Trees. Web accessed August 8, 2017.

Gorzelak, Monika A., et al. "Inter-plant Communication through Mycorrhizal Networks Mediates Complex Adaptive Behaviour in Plant Communities." *AoB Plants* 7 (2015).

Gumtow-Farrior, Daniel, and Catherine Gumtow-Farrior. "Wildlife on White Oaks Woodlands." Portland, OR: Woodland Fish and Wildlife Project, 1997.

Karban, Richard. "Plant Behaviour and Communication." *Ecology Letters* 11 (2008): 727–739.

Marosvölgyi, Marcell A., and Hans J. van Gorkom. "Cost and Color of Photosynthesis." *Photosynthetic Research* 103 (2010): 105–109.

Martin, Glen. "World's Tallest Tree, a Redwood, Confirmed." *SFGate*. September 29, 2006. Web accessed August 8, 2017.

Trewavas, Anthony. "Intelligence, Cognition, and Language of Green Plants." *Frontiers in Psychology* 7 (2016): 588.

Lectures

Feldman, Lewis J. "Plants and Fungi." Biology 1B, University of California, Berkeley, Berkeley, CA, spring 2015.

Moen, Gary. "Tree Biology: Their Structures and Their Functions." Boise Public Library, Boise, ID. Lecture, March 5, 2014.

Simmard, Suzanne. "How Trees Talk to Each Other." TEDSummit, Banff, AB, Canada, June 2016.

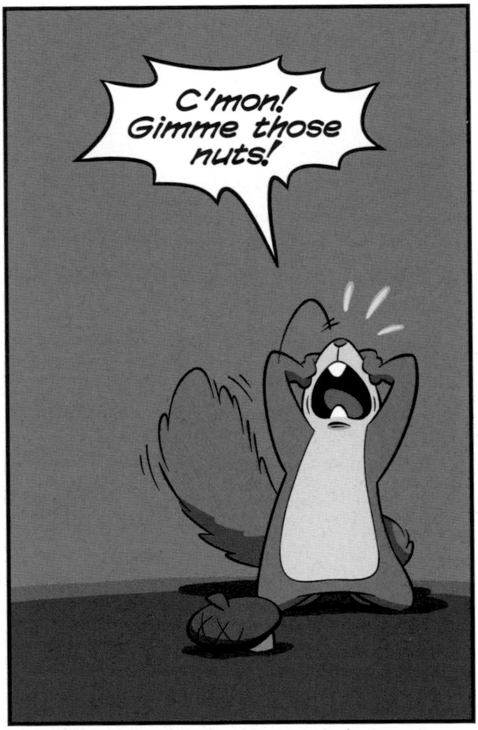
C'mon! Gimme those nuts!